Healthy or Sick?

This book analyzes how policies to prevent diseases are related to policies aiming to cure illnesses. It does this by conducting a comparative historical analysis of Australia, Germany, Switzerland, the United Kingdom, and the United States. It also demonstrates how the politicization of the medical profession contributes to the success of preventive health policy. This book argues that two factors lead to a close relationship of curative and preventive elements in health policies and institutions: a strong national government that possesses a wide range of control over subnational levels of government, and professional organizations (especially the medical profession) perceiving preventive and nonmedical health policy as important and campaigning for it politically. This book provides a historical and comparative narrative to substantiate this claim empirically.

PHILIPP TREIN is a postdoctoral researcher in political science at the Institute of Political, Historical, and International Studies (IEPHI) at the University of Lausanne and a visiting scholar at the Institute of European Studies (IES) at UC Berkeley. His research interests cover comparative public policy (coordination and integration of policies, health policy, employment policy), comparative federalism and multilevel governance (including European Studies), as well as economic voting (Germany). His research has been published or is forthcoming in the *Annals of the American Academy of Political and Social Science, European Journal of Political Research, German Politics, Journal of Public Policy, Journal of Comparative Policy Analysis: Research and Practice, Public Administration, Publius: The Journal of Federalism,* and *Regional and Federal Studies.*

CAMBRIDGE STUDIES IN COMPARATIVE PUBLIC POLICY

The **Cambridge Studies in Comparative Public Policy** series was established to promote and disseminate comparative research in public policy. The objective of the series is to advance the understanding of public policies through the publication of the results of comparative research into the nature, dynamics, and contexts of major policy challenges and responses to them. Works in the series will draw critical insights that enhance policy learning and are generalizable beyond specific policy contexts, sectors, and time periods. Such works will also compare the development and application of public policy theory across institutional and cultural settings and examine how policy ideas, institutions, and practices shape policies and their outcomes. Manuscripts comparing public policies in two or more cases as well as theoretically informed critical case studies which test more general theories are encouraged. Studies comparing policy development over time are also welcomed.

GENERAL EDITORS:

M. Ramesh, *National University of Singapore*; Xun Wu, *Hong Kong University of Science and Technology*; Michael Howlett, *Simon Fraser University, British Columbia*

Healthy or Sick?

Coevolution of Health Care and
Public Health in a Comparative
Perspective

PHILIPP TREIN
University of Lausanne

CAMBRIDGE
UNIVERSITY PRESS

University Printing House, Cambridge CB2 8BS, United Kingdom

One Liberty Plaza, 20th Floor, New York, NY 10006, USA

477 Williamstown Road, Port Melbourne, VIC 3207, Australia

314–321, 3rd Floor, Plot 3, Splendor Forum, Jasola District Centre,
New Delhi – 110025, India

79 Anson Road, #06–04/06, Singapore 079906

Cambridge University Press is part of the University of Cambridge.

It furthers the University's mission by disseminating knowledge in the pursuit of
education, learning, and research at the highest international levels of excellence.

www.cambridge.org
Information on this title: www.cambridge.org/9781108426497
DOI: 10.1017/9781108670883

© Philipp Trein 2018

First published 2018

Printed and bound by Great Britain by Clays Ltd, Elcograf S.p.A.

A catalogue record for this publication is available from the British Library.

Library of Congress Cataloging-in-Publication Data
Names: Trein, Philipp, 1981– author.
Title: Healthy or sick? : coevolution of health care and public health in a
  comparative perspective / Philipp Trein.
Other titles: Cambridge studies in comparative public policy.
Description: Cambridge, United Kingdom ; New York, NY : Cambridge
  University Press, 2018. | Series: Cambridge studies in comparative
  public policy | Includes bibliographical references and index.
Identifiers: LCCN 2018017452 | ISBN 9781108426497 (hardback)
Subjects: | MESH: Health Policy–history | Public Health–history |
  Internationality | History, 19th Century | History, 20th Century
Classification: LCC RA418 | NLM WA 11.1 | DDC 362.1–dc23
  LC record available at https://lccn.loc.gov/2018017452

ISBN 978-1-108-42649-7 Hardback

To Thenia

Contents

Figures

Tables

Acknowledgments

During the time I spent on this research project, I accumulated numerous debts to colleagues, friends, and members of my family who helped me in many ways. First of all, I want to thank Dietmar Braun, who hired me as a PhD student and teaching assistant, and helped me in many ways throughout the entire project. He diligently read my drafts, chapters, and sketches, always provided many critical and constructive comments on how to pursue this project, and – if necessary – put me back on track.

Second, my thanks go to three colleagues who read previous versions of this manuscript and commented extensively on them: Daniel Kübler who kindly provided me with many helpful comments on how to improve my manuscript – notably on how to structure the argument; Stéphane Nahrath who particularly helped me to situate my manuscript in the comparative public policy literature and re-read important aspects of my conceptualization regarding policy sectors and their relation; and of course Yannis Papadopoulos who had numerous helpful suggestions on how to improve my argument, the framing of this thesis overall, and who hired me as an assistant, always making sure that I was not overloaded with teaching duties. Eventually, I am very grateful to Martino Maggetti for giving me the freedom to work on this book alongside other tasks.

Additionally, I would like to thank the editors of the Cambridge Studies in Comparative Public Policy series and three anonymous reviewers for their very helpful comments and suggestions. I would also like to thank the Swiss National Science Foundation and the Institute of Political, Historical, and International Studies at the University of Lausanne for generous financial support at all stages of my research.

Furthermore, I want to thank a large number of colleagues who helped me with comments and suggestions on how to improve my work: Wally Achtermann, Philip Balsiger, Nils Bandelow,

Ruth Beckmann, Giuliano Bonoli, Aurélien Buffat, Fabrizio de Francesco, Patrick Farfard, Scott Greer, Fabrizio de Francesco, Ted Marmor, Johannes Marx, Julie Pollard, Claudio Radaelli, Harald Saetren, Fritz Sager, Fritz W. Scharpf, Manfred G. Schmidt, Monica Steffen, Eva Thomann, Lorenz Trein, Lars Tummers, Fréderick Varone, Thomas Widmer, the members of the WIPCAD research group at the University of Potsdam, and Stefanie Walter. My thanks also go to colleagues and friends who supported me in many other ways during the process of my PhD project. These are: Daniel Auer, Hakim Bensalah, Sandra Dolderer, Steven Eichenberger, Alain Eloka, Christian Ewert, Gerold Eyrich, Flavia Fossati, David Giauque, Edoardo Guaschino, Bob Hancké, Dorte Hering, Ewoud Lauwerier, Fabienne Liechti, André Mach, Gian-Andrea Monsch, Markus Orth, Andrea Pilotti, Delia Pisoni, Carolina Rossini, Christian Ruiz, Johanna Schnabel, Marco Silvestri, and Björn Uhlmann.

This book is dedicated to my wife Thenia for her love, patience, and support. Without her constant encouragement, I would not have been able to finish this project.

Acronyms

AAAS	American Association for the Advancement of Science
ACoSH	Action Council on Smoking and Health, Australia
AHA	Area Health Authority, UK
AHV	Alters- und Hinterlassenenversicherung, Switzerland
AMA	American Medical Association
AUSMA	Australian Medical Association
ASH	Action on Smoking and Health
AUS	Australia
BMA	British Medical Association
CACR	Centre Anti-Cancéreux Romand
CDP	Cantonal Directors of Public Health, Switzerland
CG	Central government
CHP	Community Health Program, Australia
CME	Coordinated market economy
CW	Commonwealth of Australia
DHA	District Health Authority, UK
DHHS	United States Department of Health and Human Services
DRG	Diagnosis-related groups
EHI	Etatist Health Insurance
FAZ	Frankfurter Allgemeine Sonntagszeitung
FCTC	Framework Convention on Tobacco Control
FDR	Federal Democratic Republic of Germany
FSA	Federal Security Agency, USA
GB	Great Britain
GDR	German Democratic Republic
HC	Health care
HTA	Health technology assessment
IMNA	Institute of Medicine of the National Academies, US
JPCSS	Joint Parliamentary Committee of Social Security, Australia

LME	Liberal market Economy
LTC	Long-term care
MOH	Medical officer of health, UK
NHI	National health insurance
NHMRC	National Health and Medical Research Council, Australia
NHS	National Health Service
NRW	North Rhine-Westphalia, Germany
NS	National Socialism
NSDAP	Nationalsozialistische Deutsche Arbeiterpartei, Germany
NSW	New South Wales
NZ	New Zealand
PBS	Pharmaceutical Benefits Scheme, Australia
PH	Public health
PHI	Private health insurance
PHIAC	Private Health Insurance Administration Council, Australia
PHIO	Private Health Insurance Ombudsman, Australia
QUE	Queensland
RACP	Royal Australian College of Physicians
RACS	Royal Australian College of Surgeons
SA	Southern Australia
SHI	Social health insurance
SKI	Schweizerisches Krankenhausinstitut, Switzerland
SUVA	Schweizerische Unfallversicherungsanstalt, Switzerland
TAS	Tasmania
TB	Tuberculosis
USPHS	United States Public Health Service
VIC	Victoria
VoC	Varieties of capitalism
WA	Western Australia
WHO	World Health Organization
WZB	Wissenschaftszentrum Berlin

1 | Introduction

In recent years, new policy challenges have emerged in the field of health policy. On the one hand, caseloads have increased, such as with cancer and diabetes. On the other hand, infectious diseases have returned, for example, the Ebola epidemic which recently hit countries in Western Africa. Other instances of infectious diseases include resistant influenza viruses (such as H5N1), the MERS (Middle East respiratory syndrome) coronavirus, tuberculosis, and antibiotic-resistant bacteria, all of which have become primary concerns for health policymakers worldwide (WHO, 2013b, 2014). Furthermore, preventing noncommunicable diseases (UN General Assembly, 2010; OECD, 2011; WHO, 2013a), such as cancer and diabetes, has become an important challenge for policymakers around the globe. During the last sixty years, life expectancy and the share of elderly in the population increased in many OECD (Organisation for Economic Co-operation and Development) countries. This poses a new policy challenge for many nations as a larger percentage of older people will come along with higher caseloads of chronic diseases. Consequently, there is a demand for more preventive health policies – in addition to curative interventions. These new health policies will cause additional health expenditure (Russell, 1986, 2009), but will also lead to improved health outcomes (McDaid, Sassi, and Merkur, 2015, xxi–xxiii). At the same time, health expenditures are consuming an increasing share of the national income overall in many countries. For example, in 1960, countries like the United States spent around 5 percent of their GDP on health (care and prevention) whereas in other countries, such as Australia and the United Kingdom, it was a bit less. By 2010, this share had doubled and in the United States, it had more than tripled (Figure 1.1).

To deal with these health policy challenges efficiently, health systems have to manage complex cases of multiple morbidities as well as new threats from resistant viruses and bacteria, which can travel easily in a

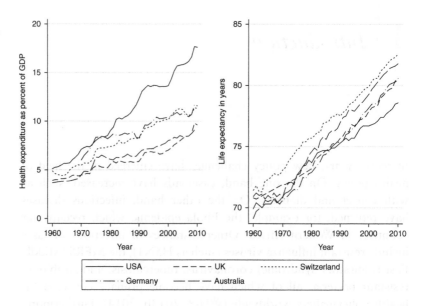

Figure 1.1 Health expenditure and life expectancy.

globalized world, along with increasing pressure for cost containment. It is the goal of this book to analyze how different health systems have dealt with these policy challenges, notably how to coordinate and integrate preventive, curative, individual, and population aspects in health policy from a comparative historical perspective.

Policy responses to the aforementioned challenges can be distinguished according to two dimensions: preventive approaches, which attempt to tackle origins of a disease before it breaks out, and cure, which comprises of policy instruments to regulate, finance, and provide treatment of sick individuals or groups. This book identifies these two approaches as health care and public health. In short, *health care* refers to policies organized along the illness or individual-based principle. Illness-based refers to the moment of intervention against a disease, which occurs when a patient is already suffering from an illness. Individual-based means that health care sector policies are designed to foster treatment of individuals by doctors who cure diseases. *Public health* focuses on policies that take a health hazard or population-based perspective. Health hazard denotes that the moment of intervention is when health is in danger, which is before the outbreak of a disease. Public health interventions are population-based, which means that they are designed to affect the entire population, or groups, rather than just individuals (Trein, 2017a).

This distinction of the two policy sectors is ideal-typical, which means that in the real world they must work together effectively to deal with policy challenges that require the coordination of both fields. For example, this is the case with chronic diseases – e.g., cancer or diabetes – which require the combination of individual cures, individual medical screening, and group- or population-focused primary prevention measures (Busse et al., 2010; Nolte, Knai, and Saltman, 2014). Nevertheless, readers should keep in mind that the proposed distinction between health care and public health is ideal-typical and serves as an analytical tool to analyze the relationship of the two principles, but that it does not describe the full range of the term's use among practitioners.

During the twentieth century, health policy has evolved toward a structural and professional dominance of the medical approach (Foucault, 1963) and, as a consequence, most of the health expenditures have gone into the cure of diseases (OECD, 2017). Nevertheless, due to the changing demands on health policymakers – notably the appearance of new infections and chronic diseases – public health (health hazard and population-focused) solutions, such as health promotion, have reappeared on the agenda of policymakers (McQueen et al., 2007). Around the world, health policymakers have dealt with this problem in many different ways to take into account the renewed demand for public health policies (Blank and Burau, 2013; Tulchinsky and Varavikova, 2014). Ideally, health care and public health would appear in a coordinated or even integrated (Chernichovsky and Leibowitz, 2010) manner in order to provide cost-effective focus on the patients' interests. Given the different legal approaches of health care and public health (Gostin, 2014), as well as the professional autonomy and power of the medical profession (Rodwin, 2011), it is not self-evident that coordination and integration of health care and public health will be implemented smoothly and conflicts are likely to occur. Given the variety of health care systems around the world (Böhm et al., 2013), there might be differences among countries regarding the capacity of the country to relate the two sectors and resolve the conflicts between them (Trein, 2017a). For these reasons, we need to know more about the relation of health care and public health and its development over time. Notably, insights from this

research could help to understand actor coalitions and the capacity
to create policies combining health care and public health in different
countries.

This research problem ties into a theoretical challenge of the
political science literature. Public policies are separated into a large
number of policy sectors or subsystems, which govern a part of the
political system with a certain autonomy (Howlett, Ramesh, and Pearl,
2009, 81–88). Nonetheless, they interact constantly with one another.
This dimension of sectoral interaction has been poorly researched
by the political science literature – especially from a comparative
perspective. Taking the viewpoint of the public policy and public
administration research, Guy Peters referred to the search for the
coordination of policy sectors as the "Holy Grail" for policymakers
(Peters, 1998, 295). Recent contributions still emphasize the need for
more empirical research on this problem (6, 2005; Tosun and Lang,
2017; Trein, Meyer, and Maggetti, 2018). Similarly, there is room
for a deeper conceptual inclusion of the concept of institutional and
sectoral coevolution in the literature (Pierson, 2000; Cusack, Iversen,
and Soskice, 2010; Steinmo, 2010; Trampusch, 2010; Thelen, 2014).

1.1 Concepts and Theoretical Priors in Brief

Starting from these practical and theoretical problems, this book
analyzes the institutional and policy relations of health care and public
health and their change over time. Therefore, this book uses a number
of concepts from the political science and public policy literature, such
as policy sectors, coevolution, coupling, distinctiveness, responsiveness, integration, and coordination. Analytically, this book starts from
hypotheses that I develop based on secondary literature to provide the
conceptual background for the following empirical analysis. In this
section, we will go through to the concepts and hypotheses guiding the
analysis. The following section will discuss the results of the analysis.

1.1.1 Concepts

This book defines health care and public health as policy sectors.
Analog to industrial sectors, policy sectors include specialization and
provision of public services, but, next to service delivery, they also
have a political component to them. The specialists (Rodwin, 2011)
and organized interests participating in the delivery of services reach

out to decision makers and form subsectors to the overall political system, similar to narrower policy subsystems (Howlett, Ramesh, and Pearl, 2009, 81). In the sense used in this book, policy sectors entail the core elements of public policy analysis, such as "sectoral" policy paradigm (Béland, 2005, 8), actors, policy instruments, and institutions (Howlett, Ramesh, and Pearl, 2009). Given the (relative) autonomy of policy sectors, conflicts between sectors might occur when sectors attempt to coordinate – in our case – population, individual, curative, and preventive elements of health policy to deal with the discussed policy challenges (Trein, 2017a).

To analyze the relation between the health care and the public health sectors and their development over time, this book refers to *coevolution*. According to the literature on evolutionary biology, coevolution is an evolutionary change in one population as a reaction to a condition of a second population, which is followed by a change in the second population (Janzen, 1980, 611). This book transfers coevolution to policy analysis to understand the mutual influence and adaptation of the health care and the public health sectors and the change of the relation between both sectors over time. In the following, I will use coevolution as a metaphor and I do not identify evolutionary theory with political analysis (Ma, 2016, 225), as other authors have proposed (Lewis and Steinmo, 2010). This book refers to coevolution in the same way as research focusing on coevolution of dyads, such as capitalism and systems of political representation (Cusack, Iversen, and Soskice, 2010) or skills and welfare (Trampusch, 2010).[1] Thereby, this book accounts for two analytical dimensions: first, an intersectoral dimension that concerns the connection between the health care and the public health sectors and, second, a temporal dimension that refers to the development of the sectors' relations over time.

To analyze the relationship between policy sectors, I hark back to the concept of coupling (Orton and Weick, 1990; Weick, 1976) and propose four forms of coupling to denote different conditions of the relationship between policy sectors. These are tight coupling, loose coupling, decoupling, and noncoupling. Tight coupling entails the conditions of "no distinctiveness"[2] and "responsiveness" between the two sectors. No distinctiveness contains the presence of formal institutional unification, i.e., the sectors share common structures that intend to set up common organizational elements and policies to merge professional practices and interventions. Responsiveness means that professionals and administrators from the two policy sectors formally coordinate political activities because they have "ideas about joint and holistic working" (6 et al., 2002, 33–34) or actors from both policy sectors engage in common discourse coalitions. For example, the medical profession (broadly defined) makes nonmedical public health policies, such as tobacco control, a political priority. Responsiveness entails also policy integration, e.g., policies that actually merge professional practices and interventions of the two sectors (6 et al., 2002, 33–34), which is different from institutional unification which entails only structural preconditions for the integration of policies. An example for political coordination is when medical associations publicly support tobacco control policies. Instances of policy integration are integrated care measures or health strategies that aim at particular diseases. The other forms of coupling follow this logic. Loose coupling combines distinctiveness with the presence of responsiveness. Decoupling includes distinctiveness and the absence of responsiveness and noncoupling refers to the combination of no distinctiveness and the absence of responsiveness (Trein, 2017c).

These four forms of coupling are ideal-typical. To make them applicable to empirical analysis, this book proposes a two-dimensional continuous space with two axes. The vertical axis runs from no responsiveness at the bottom end to full responsiveness at the top end, and the horizontal axis spans from distinctiveness on the left side to no distinctiveness on the right side. The four forms of coupling are placed in the corners of this two-dimensional analytical space: loose coupling is in the upper left corner, tight coupling in the upper right corner, noncoupling in the lower right corner, and decoupling in the lower left corner. In between these extreme points, there are a number of intermediate forms mixing the different forms of coupling (cf. Figures 1.2 and 2.1). I will use this analytical space to map the coupling of health care and public sectors in different countries at different points in time. This strategy allows me to examine the coevolution of the health care and the public health sectors from a comparative perspective (see Chapter 2).

1.1.2 Theoretical Priors and Research Design

This book not only aims to describe the relations of health care and public health over time, but also attempts to explain why the two sectors (potentially) coevolve differently in different countries. Therefore,

I start the analysis with three hypotheses. My first hypothesis holds that there is no distinctiveness (unification) of health care and public health if government is unified. Unified government means that the national government has a relatively large discretion in changing policies and parts of the formal institutional structure without having to consider the position of many veto players, such as a second parliamentary chamber, subnational governments, or find solutions among several parties in government. Examples of a unified government are centralized federations (Hueglin and Fenna, 2006), countries with few veto points (Tsebelis, 2002), majoritarian democracies (Lijphart, 2012), and strong states (Crouch, 1993; Nathanson, 2007). Countries whose political system resembles these qualities are likely to have institutional unification of the health care and public health policy sectors.

The second hypothesis states that there is responsiveness of health care and public health if professionalism in that country is high (Macdonald, 1995). High professionalism means that professional organizations – for example, the medical and legal associations – are strong and politically independent from the state; in other words, they are "free professions" (Rodwin, 2011, 321). In this instance, professional actors are active political pressure groups who defend their special interests and, in addition, lobby for problems that do not directly concern their own interests but are beneficial for the public good. For example, doctors should be interested in public health matters that concern nonmedical health policies from a professional point of view but not because public health touches on their special interests as a profession. Additionally, in the context of strong professionalism, medical organizations would advocate public health issues because they need political legitimacy clout to attract policymakers' attention. The reason for this is that strong professionalism comes along with interest group pluralism (Macdonald, 1995; Siaroff, 1999), i.e., a situation, in which not all interest groups are included automatically in the political process but need to compete with other interest groups for the access to politicians. Thus, health care actors have an incentive to demonstrate that they care about public health matters and work together with health care actors. Consequently, I expect to find responsiveness between the two sectors. To the contrary, weak (or low) professionalism (Macdonald, 1995) implies that health professions are "professions of office" (Rodwin, 2011, 321). In this case, professional organizations do not consider themselves as pressure groups that need to voice societal problems to policymakers. Obviously, professions of office are politically active, but mostly regarding their special interests as they operate in contexts where they do not need to do more, as corporatist structures of interest inclusion guarantee their political participation (Macdonald, 1995; Siaroff, 1999). Therefore, in countries with weak professionalism there should be no responsiveness between the two sectors.

The third hypothesis accounts for contextual elements. I hypothesize that the relation of the health care and public health sectors (coupling) should remain stable over time, as long as the context (most problematic illness, technology) does not change either. However, changes in the context might alter the demand for the coupling of the health care and the public health sectors. My analysis covers the time period from 1880 until 2010. Across this time span, the socioeconomic context has changed considerably and the demands for health policy along with it. In order to consider the mentioned contextual changes, this book focuses on four time periods, each of which has different contextual conditions and therefore varies in its expectations regarding sectorial coupling. The first time period (t1) covers the period from 1880 to 1918. During this period, infectious diseases were the most pressing health problem and medical capacities were limited. This context created high incentives for more responsiveness between professional organizations and policies during that time period. The second period (t2) comprises the time from 1918 to 1945. During this period, infections were still a problem, but less so than before, and medical technology had been improving. Therefore, incentives for responsiveness and policy integration remained present, but should have been weaker than in the previous time period. The third time span (t3) entails the time from 1945 until 1980. During this period, contextual incentives for responsiveness and policy integration were not present because most infections could be cured. Incentives for and unification of policy sectors have returned since the 1980s (t4) because disease patterns have changed as well. Notably, prevalences of noncommunicable diseases have increased and new infections have become a problem, for example, HIV (Baum, 2008; Tulchinsky and Varavikova, 2009).

Starting from these hypotheses, this book analyzes the coevolution of the health care and the public health sectors in five countries, namely Australia, Germany, Switzerland, United Kingdom, and the United States. I selected these countries according to their differences in professionalism and unified government (Table 1.1); other elements,

Table 1.1. *Case studies and empirical implications.*

	Strong professionalism	Weak professionalism
Fragmented government	US → *loose coupling*	Switzerland → *decoupling*
Unified government	Australia, UK → *tight coupling*	Germany → *noncoupling*

such as the nations' economic development and levels of democracy, are fairly stable. The only particularity is the United Kingdom, which is not a federal state. It serves as a control case to and allows for testing my hypotheses beyond the realm of classical federations.

My empirical analysis is a historical account of the development of coupling between the health care and the public health sectors from the mid-nineteenth century until 2010. I chose this long time span because it allowed me to trace the relationship between the two sectors from the origins of the modern state until today. I base my analysis on secondary literature, official documents (including Internet sources), and interviews. Based on a review of these sources, I record instances of institutional reforms, responsiveness between the actors, and policies of the health care and the public health sectors. An example of institutional unification is the creation of a national health service. Responsiveness entails a common advocacy between health care and public health actors, such as when the medical profession and health foundations share support for tobacco control policy or health promotion. Conflicts between the professions would also count the absence of responsiveness. An example of policy integration is a policy that combines prevention and cures regarding a certain policy challenge, such as cancer.

1.2 Main Results

The results of my analysis demonstrate that health care and public health coevolved differently between the five countries. In short, health care and public health coevolved from loose to tight coupling in Australia. In the United States, the development was similar, but the institutional distinctiveness between both fields was more pronounced. In the United Kingdom, the two sectors coevolved from noncoupling

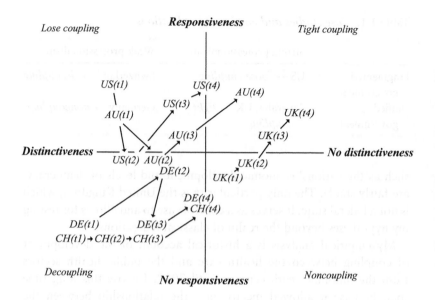

Figure 1.2 Coevolution of health care and public health.

to tight coupling. In Germany and Switzerland, health care and public health coevolved from decoupling to some degree of noncoupling, i.e., both sectors remained relatively distinct institutionally and did not enter a full relationship of noncoupling. An intriguing finding is that the two sectors coevolved toward more responsiveness in all countries in the sample (Figure 1.2).

Concerning the hypotheses that guided the analysis, my results are particularly interesting. The findings of my analysis confirm my hypothesis regarding the effect of professionalism on policy sectors' responsiveness. In countries where professions were more politically active, the medical profession tended to advocate for public health issues, such as health promotion services, immunization, and tobacco control policy, taking the role of an important pressure group in these matters. This was especially the case if the issue did not concern the group's original interests, for example, in the case of the merger of universal health care with a public health service. Responsiveness changed according to the context. In the United States, and partly in Australia, responsiveness was strong, but only at times when the most prevalent diseases demanded policy integration of the two sectors. If this was not the case, political conflicts and absence of responsiveness remained prevalent. The situation was different in the United Kingdom. The health care and public health sectors were already unified institutionally in the late nineteenth century. During the late nineteenth and the early twentieth centuries, this led to conflicts between the medical profession and public health professionals, mostly about resources. At the same time, in Australia and the United States, there were fewer conflicts, although professionalism was similar to the United Kingdom. Nonetheless, through a mutual learning process, the relationship between the health care and the public health sectors coevolved toward greater responsiveness, in all three countries. On the other hand, in Germany and Switzerland, there was no responsiveness because the medical profession was not politicized in the same way as it was in other countries; rather, it acted like a member of the administration, i.e., as professions of office, rather than a public interest organization. Consequently, health professions in Germany and Switzerland did not play the same role in the coupling of the two sectors as health professions did in the other countries.

Based on my empirical results, I need to modify my hypothesis on unified government. My analysis shows that federalism has mostly impacted the institutional relationship between the two sectors. In other words, the coevolution of health care and public health proceeded differently in federal states and in unitary states in the sample. Notably, there has been an overall centralization of health policy, which means that in all countries the two sectors coevolved toward less vertical and horizontal institutional distinctiveness and toward more unification of the various institutions. This process was slower in decentralized federations, namely, in Switzerland and the United States, than in Germany, which is a more centralized federation. In Germany, health care and public health were institutionally unified at a later time. In Australia, which has an even more centralized form of federalism, the two sectors were unified earlier at the national level due to the advocacy by health professions, especially doctors. Contrariwise, in the United Kingdom, which is a unitary state, health care and public health coevolved above all in a tightly coupled manner.

Although my analysis targets primarily democratic countries, the results show also that the difference between democratic and autocratic countries has had an impact on the distinctiveness and responsiveness of the two sectors. This book also covers the coevolution of the health care and the public health sectors during

Nazi rule in Germany. In addition, it contains some preliminary references to the GDR and the USSR. In all of these countries, autocratic government accelerated the institutional unification of health care and public health.

My results also show that a number of other elements impacted the relationship between health care and public health. Another key finding is that the two sectors coevolved toward complementarity. In other words, independently from the starting point, responsiveness between the policy sectors increased over time (Figure 1.2). Changing contextual elements played an important role in that outcome. Similar to capitalist institutions, policy sectors emerged randomly and co-evolved to complementarity (Crouch et al., 2005). In complementarity, two sectors generate policy outputs that complement one another and they attempt to provide better outcomes than any single sector's instruments can provide. For that outcome, changing context played an important role regarding health care and public health. Once contextual conditions changed, i.e., noncommunicable diseases increased and infections returned since the 1980s, governments in all of the countries in this sample passed policies that integrated health care and public health policies, although at different speed. This finding points to the importance of policy learning in the coevolution of policy sectors. I hypothesized that the absence of responsiveness led to less policy integration between the two sectors. However, my results show that in countries with little actor responsiveness (for example, Germany) there was also policy integration between the two sectors. Instead of learning from politicized professions, national policymakers followed the examples set by other governments about integrating health care and public health. For that outcome, changing contexts played an important role. Another explanation for this result is that policymakers from both sectors learned from one another over time regarding policy design – even against the backdrop of non-politicized professions. Thus, the increase of policy integration of health care and public health signals policy learning or emulation between the two sectors.

The design and the placement of this analysis are in some ways unusual because it is situated at the intersection of comparative public policy and comparative politics. I use concepts from the public policy literature, such as sectors (Howlett, Ramesh, and Pearl, 2009; Trein, 2017a) and their coordination (Peters, 1998), and I apply them to a longitudinal comparative historical analysis of five countries, which is usually done in the qualitative comparative politics literature (Steinmo, 2010; Thelen, 2014). The consequence of this hybrid approach is that such an analysis does not have as much detail as is usually found in public policy analyses, which focus on an in-depth understanding of agenda-setting, decision-making and/or implementation processes (Howlett, Ramesh, and Pearl, 2009; Knoepfel et al., 2011; Saetren, 2005) across the entire time frame that this book covers. Nevertheless, my approach is innovative and interesting because it researches the historical background of policy sectors – namely their main stakeholders, institutions, and policy instruments – in a clearly comparative perspective. Thereby, this book makes a number of contributions to the political science literature, which will be discussed in the following section.

1.3   Lessons from this Research for the Political Science and Health Policy Literature

Overall, this book contributes to the scholarly literature in three ways. First, this book speaks to the health policy and public health literature in general. The second and third contributions are on theoretical and conceptual elements that are relevant to the political science and public policy literature.

1.3.1   Health Care and Public Health

This book clearly contributes to health policy research. My results are indeed interesting for the literature on both health care and public health because my analysis connects policies from health care, which focus on sickness, to public health policies, which aim at preventing diseases. In the comparative health policy literature, researchers focus often on health care systems and the differences between them (Freeman and Rothgang, 2010; Rothgang, 2010; Böhm et al., 2013) taking a comparative political-economic approach to the study of health policy. On the other hand, the public health literature focuses on public health (population health) problems (Nathanson, 2007) and politics from a broad perspective, which usually includes individual health care into the public health perspective (Tulchinsky and Varavikova, 2014; Baum, 2016). Another line of research that has emerged from public health has focused on health promotion (McQueen et al., 2007) and the politics and political science aspects that are relevant to it (Clavier and De Leeuw, 2013).

This book contributes to the health policy and the public health literature by forging an explicit connection between health care and public health from a comparative public policy and a comparative politics perspective. Previous researchers have rarely pursued such an approach to the analysis of health policy (Blank and Burau, 2013). Therefore, this analysis fills a gap in the health policy literature. This book makes a general conceptual contribution to the health policy literature by distinguishing health care and public health as two distinct but overlapping policy sectors. Furthermore, since this book connects an institutionalist approach with a public policy approach to the analysis of health policy, it allows readers to draw some hypotheses that could explain differences in expenditure for health promotion and prevention in general, as well as the adoption of different strategies on integrated health policies (Trein, 2017a). Eventually, this book takes a historical perspective on health policy that starts in the second half of the nineteenth century when modern health policy emerged (Foucault, 1963) and extends until the third public health revolution and its implications in the late twentieth and the early twenty-first centuries (Potvin and McQueen, 2007, 17–18).

1.3.2 Professional Activism and Institutional Evolution

This book also contributes to the (new) institutionalist literature that has become very prominent across the political science literature (DiMaggio and Powell, 1991; Mahoney, 2000; Pierson, 2004; Shepsle, 2006). This literature has analyzed from different theoretical angles how institutional contexts shape the way individuals construct and express their preferences and how mutual understanding and aggregation of these preferences are rendered complicated (Immergut, 1998, 25). For example, from a historical institutionalist perspective, authors have focused on how historical events and contexts affect changes in institutions (Streeck and Thelen, 2005; Thelen, 2004; Mahoney and Thelen, 2010) or the evolution of entire states (Steinmo, 2010). Another strand of the institutionalist literature has focused on different institutional configurations (Crouch et al., 2005) and the coevolution of different institutional configurations (Trampusch, 2010; Thelen, 2014).

This book contributes to the historical institutionalist literature by emphasizing the role of professions and their political activity for institutional development. Specifically, my analysis connects the development of institutions and policy innovations to the political activism of professional actors, notably the medical profession. The literature on professions and the sociology of professions (Rueschemeyer, 1973b; Freidson, 1983; Macdonald, 1995; Rodwin, 2011) points out that there is a difference between the political activity of professional actors across countries, since there are variances in how the state governs professional education, training, standards, and its relation to these groups (Rueschemeyer, 1973a, 63–122; Freidson, 1983, 23–26; Rodwin, 2011, 321). This book uses this literature to demonstrate how in the context of "free professions," health professions make nonmedical health policies a political priority, which results in responsiveness of the health care and public health policy sectors. Examples for this finding are Australia, the United Kingdom, and the United States. On the other hand, this book argues that in countries such as Germany and Switzerland, "weak" professionalism or "professions of office" (Rodwin, 2011, 321) result in less responsiveness between the two sectors. Against this backdrop, health professions are included in the political process rather automatically and also through corporatist interest intermediation. They consequently do not need to gain legitimacy clout by advocating publicly on policy problems beyond their special interests, such as public health matters in the case of the medical profession. On the other hand, in countries with strong professionalism and pluralist interest intermediation, health professions are more free from state intervention but need to develop a stronger political profile to defend their special interests. Therefore, it is in their interest to support public health, including non-medical interventions. It is important to note that the political activity of health professions is also related to the broader structure of interest intermediation within a country, given that the countries with "strong" professionalism have a liberal and pluralist interest intermediation (Australia, UK, and the US) whereas the countries with "weak" professionalism (Germany and Switzerland) have relatively more corporatist interest intermediation (Lijphart, 2012).

1.3.3 Policy Integration, Coupling, and Coevolution of Policy Sectors

This book contributes to the public policy literature, notably on the research that regards coordination and integration of policies and public sector organizations (6, 2004; Christensen and Lægreid, 2007; Peters, 2015; Trein, Meyer, and Maggetti, 2018). More recent theoretical contributions to this literature have emphasized that the connection of policy sectors can take the form of regimes, specifically boundary-spanning policy regimes, which denote the durability of the integration of different fields. Examples for boundary-spanning policy regimes are drug policy, pollution abatement, or homeland security (Jochim and May, 2010). Another concept that researchers have recently elaborated on is functional regulatory spaces, which build on boundary-spanning policy regimes and add a territorial, as well as a federal dimension, arguing that we need to understand public policymaking in a three-dimensional space combining different policy sectors, different levels of government, and territories (Varone et al., 2013). However, this literature falls short on describing different degrees in the connection on policy sectors and their changes over time. For instance, in decentralized countries there should be a different type of boundary-spanning policy regime than in centralized nations. Rather than proposing another concept to understand the conceptualization of the institutional relations among different policy fields, this book focuses on comparing the degree to which existing sectors are related. We look at different degrees of coupling between the health care and the public health sectors. The different forms of coupling proposed in this book could be used to compare different boundary-spanning policy regimes or functional regulatory spaces concerning how they are coupled in order to denote to what degree they provide integrated policy solutions (6 et al., 2002, 33–34).

In addition to coupling, this book contributes to the literature on policy integration and public sector coordination by transferring coevolution from the comparative political economy literature to comparative public policy research. Notably, this book shows that despite the presence of different forms of coevolution, health care and public health moved toward complementarity, i.e., more policy coordination, of health care and public health. My analysis demonstrates that the two policy sectors, which have emerged randomly, coevolved toward complementarity: that is, the coordination of both fields to improve the common output, similar to the way in which the literature on institutional complementarity had demonstrated it regarding capitalist institutions (Boyer, 2005; Crouch et al., 2005).

The analytical framework and terminology used in this book can be transferred to the analysis of other new policy challenges that span existing policy sectors; notably I suggest two examples. First, homeland security and politics of domestic security have become important issues of the domestic political agendas and for research in political science. The problem has been researched, covering various countries, in case studies (May, Sapotichne, and Workman, 2009; May, Jochim, and Sapotichne, 2011; Wolf and Pfohl, 2014) as well as in cross-national studies (Wenzelburger, 2013). Homeland security involves various types of policy sectors that can possibly be involved. For instance, in the case of the United States, various sectors or subsystems take part in the provision of homeland security (May, Jochim, and Sapotichne, 2011). A comparative study of countries and the degrees of coupling between involved policy sectors, as well as the levels of government, could contribute to our understanding of the presence or absence of institutional cohesiveness on the one hand and the responsiveness and interaction between actors on the other. Second, migration and refugee policy has emerged as a key policy challenge for many governments around the world. To deal with this policy problem, governments will need to at least coordinate or even integrate (Scholten, Collett, and Petrovic, 2016) different policy instruments that are needed to resolve the problem of migration – such as social assistance, employment promotion, and housing – to address the challenge of immigrant integration.

1.4 Outline for this book

In order to pursue the planned analysis of the coevolution of the health care and the public health policy sectors in five countries, this book will proceed in the following manner. Chapter 2 defines health care and public health as two different policy sectors. Notably, I will explain how they differ regarding ideas, actor constellations, policy instruments, and conflicts. Chapter 3 discusses my theoretical priors and develops hypotheses concerning the horizontal relations of health care and public health. I will discuss how both sectors can be coupled by developing different forms of sectorial coupling. Subsequently, I discuss why I expect differences in sectorial coupling between countries and over time, particularly as a result of differences in the political activity of health professions and fragmentation of government. Contextual elements – namely pressing problems for changes in health policy, i.e., due to new diseases – lead me to expect differences of sectorial coupling over time. Chapter 4 elaborates on the contextual dimension. I discuss how patterns of diseases, the technological development over time, broad ideas, and the economic development create demands for responsiveness between policy sectors. Chapter 4 concludes with the study's research design, case selection, and material used for the analysis in addition to providing the respective empirical expectations for the five countries.

Chapters 5 to 9 comprise the case studies for the five countries. Each case study reviews the coevolution of both sectors, strictly along the two main analytical dimensions (actor–policy responsiveness and institutional distinctiveness), in each of the four time periods. Each chapter concludes with a summary of the results and a discussion of the hypotheses (professionalization, governmental fragmentation, and contextual elements) in light of the empirical analysis' findings. Chapter 10 presents a comparative evaluation of the results. Therein, I summarize my main results, compare the coevolution of the sectors, and present a revised argument with more specific causal pathways in order to account for other theoretical elements as well.

2 | Sectoral Coupling of Health Care and Public Health

This chapter defines health care and public health as two different policy sectors. Harkening back to the concept of sectoral paradigms, the chapter discusses how health care and public health can be conceptualized as two different policy sectors, which overlap on important policy challenges. To analyze the horizontal relations of policy sectors comparatively and to find different forms of sectoral overlap, the chapter defines different degrees of sectoral coupling based on the literature on coupling in organizational systems, public policy and institutional analysis. It then organizes the different forms of sectoral coupling into a two-dimensional ideal-typical analytical space with four different degrees of sectoral coupling – namely tight coupling, loose coupling, decoupling, and noncoupling – at the extreme corners of the analytical space.

2.1 Health Care and Public Health as Two Different Policy Sectors

The basic units of analysis in this book are policy sectors. Comparable to industrial sectors, policy sectors entail specialization and provision of public services, but in addition to service delivery, they also have a political dimension. The specialists (Rodwin, 2011) and organized interests participating in service delivery reach out to decision makers and form subsectors to the overall political system, similar to policy domains (Burstein, 1991) or more narrow policy subsystems (Howlett, Ramesh, and Pearl, 2009, 81). This book uses a notion called *policy sector*, which contains the core elements of public policy analysis, such as sectoral paradigms (Béland, 2005, 8), actors, policy instruments, and institutions (Howlett, Ramesh, and Pearl, 2009). Given the (relative) autonomy of policy sectors, conflicts between sectors might occur since many policy challenges require policy sectors to coordinate (i.e., establish continuous and committed relationships between one another) (Peters, 1998) or integrate policies (Candel and Biesbroek, 2016) in case there is a demand for this (Trein, 2017a). The remainder of this chapter discusses in depth the implications of this distinction for the analysis of health care and public health. Table 2.1 applies the definition to health care and public health, and connects it in an ideal-typical way to the dimensions of the sectoral paradigm, actors, institutions and public sector organizations underlying them (Howlett, Ramesh, and Pearl, 2009), substantial but specific policy instruments (Howlett, 2005), and different actor categories in public policy analysis (political administrative actors, beneficiaries, and target groups) (Knoepfel et al., 2011). The book adopts a broad definition of institutions. These can be the main policies and laws for health governance, such as a health insurance law, and the public sector organizations related to these policies and laws. The difference between a simple policy and an institution is that policies become institutions over time, if they come to play an important role in defining actors' reform preferences in the future (Hacker, 1998). Furthermore, institutions are also public organizations and jurisdictions (parliament, levels of government) that make up the state. The following distinction is an approximate generalization of the connection of the two policy sectors which summarizes all the policies that are part of the respective sectors explained in the following. Some actors appear in two categories because they might take different roles depending on the exact policy problem – given that each sector consists of several policies. Of course, the following distinction is ideal-typical and there are differences between countries that will be analyzed in the empirical parts of this book.

2.1.1 Health Care

This book defines the sectoral paradigm of the *health care* sector as *illness-* or *individual-based*. Illness-based health care refers to the moment of intervention against the disease, which is when the patient is already suffering from an illness. Individual-based health care means that, in the health care sector, policies are designed to foster treatment of individuals by doctors responding to their individual needs. Policies and institutions in the health care sector are often of a distributive or redistributive nature. This implies that financing individual health care is the most important issue in health care policy, considering the budgets in different OECD countries (OECD, 2017). Although cost

Table 2.1. *Ideal-typical distinction of health care and public health as two different policy sectors.*

	Health care	Public health
Sectoral paradigm	Illness- or individual-based	Health hazard- or population-based
Policy instruments	Mostly distributive policies, such as medical care, organization, and financing of hospitals and pharmaceutical policies, short-term goals; regulative policies less important	Regulative policies of central importance, such as sanitary legislation, regulation of epidemics, higher tobacco taxes, long-term goals; population based primary and secondary prevention
Political administrative actors (in sector-specific institutions)	Department of health, social insurance department, treasury (medical profession or interest groups)	Department of health, public health services, medical authorities, local health departments (medical profession or interest groups)
Actors – beneficiaries	Individual patients. *Positively affected third parties: doctors, nurses, health insurance, pharmaceutical industry, hospitals*	Population or group. *Positively affected third parties: public health doctors, epidemiologists, health foundations (Cancer Foundation, Heart Foundation), pharmaceutical industry*
Actors – target groups	Doctors, nurses, health insurance, pharmaceutical industry, hospitals. *Negatively affected third parties: nurses, health insurance, pharmaceutical industry, hospitals*	Population or group, tobacco industry, alcohol industry, fast food producers, producing industry, chemical industry. *Negatively affected third parties: tobacco industry, alcohol industry, fast food producers, chemical industry*

containment is a recurring issue in health policymaking (Rothgang, 2010), individual health care expenditure remains relatively stable in many OECD countries (Wagschal and Wenzelburger, 2008). Furthermore, regulatory policies are also part of the health care sector as they are targeting and protecting industries, such as the pharmaceutical industry and the health insurance industry (Braun and Uhlmann, 2009).

The political administrative actors that are part of the health care sector are the groups operating the main institutions of the political system, such as members of government, parliamentarians, and the bureaucrats involve in health policymaking. In the health care sector, these groups consist of actors associated with the following institutions and organizations: the department of health, if it exists at the national level; the department of social insurance; and health departments at the level of the member states and local governments. Depending on the political system of a country, institutions in the health care sector can be distributed over different levels of government. The medical profession and interest groups can also become part of the political administrative apparatus if they participate in health care governance, for example, in the context of a self-governance system, such as the corporatist administration of health policy in Germany (Webster, 2002; Jonas, Goldsteen, and Goldsteen, 2007; Duckett, 2007; Rosenbrock and Gerlinger, 2009).

Concerning the end beneficiaries of health care policies, the most important group is individual patients who suffer from a certain illness. It is for this group, above all, that health care policies are made. However, there is a long list of actors, including powerful interest groups and professions, that indirectly benefit from health care policies. More specifically, these are health insurance companies, the pharmaceutical industry, producers of medical appliances, and health professionals such as doctors and nurses. These groups have powerful material and ideational interests and often benefit indirectly from health care policies. Due to their professional situation and reputation, doctors are the most important actors in the health care sector. The differences between the medical profession and other professions is that doctors have a prolonged training of very specialized abstract knowledge, a common ethical code of behavior, and a commitment to community services and values. These interests are often superior to interests of material self-gain because they are rooted in medicine as a calling, rather than a day job (Saks, 1995, 29). What is more, given their possibility to decide when someone is sick and how a strategy for a cure is chosen, the medical profession virtually enjoys power over life and death. Different from other professional groups, doctors hold considerable power that goes beyond immediate application of their knowledge (Gottweis et al., 2004). The special role of doctors has been confirmed in the literature on the sociology of professions (Dingwall and Lewis, 1983; Macdonald, 1995), including the medical profession especially (Freidson, 1970; Hassenteufel, 1997; Lupton and Najman, 1995; Willis, 1989; L. Hancock, 1999).

Nevertheless, research has shown that the political system limits the influence of the medical profession on health policymaking (Immergut, 1990). This finding underlines that, despite their powerful status, all professional and corporate interest groups of the health care sector, including the medical profession, can become target groups for political action as well as negatively affected third parties. There are, of course, differences between various reforms in different subsystems of the health care sector, such as hospital financing or health insurance, because a group cannot be a target group and a benefiting third party at the same time in a specific reform (Knoepfel et al., 2011). Degrees of regulation and targeting of these actors vary among health care systems (Wendt, Frisina, and Rothgang, 2009; Rothgang, 2010). For instance, public health care systems, such as the National Health Service in England, directly regulate the medical profession (Webster, 2002), as does the Pharmaceutical Benefits Scheme for the drug market in Australia (Duckett, 2007). Furthermore, during the 1990s, there were reforms that strengthened choice eligibility for consumers and reduced the benefits of professional and corporate interest groups in many countries. Notably, governments introduced managed competition and strengthened the rights and the choice of consumers, who are the actual beneficiaries of the health care system (Enthoven, 1988, 1993), in some countries such as Germany (Böhm et al., 2012).

2.1.2 Public Health

In the *public health sector*, the sectoral paradigm is *health hazard-* or *population-based*. Health hazard-based health care denotes that the moment of intervention is when health is endangered, which is earlier in time than the possible intervention of the health care sector. Thereby, interventions are population-based, which means that they are designed to affect the entire population or population groups rather than just individuals (Baum, 2008; Rosenbrock and Gerlinger, 2009, 2014).

These are completely different interventions than in the health care sector. Public health policies and institutions are mostly regulative and redistributive policies, such as those that prevent people from smoking in public, that levy taxes on smoking, or that introduce mandatory screening for cancer. At the same time, they aim for long-term goals, which means that it is difficult to explain their immediate payoff (Tulchinsky and Varavikova, 2009). A large part of public health policy is related to disease prevention. However, regarding prevention, it is necessary to distinguish among different forms of prevention, specifically primary, secondary, and tertiary prevention (Holland, 2004; Egger and Oliver, 2012). Primary prevention focuses on avoiding health hazards in the population, or at least reducing the likelihood that they will occur. It entails policies such as smoking bans and sales bans of unhealthy products, but also immunization laws. Primary prevention can occur at three levels: the individual level, the setting level, and the population level. Individual measures are, for instance, health counseling by doctors. Policies in settings entail health counseling in schools, for instance, about the risks of tobacco. Population-wide preventive health policies entail campaigns demanding healthier nutrition or less smoking (Rosenbrock and Gerlinger, 2014). Secondary prevention means to recognize early stages of diseases, for instance, by screening patients. Finally, tertiary prevention aims to slow down the disease and its course. It could also entail rehabilitation measures after a heavy coronary heart disease event (Egger and Oliver, 2012). As to at the distinction of the two sectors (Table 2.1), primary prevention at the setting and population level, as well as population-wide screening programs, fall into the category of public health. On the contrary, individual primary prevention is a case of sectoral overlap because it entails individual counseling to prevent further diseases. Concerning tertiary prevention, there is even more sectoral overlap because it overlaps a lot with curative health care (Jonas, Goldsteen, and Goldsteen, 2007).

The political administrative group of actors in this sector is different than in the health care sector; however, both sectors can be unified in the same ministry or administrative unit (see below and Chapter 3). Specifically, the political administrative actors of the public health sector can be situated in public health departments, medical authorities, and local health departments. These can be institutionally and organizationally unified (Achtermann and Berset, 2006) with the health care sector or completely separated (M. Lewis, 2003b; Porter, 1999). A third option is that both sectors are formally under the same institutional and organizational umbrella, but one is in a different region and operates independently of the main ministry, such as a public health agency. Nonetheless, it remains hierarchically subordinate to the main ministry of health (Rosenbrock and Gerlinger, 2009; see below for more details).

With regard to private actors, the main beneficiaries (those who should benefit from public health policies) are primarily populations and groups. However, along with them comes a number of third parties that are positively affected by public health policies because they profit from them materially or ideationally. Specifically, these are individuals who have a master's degree or a doctorate in public health (MPH or DPH) as well as epidemiologists (D. Braun, 1994), who work either in public health departments or in health foundations, such as a cancer and heart foundation (Brößkamp-Stone, 2003). In the public health sector, benefiting third parties do not entail as many corporate interest groups as in the health care sector. Most notably, it is the pharmaceutical industry that benefits, for instance, from large immunization campaigns (Rosenbrock and Gerlinger, 2014).[1] Compared to the health care sector, however, the possibilities for economic profits are considerably lower in the field of public health. This is due to the fact that most of the activities aim at preventing diseases, which means that little medication is needed. On the other hand, most job opportunities in the public health sector are in public health services, which often are not as well paid and provide fewer career prospects than in individual health care. In the latter, ambitious candidates can specialize much more and earn more money as private practitioners and leading doctors in hospitals (Starr, 1982, 2009; Fee, 1994, 2008). Nevertheless, it is important to keep in mind that the professions of the public health sector do not have the same reputational and medical power as the medical profession, which is the dominant profession in the health care sector (Potvin and McQueen, 2007, 15).

Concerning target groups, public health policies focus also on the population, or certain parts of it, such as smokers, because their behavior might need to change in order to improve overall population health. At the same time, regulative public health policies target a number of corporate interests, which in turn are opposed to these public health policies – especially the tobacco industry (Hirschhorn, 2000; Bornhäuser McCarthy, and Glantz, 2006; Givel, 2007). Although the tobacco industry is an extreme example, opposition to regulation might also occur from other industries, such as the chemical or the lead industries (Bero, 2003), energy suppliers, or the alcohol and food industries (Bell, Salmon, and McNaughton, 2011), which might also be opposed to public health policies.

2.1.3 Power Asymmetry of Health Care and Public Health

Before turning to the analysis of the horizontal relations of the health care and the public health sectors, it is important to note that there is a power asymmetry between the health care and the public health sectors. According to the critical sociology and public health literature, the curative clinical approach to dealing with illness and health has become dominant in health policy during the last 150 years. This becomes visible in the change of the use of knowledge in medicine and clinics (Foucault, 1963) that helped the medical profession to become very influential and that resulted in a powerful biomedical industry (Starr, 1982). The German sociologist Niklas Luhmann referred to the functional code of the German health insurance system as ill/healthy because it approaches health only through a perspective of illness and only a patient that has been declared sick is entitled to benefits (Luhmann, 1990). The critical public health literature has pointed out how the scientific medical approach has entered public health practice (Lupton, 1995). Thus, scholars of public health aim at improving the theoretical approach to health promotion and public health (Foucault, 1963). Against this background this book develops an empirical analytical approach to the coevolution of health care and public health that analyzes the differences in the dominance of the biomedical paradigm and how policymakers hvae reformed health systems to strengthen nonmedical approaches to health policy. We will discuss the dominance of the biomedical approach and the return of "public health" in Chapter 4.

2.2 Horizontal Relations of Policy Sectors

Since this book is going to compare the coevolution of health care and public health in five countries, it is necessary to have an analytical concept that allows to account for differences in the relations between both sectors, as well as their dynamics over time. To deal with the sectoral dimension, this book proposes a typology that distinguishes different degrees of coupling between policy sectors. Originally, the educational scientist Karl Weick proposed coupling as an analytical concept to analyze the relations of constituting parts of organizations. Loose coupling emphasizes that organizations have different parts that interact in order to ensure that the organization keeps on functioning, but they are also different enough to ensure adaptability and effectiveness (Weick, 1976; Orton and Weick, 1990). Coupling has been used before in political science research, for example, in the literature about Europeanization (Benz and Eberlein, 1999; Börzel, 2010; Papadopoulos, 2007), federalism (Benz, 2013), and neo-institutionalism (Mayntz, 1993; Mayntz and Scharpf, 1995; Scharpf, 1997; Blatter, 2001).

From the outset, coupling is relatively underspecified, which makes it possible to apply the concept to a variety of contexts. Yet, it requires a specific definition when being put into a conceptual framework, as Karl Weick has admitted himself (Orton and Weick, 1990). Researchers refer to loose coupling in many different ways and contexts, sometimes even with contradictory meanings. For instance, Askim holds that loose coupling could also be understood as the absence of learning (Askim, Johnsen, and Christophersen, 2008), which is perfectly fine if we take into consideration that, according to the original text, such a reading would be possible (Weick, 1976). Specifically, there are two main understandings in which coupling has been used. On the one hand, scholars have distinguished tight coupling and loose coupling as two poles of a linear continuum, which is mostly how political science authors have been referring to the concept. The degree of coupling means the extent to which organizational parts, ideas, hierarchies, organizations, and environments as well as intentions and actions are coordinated or communicated (Weick, 1976; Orton and Weick, 1990). On the other hand, researchers define coupling as a dialectical concept described on a two-by-two matrix, depending on distinctiveness and responsiveness of the organizational elements (Czarniawska, 2005). In their article regarding the reconceptualization of coupling, Orton and Weick hold that, "If there is neither responsiveness nor distinctiveness, the system is not really a system, and it can be defined as a non-coupled system. If there is responsiveness without distinctiveness, the system is tightly coupled. If there is distinctiveness without responsiveness, the system is decoupled. If there is both distinctiveness and responsiveness, the system is loosely coupled" (Orton and Weick, 1990, 205).

This book starts from this citation concerning a dialectic of distinctiveness and responsiveness to define four forms of coupling which will be useful for comparing differences in the relationship between policy sectors over a longer time period.[2] Specifically, this book is going to differentiate institutional/organizational-, actor- and policy-related elements to establish distinctiveness and responsiveness between policy sectors. The aforementioned definition of a policy sector includes a sectoral paradigm, institutions, policy instruments, and private actors, which are negatively and positively affected by the policy. To make use of coupling, the following subsections connect distinctiveness to the institutional/organizational dimension of policy sectors and responsiveness to the dimension of private actors and policy instruments.

2.2.1 Distinctiveness

Distinctiveness between policy sectors is present if it is possible to allocate them to different institutions, private actors, and policies. Concerning the institutional/organizational dimension, this means that they are horizontally separated into different ministries and administrations (Grant and MacNamara, 1995). However, it can also entail that the two sectors are located at different levels of government, for instance, that one sector sits on the national level and the other one on the subnational layer of government, such as in federal states (Hueglin and Fenna, 2006). On the other hand, distinctiveness is absent if the two sectors are institutionally/organizationally unified or merged, i.e., horizontally merged in the same institutional and organizational arrangement and vertically merged at the same level of government (6, 2005, 89).

2.2.2 Responsiveness

Responsiveness between two policy sectors is present if there is collaboration between the actors in the two sectors with regard to policy output and/or policy coordination. Responsiveness can be interaction between individual and collective actors, such as interest groups, professions, or nonprofit organizations, with regard to a specific policy. This can be communication in order to support a certain policy (Zafonte and Sabatier, 1998) or mutual learning between different interest groups in the sense of substantial policy learning (Bennett and Howlett, 1992; May, 1992). Another kind of responsiveness entails mutual support in putting issues on the political agenda (Kingdon, 1995; Howlett, Ramesh, and Pearl, 2009; 6 et al., 2002, 33–34), which can occur by direct interaction and coordination of the different groups or indirectly in "discourse coalitions" wherein various actors support the same policy ideas publicly without actually exchanging information about a common strategy (V. Schmidt, 2008, 310). Thereby, interest groups and professions from different sectors work together regarding a specific policy and support it in public. This is especially relevant if the actor constellation for a specific policy naturally has little support from strong interest groups, for example, because the end beneficiaries have no powerful political agenda. In this case, the support of interest groups or professions that originally were concerned with other problems can be crucial for the stakeholders of certain policies.

Another way responsiveness might occur is policy integration (Candel and Biesbroek, 2016). In this case, responsiveness is present if there is some kind of a common output, such as a policy instrument or common strategy, that explicitly connects the two sectors (Metcalfe, 1994; Jordan and Schout, 2006; D. Braun, 2008), for example, connecting health and environmental policies. A common policy output is different from an institutional and organizational merger (6, 2005, 89), such as a boundary-spanning policy regime (Jochim and May, 2010), which would be an indicator for institutional/organizational unification. Consequently, it is possible to use policy integration as a form of responsiveness between both sectors. By the same token, this includes the dimension of political administrative actors in the relationship between two policy sectors. Responsiveness is absent if there are conflicts between interest groups of the two sectors, no interaction between private actors, competition and conflicts, or only negative coordination among public actors.[3] Conflicts between sectoral actors can be ad hoc about political issues; however, they can also become more institutionalized as a result of transgression (Bednar, 2009) of one sector into the space of another sector. For instance, if sector x begins to provide a function or service that originally was assigned to sector y, this is absence of responsiveness. A more specific example is if diplomacy is done not by the diplomatic corps, but by the military or private actors.

2.2.3 Combining Distinctiveness and Responsiveness

In order to make these concepts useful for the analysis in this book, I suggest a continuously differentiable space, in which the first axis spans from "distinctiveness" to "no distinctiveness" and the second axis from "no responsiveness" to "responsiveness" (Figure 2.1). Against this backdrop, it is possible to develop ideal-typical expectations for the coupling of policy sectors in general. At the extreme corner of "responsiveness" with "no distinctiveness," there would be tight coupling of policy sectors, which entails full institutional/public sector organizational unification and encompassing interaction of actors – in the sense that they politicize and advocate common policy intentions very actively and frequently (6 et al., 2002, 33–34). Consequently, policy integration of health care and public health is very likely.

At the extreme angle of "responsiveness" with "distinctiveness," there would be tight coupling of policy sectors. This contains complete institutional/public sector organizational separation but full interaction of actors. Thus, policy integration is likely. At the extreme corner of "no responsiveness" with "distinctiveness," we find complete institutional and organizational separation of the sectors and absolutely no interaction between actors. Consequently, policy integration is unlikely. Finally, at the extreme angle of "no responsiveness" and "no distinctiveness," we find full institutional/public sector organizational unification combined with complete absence of actor interaction. Again, policy integration is unlikely.

In between the four ideal-typical corner solutions, we would find a variety of intermediate arrangements. Between distinctiveness and no distinctiveness as well as responsiveness and no responsiveness, there should be a variety of intermediate arrangements. Concerning distinctiveness, some parts of the two sectors can be unified institutionally/public sector organizationally, for example, through common administrative services or legal frameworks that apply only to some part of a sector. On the other hand, there can be some degree

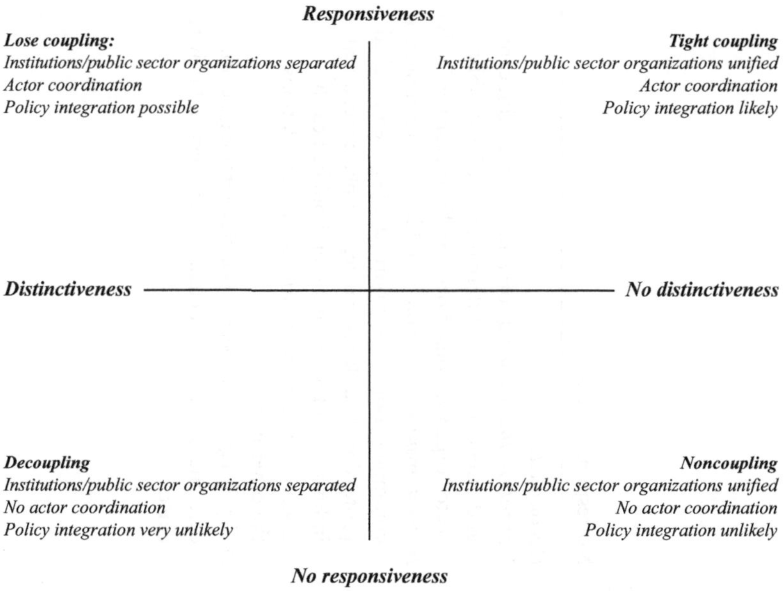

Responsiveness

Lose coupling:	*Tight coupling*
Institutions/public sector organizations separated	*Institutions/public sector organizations unified*
Actor coordination	*Actor coordination*
Policy integration possible	*Policy integration likely*

Distinctiveness ———————————|——————————— **No distinctiveness**

Decoupling	*Noncoupling*
Institutions/public sector organizations separated	*Instiutions/public sector organizations unified*
No actor coordination	*No actor coordination*
Policy integration very unlikely	*Policy integration unlikely*

No responsiveness

Figure 2.1 Ideal-typical coupling of policy sectors.

of responsiveness, for example, interaction of some beneficiaries or stakeholders from different sectors. Readers should keep in mind that this distinction is ideal-typical and that the application of the typology needs to be put in the context of the specific empirical example. In the following, I will do this for health care and public health.

2.2.4 Implications for Health Care and Public Health

I will now turn to a discussion on the implications of the typology that I discussed previously for the health care and the public health sectors. Table 2.2 presents the implications of the different ideal types of sectoral coupling for the health care and the public health sectors and shows what needs to be observed empirically for each of the different forms of coupling. *Loose coupling* of health care and public health implies that both sectors are separated institutionally/public sector organizationally from one another because they are located in different institutional and organizational frameworks, such as ministries and administrations, or at different levels of government. At the same time, there should be responsiveness of private actors, which means that interest groups and professions from the health care and the public

Table 2.2. *Ideal-typical coupling of health care and public health.*

	Responsiveness	No responsiveness
Distinctiveness	*Loosely coupled:*	*Decoupled:*
	Institutions/public sector organizations: health care and public health in different institutions/public sector organizations (horizontally and/or vertically)	*Institutions/public sector organizations*: health care and public health in different institutions/public sector organizations (horizontally and/or vertically)
	Interest groups/professions: learning, communication, support, etc. between medical profession, health insurance, and pharmaceutical industries on the one hand and public health doctors' organizations and health foundations on the other hand	*Interest groups/professions*: conflicts, no learning, no communication, no support, etc. between medical profession, health insurance, and pharmaceutical industries on the one hand and public health doctors' organizations and health foundations on the other hand
	Policy integration: specific policies entailing health care and public health elements possible	*Policy integration*: specific policies entailing health care and public health elements are very unlikely to exist

No distinctiveness	*Tightly coupled:*	*Noncoupled:*
	Institutions/public sector organizations: health care and public health unified institutionally/organizationally (under the same "institutional/organizational umbrella") (horizontally and/or vertically)	*Institutions/public sector organizations:* health care and public health unified institutionally/organizationally (under the same "institutional/organizational umbrella") (horizontally and/or vertically)
	Interest groups/Professions: policy learning, communication, support, etc. between medical profession, health insurers, and pharmaceutical industries on the one hand and public health doctors' organizations and health foundations on the other hand	*Interest groups/Professions:* conflicts, no learning, no communication, no support, etc. between medical profession, health insurance, and pharmaceutical industries on the one hand and public health doctors' organizations and health foundations on the other hand
	Policy integration: specific policies entailing health care and public health elements are very likely to exist	*Policy integration:* specific policies entailing health care and public health elements are unlikely to exist

health sectors communicate, learn from one another, and cooperate in policy advocacy. With regard to integration of specific policy instruments, it is possible that there are common policies between health care and public health because there is strong responsiveness between private actors in both sectors. This should especially be the case if interest groups and professions assigned to the health care sector support public health policies because the interest groups that are part of the health care sector ought to be politically more potent. For example, if the medical profession, which is part of the health care sector, advocates a public health policy, such as immunization programs or tobacco control policy, these policies have much stronger support than if they only received support from actors belonging to the public health sector.

On the other hand, if health care and public health are decoupled, the conditions of the institutional and public sector organizational relations between the two sectors are the same as in the case of loose coupling. However, there are differences with regard to responsiveness. First of all, concerning private actors, this condition entails conflicts between interest groups and no or little communication and policy advocacy. For example, there could be serious conflicts between medical doctors and public health doctors instead of mutual policy learning in the sense that the medical profession considers findings of medical sociology or public health research to be interesting and important. What is more, in this situation there should be transgression (Bednar, 2009), for instance, when prevention is mostly executed by medical doctors rather than public health departments. Concerning policy integration, I do not expect common policy outputs to occur in this configuration mainly for two reasons. First, both sectors are separated institutionally and organizationally, which already reduces interaction between them and makes a hierarchical decision to integrate both fields more costly. Second, due to conflicts and lack of cooperation between private actors, policy integration becomes even less likely (but not impossible).

Contrary to loosely and decoupled sectors, *tight coupling* of policy sectors entails institutional and public sector organizational unification of the sectors. Concerning the relationship of health care and public health, this means that both fields are organized by and large in a single ministry of health, or a national health service, and not in horizontally or vertically different levels of government, nor with extensive delegation of power to interest groups or the market (Burau and Blank, 2006; Wendt, Frisina, and Rothgang, 2009; Böhm et al., 2013). At the same time, there is responsiveness between private actors of the two sectors, in the sense that doctors or health foundations connect the paradigms of the two sectors in the agenda-setting process or that medical organizations actively support the agenda setting of public health policy issues. Due to the institutional and organizational connection and private actor responsiveness, policy coordination between the two sectors is very likely to occur.

The fourth category refers to *noncoupling* of policy sectors. It entails that both sectors are located in the same institutional and organizational environment, such as a ministry of health or in a common legislative framework. However, with regard to the interaction between private actors, there is a similar situation as discussed concerning noncoupling. There should be mainly conflicts about resources or specific policies, such as managed care programs, and no policy learning between the groups that belong to each of the policy sectors. Rather than communication, adjustment of preferences, and support in agenda-setting, unilateral action and transgression between the sectors dominate. With regard to common policies, I have the same expectations as for decoupling, namely the absence of policy integration. From the perspective of the absence of responsiveness of private actors, this logic makes sense. However, a possible objection is that the institutional and organizational unification of both fields might be an incentive for political administrative actors to integrate policies. This is indeed possible, but with the expected opposition of private actors, there are some powerful obstacles to substantially integrated policy output.

2.3 Summary

To sum up, this book puts forward different degrees of sectoral coupling, based on the concept of coupling developed by Karl Weick. To make different degrees of coupling applicable to comparative public policy analysis, this book connects coupling to the previously defined dimensions of policy sectors, notably by distinguishing between private actors on the one hand and institutions (broad policies), political administrative actors (e.g. public sector organizations), (e.g. public sector organizations) on the other hand. This chapter conceptualizes four ideal-typical forms of coupling that allow for the analysis of the connection between policy sectors on the dimensions of political and administrative institutions and organizations, private actors, and policies. Tight coupling refers to unified institutional and organizational elements and responsiveness between private actors, such as professions. Loose coupling entails institutional and organizational distinctiveness and actor responsiveness. Noncoupling combines institutional and organizational unification with the absence of responsiveness and decoupling with institutional and organizational distinctiveness and no responsiveness of the two sectors. Concerning policy integration, I have been arguing that responsiveness of private actors, such as professions, is important and makes policy integration more likely. However, institutional and organizational unification of the two fields might also catalyze the integration of policies. To make the four different forms of coupling applicable to comparative public policy analysis, I put them into a continuously differentiable space that allows to account for intermediate forms of distinctiveness and responsiveness.

3 | *Theoretical Priors*

This chapter sets out the theoretical foundations of the argument that this book proposes to explain differences in the coevolution of health care and public health. In short, I contend that professionalism and interest intermediation, unified government, as well as contextual elements such as technological novelties or economic development, need to be taken into account to understand the coevolution of health care and public health. The chapter has two parts: first, an elaboration of on the argument in general terms; second, a discussion of the implications for health care and public health. In each part, I start with a discussion of the standard institutionalist approach and then turn to the literature of the politicization of professions and interest group inclusion, unified government, and contextual conditions. I am harkening back to the research on the politicization of professions and interest group inclusion to develop a hypothesis on the responsiveness between policy sectors. To hypothesize on the institutional relations of policy sectors, I am employing the notion of unified government (veto players and federalism).

3.1 The Argument in General Terms

3.1.1 Prelude: Standard Institutional Analysis

In an analysis of the coevolution of policy sectors, the most obvious theoretical references are theories related to institutional analysis, especially to the branch of historical institutionalism and related concepts of institutional evolution. The argument of this book takes a different analysis. Nevertheless, as the goal here is to understand the institutional coevolution of health care and public health over a long period, I start by mentioning the implications for this analysis of the literature on historical institutional analysis because the findings of this book do also speak to this research. Before explaining the main argument, this section reminds the reader of four key theoretical dimensions that emerge from the historical institutionalist literature and presents their implications for the health care and the public health policy sectors.

1. *Contingent events and increasing returns* (Mahoney, 2000; Pierson, 1994, 2000, 2004; Skocpol, 1979): With regard to the coevolution of policy sectors, this theoretical dimension implies that minor events might impact on how the health care and public health sectors are coupled. Once established, the relationship of two sectors should remain rather difficult to change.
2. *Gradual institutional change* (Streeck and Thelen, 2005; Mahoney and Thelen, 2010): Concerning the coevolution of policy sectors, this dimension entails that the relationship of policy sectors changes slowly, if at all.
3. *Different types of institutions and countries* (Steinmo and Watts, 1995; Steinmo, 2010; Thelen, 2004, 2014): Regarding the coevolution of policy sectors, this implies that the endogenous qualities of different constellations of policy sectors determine how they change.
4. *Convergence and complementarity* (Boyer, 2005; Campbell, 2011; Crouch et al., 2005; Deeg, 2007; Hall and Soskice, 2001; Streeck and Yamamura, 2001; Yamamura and Streeck, 2003): This theoretical dimension implies for the coevolution of policy sectors that they emerge randomly and in an uncoordinated way, but, over time, they should coevolve toward more coordination and complementarity.

This book's argument departs from these four dimensions. I hold that the coevolution of policy sectors – i.e., sectorial coupling and its development over time – depends on the politicization of professions and interest group inclusion, unified government, and contextual factors. In short, the presence of unified government leads to institutional unification of the two sectors. Politicized professions and the presence of a pluralist system of interest group intermediation lead to political activity of the medical profession with regard to public health issues and there is responsiveness, i.e., the presence of a discourse coalition (V. Schmidt, 2008, 310), between actor groups of the two sectors in the political process as well as integration of policy instruments. Thus, the impact of political activism by professions varies according to contextual factors such as policy ideas, technological development, and economic factors.

3.1.2 Professionalism and Interest Group Inclusion

To develop theoretical expectations and a hypothesis on the responsiveness of policy sectors, I am referring to previous research on the
politicization of professions and the inclusion of interest groups. A
standard argument in the sociological literature is that professions are
important; most prominently, Max Weber proposed that professionalization is an important factor for the rationalization of society. Professional roles and organizations are important in the societal structure.
Due to the competition among them, they are an important part of
the inherent conflict in every society. As such, professional groups
pursue economic interests, but this is not their only goal. Members of
professions also seek social status. According to Weber, professions are
important to the societal class system because they can create income
based on their knowledge and qualifications. In comparison, other
groups fulfill this function based on the powers of labor or capital.
Consequently, professions play an important social role in society
(Larson, 1977; Weber, 1980; Macdonald, 1995, 30). Professionalism
and the sociology of professions have become important elements
in the social sciences literature in general, and have focused on a
number of important professional groups, such as lawyers, doctors,
and accountants (Abbott, 1988, 2005; Barber, 1963; Carline and
Patterson, 2003; Dingwall and Lewis, 1983; Döhler, 1993, 1997;
Heinz and Laumann, 1978; Macdonald, 1995; Rueschemeyer, 1973b;
Saks, 1995; Surdez, 2005; Dingwall and Lewis, 1983).

Empirical research on the sociology of professions has distinguished
different degrees of professionalization between countries. This means
that professions do not function as the same link between society
and the state in all nations. For instance, in some countries, such as
the United Kingdom and the United States, belonging to a profession
is important for citizens due to economic reasons but also to form
individuals' professional identity. On the contrary, in other countries
such as Germany, professional identities play a secondary role in comparison to a high school, occupational, or university degree, which are
crucial elements of the "Bildungsbürgertum." In countries with low
professionalism, a general degree of education is more important
for personal development and the signaling of personal status than
belonging to a profession (Freidson, 1983, 23–26; Rueschemeyer,
1973a, 63–122). This has consequences for the importance of

professional organizations in the political process. In countries with strong professionalism, professional organizations play an important role as intermediary instances (D. Braun, 1993), which politicize problems and put them on the political agenda. On the contrary, in countries with low professionalism, professional organizations are also important – not so much to politicize problems, but rather as a forum for the exchange of knowledge and scientific innovations. In this case, politicization occurs mainly by other actors, such as political parties.

The role of professionalism is linked to institutions of capitalism and interest intermediation. Interestingly, countries that the literature on the sociology of professions denominates to have high professionalism – in this sample, Australia and the United States – are at the same time liberal market economies, whereas those with low professionalism are coordinated market economies (Germany and Switzerland) (Hall and Soskice, 2001, 1–68). In liberal market economies it is extremely rewarding economically to belong to a profession, such as law, medicine, science, or accounting. Due to the liberal employment and wage-bargaining system as well as the lack of an apprenticeship system, membership in a profession implies a stable route to economic security. In coordinated market economies, however, the encompassing wage-bargaining and apprenticeship system also guarantees education and social benefits to those who are not members of an extremely specialized profession. A professional identity and formation have advantages, but are not as necessary for economic security as they are in liberal market economies. In other words, a liberal economy comes along with "free professions" where the state takes a rather passive role in regulating and educating professions, whereas in coordinated economies there are "professions of office" (Rodwin, 2011, 321) that are more regulated. These differences in the economic structures impact on the politicization of professions. In liberal market economies, professions are more politically active; they need to protect the economic interests of their members because the general labor market regime is much more unregulated. In contrast, professional organizations are less politicized in coordinated market economies than in liberal market economies because labor market protection is more institutionalized.

The third strand of the literature that is relevant to this argument is the research concerning corporatism (Schmitter, 1974; Lehmbruch,

1977; Siaroff, 1999), which helps to justify why professions that are more politically active lobby on issues beyond their special interests, such as tobacco advertising restrictions. The term "corporatism" refers to an institutional arrangement in which the state "grant[s] a deliberate representational monopoly" (Schmitter, 1974, 94) to interest groups. According to Lehmbruch, this form of interest intermediation has developed into an "institutionalized pattern of policy-formulation in which large interest organizations cooperate with each other and with public authorities" (Lehmbruch, 1977, 94). A more recent empirical analysis by Alain Siaroff brought together these dimensions and defined a scale to measure corporatism in different countries (Siaroff, 1999). This literature is important for the argument in this book because coordinated market economies are accompanied by corporatist forms of interest intermediation, whereas liberal market economies tend to be more pluralistic regarding interest group inclusion (Hall and Soskice, 2001).

Therefore, I argue that *against the background of politicized professions and a pluralist form of interest group inclusion – which is the case in Australia, United Kingdom, and the United States – we should find responsiveness between policy sectors.* In this case, professional organizations play a politically important role as intermediary agencies that link policy sectors. This implies that professions either forge explicit alliances or join discourse coalitions with collective actors from other policy sectors. The goal of these alliances is to solve a specific policy problem or to argue against powerful target groups of regulative policies. Although professions are prone to enter into conflicts with other professions if the interests of their members are at stake, professional organizations have an interest to act this way for the following reasons: first, they have the organizational capacity and political experience to do this, as they need to defend their members against market pressures. Second, they have an interest to act this way as it increases their political legitimacy clout if they are active politically for other matters than their proper sectoral interest only.

However, *in the instance of unpoliticized professions and a corporatist form of interest group inclusion, which is the case in Germany and Switzerland, we should find little responsiveness between policy sectors.* Professions are less likely to take the role of politically relevant intermediary agencies that connect policy sectors. They are less likely to forge alliances or enter discourse coalitions that span over policy sectors. The reasons for this are that they are a less powerful pressure group because they do not represent the interests of their members in a free market. They do not need additional legitimacy or clout, which they would attain by focusing on matters that go beyond their proper interests. Therefore, I propose the following hypothesis:

> **Hypothesis 1:** *In countries with politicized professions and pluralist institutions of interest intermediation, there should be responsiveness between professions and interest groups from different sectors.*

3.1.3 Unified Government

To propose theoretical expectations and a hypothesis on the institutional relations between policy sectors, I refer to the structure of government and as to what extent the national government is "unified." I am therefore leaning on the seminal work by Lijphart (Lijphart, 1999, 2012) who suggested that two main dimensions affect policymaking in developed democracies: the executive-party dimension, i.e., the horizontal division of powers, and the federal-unitary dimension, i.e., the vertical division of powers. In following Lijphart, I am starting from the assumption that these two dimensions have an impact on the institutional relations of policy sectors. Unlike than Lijphart, I refer to these two dimensions as federalism and veto powers. I use a different label for the horizontal dimension of power sharing to underline the importance of veto points, which is significant for the development of this argument.

1. *Federalism:* The federalism dimension refers to jurisdictionally shared powers between the central and subnational governments. Some areas of legislation are in the hands of the national governments, whereas others are in the discretion of the member states. Federal states are different from confederations, where the business of the supranational level is dealt with mainly by the governments of member states, such as in the European Union. However, federations differ from unitary states, which do not have subnational governments with the qualities of a state (*Staatsqualität*), as, for instance, the states in the United States, the cantons in Switzerland, or the German *Länder* (Hueglin and Fenna, 2006). The literature on comparative federalism is vast and has put forward a variety of dimensions to distinguish federal countries. Such

dimensions include different degrees of centralization of legislative, administrative and especially fiscal powers; federations with shared powers versus those with separated powers; federations that are holding together and coming together (D. Braun, 2000; Braun and Trein, 2014; Burgess, 2006; Hooghe et al., 2016; Stepan, 1999; Watts, 1996).

2. *Veto Points/Players:* The second theoretical dimension refers to the idea of veto points or veto players. This argument has been framed in an institutional as well as in a rational-choice version. In the former, authors have insisted that in countries with many institutionalized veto points in their political system, it is easier for interest groups and political parties to veto a certain policy and influence the decision-making process (Henisz, 2000). In the literature, the authors have referred to this problem as "divided government." This can be the division of power between parliament and presidency or two chambers with similar powers in national parliament. Another feature of divided government is a strong proportional representation, which results usually in arrangements of shared government. In the rational-choice version of the argument, George Tsebelis refers to veto players who seek to maximize their influence and utility in the policy process (Tsebelis, 2002). He argues specifically that alongside the number of veto players, the ideological distance between them is especially important for whether they will block political decisions, effectively slowing down the decision-making process (Tsebelis, 2000, 463).

These two dimensions imply for this book's argument that the degree to which the government is unified impacts on the distinctiveness of policy sectors. In countries with strong decentralization of the legislative competences in one or both sectors that are under observation, it is less likely that both sectors are institutionally unified at the national level, for instance, in the same ministry or the same legislative framework. The same holds true for policy integration. However, if the competences of both sectors are located at the subnational level, it could be possible that they are integrated at the subnational level of government (although this is not the main focus of this argument). The argument is the same as far as political institutions and veto points are concerned. If the government is divided, or if there are many veto players with different interests in the political game, it is more likely that policy sectors are institutionally distinct from one another and that policy integration also becomes less likely. Consequently, this book proposes as a second hypothesis:

Hypothesis 2: In countries with unified government, it is less likely that policy sectors are institutionally unified and that policies are integrated.

3.1.4 Contextual Elements

The extent to which responsiveness between private actors might occur is not the same for every policy problem. Notably, there are some situations in which conflicts are possible between professions. It is thereby necessary to entertain the possibility that such conflicts might become particularly visible if professional organizations are strong and politically active. Conflicts between professions could appear especially with regard to economic issues, such as the allocation of resources to a policy that would make them beneficiaries. The same could be said for responsiveness between political administrative actors of different sectors, such as members of the administration. They might come into conflict about resources, but they might cooperate with regard to problem pressures. I have so far mentioned these possibilities of conflicts, but have not yet considered a theoretical element that accounts for situations in which conflicts between policy sectors might appear.

Therefore, this book introduces an intervening variable in the presented theoretical model, namely contextual elements. The term context is not very specific and can refer to many things. In the worst case, it could become a redundant proxy for theoretical elements that are not properly defined and refer to something very unspecific that serves to explain some of the variance in the dependent variable, which cannot be uncovered by existing theories in the field. Yet, this does not need to be the case. Researchers have recently made a significant effort to specify contextual elements and their role for the study of politics. Most notably, and encompassing in this sense, is the *Oxford Handbook of Contextual Politics*, which specifies a series of possible elements that can be understood as contextual factors for the analysis of politics and policy (Goodin and Tilly, 2006).[1]

However, the way in which context plays out concerning the coevolution of policy sectors needs to be discussed separately with regard to the empirical examples. Otherwise there is the risk of randomly selecting some elements without having a substantial justification at hand. Thus, this book will specify this for the health care and the public health sectors in the following section and only formulate a very general hypothesis at this point.

Hypothesis 3: Responsiveness between policy sectors depends on contextual factors.

3.2 Implications for Health Care and Public Health

This book has, up to now, presented its argument in a very general way. To put the discussed hypotheses to an empirical test, it is necessary to present their implications for the empirical example that will be employed in the following. This book focuses on the coevolution of the health care and the public health sectors. The remainder of this chapter explains the implications of the general argument for this example.

3.2.1 Standard Institutional Analysis and the Coevolution of Health Care and Public Health

To begin with, I will present the implications of the standard institutional analysis for the coevolution of the health care and the public health sectors. According to the historical institutionalist literature on health policy, contingent events and increasing returns, gradual institutional change, different types of institutions and countries, as well as convergence and complementarity have important implications for the analysis of the health care and the public health sectors.

1. *Contingent events and increasing returns:* In the health policy literature, especially the literature on health insurance models, some authors underline the fact that specific contingent events are responsible for institutional emergence and that they create increasing returns for certain groups. Jacob Hacker shows this in his comparative analysis of health insurance legislation in Canada, United Kingdom, and the United States. According to Hacker, we need to look at path dependencies in order to understand why England has a National Health Service and why the United States did not succeed until the end of the 1990s to introduce a comprehensive health insurance program (Hacker, 1998). The

same point has been made with regard to public health policy. Some authors refer to contingent events that are crucial for public health policymaking and have influenced the further development of this policy field. For example, some researchers argue that the fact that the Nazi government had enacted many public health policies, such as tobacco control, is one reason for the weak public health regime in postwar Germany (Proctor, 1996; Schneider and Glantz, 2008; Weindling, 1989). These premises imply for the dependent variable of this book that the coupling of health care and public health might also depend on specific contingent events.

2. *Gradual institutional change:* A second important insight from historical institutionalism is the different ways in which institutions change.[2] Specifically, institutional drift and conversion have been analyzed regarding the reforms of health policies. They show that formal legislative reforms have proven difficult in the sector of health care policy (Hacker, 2004a, 2004b, 2005) and therefore the main forms of institutional change are drift and conversion.[3] With regard to public health, concepts of gradual institutional change have not been applied. The implication of the theory of gradual institutional change for this book is that the coupling of the health care and the public health sectors should be subject to institutional drift and conversion rather than layering or displacement.

3. *Different types of institutions and countries:* Another point that we can derive from the literature on historical institutionalism is that institutional dynamics depend on the specific types of institutions. This argument has also been put forward regarding health policy. Explicitly, Sven Steinmo has held that, rather than contingent events (Hacker, 1998), the specific institutional design is the reason for success or failure of health policy reform (Steinmo and Watts, 1995). The hypothesis that different types of institutions explain variance in health policy outputs can be related to the literature on different health care system types. In the comparative research on health systems, authors have broadly distinguished between statist, corporatist, and private health care systems (Field, 1973; Terris, 1978; Frenk and Donabedian, 1987; OECD, 1987; Alber and Bernardi Schenkluhn, 1992; Moran, 1999; Burau and Blank, 2006; Wendt, 2006; Blank and Burau, 2007; Freeman and Rothgang, 2010; Rothgang, 2010) and stressed the convergence of health care systems toward mixed systems (Saltman, Busse, and

Figueras, 2004; Burau and Blank, 2006; Blank and Burau, 2007; Wendt, Frisina, and Rothgang, 2009; Rothgang, 2010; Schmid et al., 2010).[4] The institution-type argument has also been made regarding public health policies. For instance, some authors have made the point that in each country there is a specific way of pursuing public health policy that is not comparable with other countries (Baldwin, 1999, 524–525). This implies for the argument in this book that coupling of health care and public health follows a distinct path in each country and cannot be easily compared with other nations.

4. *Convergence and complementarity:* The convergence argument, which says that institutions converge over time, has not been applied with regard to health policy institutions in a country. However, it has interesting implications for the example in this book. Transferred to the health care and the public health sectors, we can expect that complementarity between both fields increases over time. This means that actors from both sectors learn from one another and that the likelihood for coordinated policy outputs becomes bigger, irrespective of sectorial coupling.

As outlined in the general theoretical discussion, this book's main argument departs from these four hypotheses. In short, I hold that the coevolution of health care and public health depends on the politicization of professions, interest group inclusion, unified government, and contextual factors. It is nevertheless important to keep the implications of the four institution-related arguments in mind as they might invoke important secondary insights on the coevolution of health care and public health.

3.2.2 Professions, Interest Group Inclusion, and the Relation of Health Care and Public Health

The first hypothesis (H1) implies that the responsiveness between the two sectors depends on the professionalism in the field of health policy in general. Specifically, this means that in countries where professions are per se politicized, the potential for responsiveness of private actors, particularly the medical profession and the public health organizations, should be high.

The following points are important to this argument: it is important to mention that both fields have different professional roles. The most important professions in the health care sector are doctors and nurses (Döhler, 1993; Freidson, 1970; Saks, 1995). The medical profession is therefore subject to conflicts of interests, which are inherent in professional roles. Doctors generally ought to have a public interest because of their professional oath to help sick individuals. However, due to their specialized professional formation and knowledge regarding life and death, they potentially can earn high salaries on a free market (Barr, 2012, 243), which results in a potential conflict of interest between economic gains and the professional responsibility. A large literature discusses this conflict between morals and personal economic interest of the medical profession (Döhler, 1993; Freidson, 1970, 1986, 1990; L. Hancock, 1999; Lupton and Najman, 1995; Rodwin, 2011; Saks, 1995; Starr, 1982).

In the public health sector there is no profession that is as comparable and influential as the medical profession in the health care sector (Potvin and McQueen, 2007, 15). The most important professional actors are public health doctors, but also engineers who are specialized in areas related to health and sanitation (Carline and Patterson, 2003; Starr, 2009). In addition, many authors have argued that community action is important with regard to public health policies. They refer to the capacity to organize local support for public health policies by interest groups and professions (Chapman and Wakefield, 2001; Givel, 2007; Nathanson, 2007; Princen, 2007).

The discussed argument implies that in countries where professions are politicized and interest groups compete in pluralist arenas for political influence, there should be responsiveness between actors from the health care and public health sectors. Regarding policy issues without strong interest conflicts (public funds), we can expect to find discourse coalitions and other forms of cooperation regarding policy issues, for example, concerning tobacco advertising restrictions. These expectations apply to Australia, United Kingdom, and the United States. To the contrary, in countries with less politicized professions and corporatist forms of interest intermediation, we ought to find no or little responsiveness between policy sectors' organizations and actors and conflicts should be the prevailing form of interaction.

3.2.3 Unified Government in Health Care and Public Health

The second hypothesis (H2) accounts for the degree of the unification of government, especially whether a country is a federal state and if there are many veto points in government. This implies, for the coevolution of the health care and the public health sectors, that distinctiveness of both sectors is more likely to occur in countries with a fragmented government, such as in federal states, and/or countries with many institutional veto points, such as multiparty governments or a presidential political system.

The literature on health care as well as public health has emphasized the importance of veto points and federalism. Regarding health care, political scientists have argued that veto points are an important factor that explains to what extent governments are able to pass far-reaching reforms such as cost-containment programs (Hacker, 2004a, 2004b, 2005). Other authors have insisted that institutional veto points, for instance, divided government, impact health policy outputs rather than the medical profession's strength (Immergut, 1990, 1992). Other researchers have underlined the importance of veto players in parliament and the distance between them for the understanding of health care reforms, taking Switzerland as an example (Braun and Uhlmann, 2009). In federal countries, such as Germany, Switzerland, or the United States (Watts, 2008), divided government comes along with federalism. This understanding of federalism emphasizes the retarding effect of federal systems on policymaking. If federalism and many veto points are so highly correlated, why is it then necessary to take into consideration both elements? The answer is that some federal countries have more nationalized policy regimes, such as national unemployment insurance or fiscal powers, than others (Hueglin and Fenna, 2006).[5] Therefore, institutional unification is possible despite the presence of federalism.

The literature on public health has emphasized the importance of veto points and federalism. One finding is that a strong (or unified) government makes it more likely that public health policies can be passed easily (Nathanson, 1996, 2007; Mackenbach and McKee, 2013). Others have underlined that the more veto points exist in the political system, the more difficult it is to pass public health policies because powerful interest groups have more venues to voice their opposition (Mayes and Oliver, 2012). Regarding federalism, some authors have argued that, due to the general separation of powers in federal countries, competences for social policies are likely to be separated or shared between levels of government, which might lead to more policy innovations regarding public health at the subnational level, but impede reforms at the national level (Shipan and Volden, 2008; Trein, 2017b).

Regarding the coupling of health care and public health, these considerations imply that there should be distinctiveness between both sectors in countries with divided government. Due to separated competences between levels of government, many veto points, or multiparty governments, it is more likely that both sectors are institutionally separated from one another. Health care and public health are therefore more likely to be organized in different ministries or at different levels of government. For example, a possible scenario would be that public health departments are at the level of subgovernments and health insurance and public hospital administration in the discretion of the national governments.

Table 3.1 shows the implications of the argument for the coupling of the health care and the public health sectors. Thereby, unified government comes along with the absence of institutional distinctiveness of both sectors. Transferred to the relation of the two sectors under study here, this means that institutions that are commonly associated with the health care sector, such as health insurance administration or the subsidies thereof, are regulated on one level of government, such as subnational governments. Institutions that belong to the public health sector, such as public health departments, are connected to another level of government, such as the national government.

If health professions are politicized and there is a pluralist interest intermediation, responsiveness of sectors should be high. This means for the example of the health care and the public health sectors that professions from both sectors, such as medical doctors and public health doctors, learn from one another (in the sense of policy and political learning), form discourse coalitions, are politically active, and advocate for the positions and problems of the other sector. This occurs not only for selfish reasons but also because professions need to merit their legitimacy clout in the pluralist system of interest intermediation. Thus, doctors publicly advocate problems beyond their special interests, such as issues related to preventive health. In case health professions are less politicized and corporatist institutions of interest intermediation are present, conflicts are likely to be the main form of interaction between both sectors, instead of common advocacy and discourse coalitions. In these contexts, professions are more regulated and doctors and medical organizations – similar to

Table 3.1. *Professionalism, interest intermediation, type of government, and coupling of health care and public health.*

	Strong professionalization/Pluralist interest intermediation	Weak professionalization/Corporatist interest intermediation
	(I) Loosely coupled:	**(II) Decoupled:**
Fragmented government	Public health (i.e., public health departments) and health care (i.e., administration of health insurance, hospitals, pharmaceutical regulation) institutions and organizations likely to be vertically and/or horizontally separated	Public health (i.e., public health departments) and health care (i.e., administration of health insurance, hospitals, pharmaceutical regulation) institutions and organizations likely to be vertically and/or horizontally separated
	Professions (medical and public health doctors) and interest groups (health foundations, health insurance) probably learn from, communicate with, or support the other sector and form a discourse coalition	Professions (medical and public health doctors) and interest groups (health foundations, health insurance) actors do not learn from, communicate with, or support the other sector and there is no discourse coalition
	Policy integration of curative and preventive policies (e.g., with regard to risk factors, such as alcohol and tobacco, but also diseases, for instance, cancer or diabetes) possible	Policy integration of curative and preventive policies (e.g., with regard to risk factors, such as alcohol and tobacco, but also diseases, for instance, cancer or diabetes) very unlikely

Table 3.1. (*cont.*)

	Strong professionalization/Pluralist interest intermediation	Weak professionalization/Corporatist interest intermediation
	(III) Tightly coupled:	**(IV) Noncoupled:**
Unified government	Public health (i.e., public health departments) and health care (i.e., administration of health insurance, hospitals, pharmaceutical regulation) institutions and organizations likely to be vertically and horizontally unified Professions (medical and public health doctors) and interest groups (health foundations, health insurance) probably learn from, communicate with, or support the other sector and form a discourse coalition Policy integration of curative and preventive policies (e.g., with regard to risk factors, such as alcohol and tobacco, but also diseases, for instance, cancer or diabetes) likely	Public health (i.e., public health departments) and health care (i.e., administration of health insurance, hospitals, pharmaceutical regulation) institutions and organizations likely to be vertically and horizontally unified Professions (medical and public health doctors) and interest groups (health foundations, health insurance) do not learn from, communicate with, or support the other sector and there is no discourse coalition Policy integration of curative and preventive policies (e.g., with regard to risk factors, such as alcohol and tobacco, but also diseases, for instance, cancer or diabetes) unlikely

other interest groups – do not need to earn their legitimacy clout by demonstrating that they are interested in more than their own special interests.

Another form of responsiveness that should occur in case of high professionalism is policy integration, i.e., the integration of policy instruments of both policy sectors, such as integrated strategies that combine curative and preventive elements, for example, to combat infectious diseases and noncommunicable illnesses. Due to the – possibly – broad support by private interest groups, integration of health care and public health policies becomes more likely. Institutional unification of both sectors should reinforces this effect as the common institutional framework makes the coordination of public actors more likely.

3.2.4 Contextual Elements in Health Care and Public Health

So far, I have discussed the implications of my argument with a focus on the horizontal relation between health care and public health. Yet, coevolution also has a temporal dimension and it is therefore necessary to account for time dynamics as well. According to the previously discussed hypotheses, coupling of sectors might change over time if the structure of government or professionalism change.

In addition, I propose a third hypothesis that takes into consideration contextual elements. Up to now, I have not specified these elements in detail because this needs to be done with regard to a specific policy problem in mind. Concerning the coevolution of health care and public health, three dimensions are important if we want to understand the relationship between these two sectors, notably how they are coupled.

- *Problem pressure and ideas:* To understand the evolution of health policy over a long time period, it is necessary to account for changing patterns in diseases as well as changing general ideas about health policy. The pattern of disease prevalence significantly changed between the late nineteenth and the early twenty-first centuries. Infectious diseases were the most pressing health problem in the late nineteenth century. This changed during the twentieth century toward more noncommunicable diseases, such as cancer and diabetes (especially in developed democracies) (Baum, 2008; Rosenbrock and Gerlinger, 2014; Tulchinsky and Varavikova, 2009). Depending on the prevalent type of diseases, we should expect different priorities concerning health policy. In case infections are the most important problem, coordination and integration of preventive and curative measures should be much higher on the agenda of policymakers than if noncommunicable diseases are the most salient issue. Consequently, policymakers should develop different ideas – in the sense of problem solutions – for these two scenarios.

- *Technology:* The second important contextual element is technological developments. These can be new arms, new medicine, or capacities to gain knowledge and information regarding the consequences of certain actions (Bijker, 2006). The development of drugs and medical equipment is a very important contextual factor in the coevolution of health care and public health. For instance, with new medical technologies the cure of some diseases becomes possible, which before could only be prevented (Rosen, 1993 [1959]; Porter, 1999). This might entirely change the priority of health policymaking with regard to the relationship of the health care and public health sectors. Notably, the combination of health care and public health policies might become less necessary.
- *Economic and fiscal development:* Another contextual element that might be important for the analysis of the coevolution of the health care and the public health sectors is the economy. The literature on health care emphasizes that the economic situation of a country is an important factor for health policymaking (Hacker, 1998; Feldstein, 2011). Regarding the relations between the health care and the public health sectors, this finding implies that in case of economic hardship when budgets of governments are tight, conflicts between both sectors become more likely. In this case, high professionalization and strong professional organizations might come along with strong conflicts between private organizations regarding the distribution of tax money.

In order to introduce context in the argument, this book combines these three contextual elements. Specifically, there are two conditions that specify the conditional effect of context as formulated in the third hypothesis: First, a favorable context for responsiveness between policy sectors and second, a less favorable context for sectorial responsiveness.

1. *Context favors responsiveness (Cx):* The first condition refers to a favorable context for sectorial responsiveness. This can be the case due to problem pressure, such as the prevalence of a new infection or rising cancer rates, and ideas that create a demand for the coordination of health care and public health. The lack of technical – respectively pharmaceutical – means is another contextual condition that might create a demand for more integration. Eventually, if the economic and fiscal context does not impose cost-containment pressures on policymakers, it is less likely that conflicts will break out between the two sectors' actors.

2. *Context does not favor responsiveness (Cy):* The second condition refers to a less favorable context for responsiveness between sectors. In this case, the problem pressure, namely the most important disease pattern that needs to be addressed, does not create a demand for policy integration – for instance, because noncommunicable diseases are the most prevalent problem. At the same time, if the medical and pharmaceutical context allows for the cure of the most important diseases, prevention is not as important and consequently reduces the demand for responsiveness between the sectors. Eventually, in times of economic slump or fiscal retrenchment, distributional conflicts are likely to occur between the actors of the two policy sectors.

These two conditions are not mutually exclusive. There could be a contextual condition that favors sectorial responsiveness, such as a disease problem pressure that needs to be addressed by a combination of preventive and curative measures. Yet, at the same time the fiscal and economic situation could be difficult and therefore lead to conflicts between both sectors. Some of the discussed contextual elements should be strongly correlated, especially the problem pressure and ideas as well as the technological context. It is nonetheless important to consider both elements as they might cause responsiveness between policy sectors in different ways and for different reasons. How they play out exactly remains to be seen in the following empirical chapters.

Figure 3.1 combines the two contextual conditions with unified government, professionalism, and corporatist institutions, although the figure mentions only professionalism for the sake of

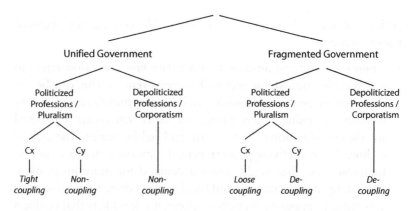

Figure 3.1 Overview of the argument.

comprehensiveness. The crucial point of the argument is that to achieve responsiveness of policy sectors, stakeholders need to recognize contextual pressures that hold the existing policy monopolies in order to appear on the political agenda (Baumgartner and Jones, 2009, 27). In the case of high professionalism and pluralistic interest intermediation, professional organizations ought to play an important role in defining the agenda concerning the relationship of health care and public health. If the problem under observation does not entail substance for conflicts between professions, for example, regarding distribution of resources, this should lead to responsiveness between sectors because private actors will cooperate to politicize issues. However, if professionalism is low and corporatist institutions of interest intermediation are present, professional organizations are not important for politicizing the problem, which will be done by other actors, such as political parties. Professional organizations will mostly serve as arenas for scientific debates, but they will not be important for the politicization of health problems. There will therefore be little visible cooperation for certain activities, such as agenda setting.

The figure shows the same links as those discussed in the prior section, namely that low professionalism and corporatist interest intermediation lead to noncoupling of sectors when co-occurring with unified government and to decoupling in combination with fragmented government. If professionalism is high and interest intermediation pluralistic, there will be responsiveness and consequently tight or loose coupling. However, this depends on the context. In the case of Cx, context is favorable to cooperation between actors and will lead to responsiveness. If Cy is present, there will be conflicts due to shortage of resources. With responsiveness present, policy integration also becomes more likely, especially in the case of the unified government. In case of low professionalism, context does not matter because professional organizations do not play an important role in the politicization of problems in health policy. Consequently, there will be no responsiveness between private actors regarding health care and public health. Problems enter the political arenas by other actors, such as political parties. Policy integration of health care and public health is still possible but less likely because problems are more politicized from a sectorial perspective. This is an unfavorable situation, especially from the perspective of public health, because it lacks the professional support from organizations for doctors, which is an important counterweight to the strong target groups in this sector.

3.3 Summary

This chapter presented the theoretical background of this book's argument. Notably, I argue that if a country has a unified government, the health care and public health sectors should be relatively and organizationally unified institutionally whereas in case of a fragmented government, disctinctiveness of policy sectors is more likely. The reason for this is that in countries with unified governments, there are fewer veto players and levels of government and therefore the departments and institutions belonging to each sector are more likely to stick together. Whether there will be responsiveness in the sense of common political advocacy of private actors and professions of both sectors depends on professionalism and institutions of interest intermediation in the society. Politicized professions and pluralist institutions of interest intermediation should come along with the presence of responsiveness between sectors, e.g., of professional organizations and interest groups. In countries with politicized professions, professional organizations play an important political role, above all because they need to protect their members' interests in politics. Thus, they support issues beyond their special interests to gain additional legitimacy clout, for example, the medical profession should actively campaign for public health issues.

If professional freedom is low, on the other hand, health professions are less politicized and corporatist institutions of interest intermediation are present; professional organizations are not as important for politicizing problems beyond their special interests, and therefore sectoral responsiveness is absent. Professional organizations in these cases are forums of scientific conflicts between health professions, but the politicization of health policy problems that are beyond professions' narrow special interests occurs with other actors, such as political parties, although whether strong professionalism actually leads to responsiveness depends on contextual factors, especially since professions are prone to conflicts, particularly around distributional issues that might touch upon the interests of their members, i.e., to defend free doctoral practice.

Therefore, this book argues that it is necessary to supply a introduce contextual conditions into for the argument, namely the differential between two contextual conditions: one that is favorable to sectorial responsiveness and a second one which is not. In the former, problem pressure and medical technology make the coordination and integration of both sectors necessary. In the latter, the opposite is the case, and there might only be distributional conflicts between the professional organizations of the two sectors. Only if the context is favorable and professionalism is high can we expect responsiveness between policy sectors. There might otherwise be conflicts and responsiveness should be absent. Furthermore, without strong professionalism, context does not matter all that much because professions do not play an important role in politicizing important problems.

4 | Global Context and Case Selection

This chapter discusses the historical context for the case studies, justifies the country selection, and presents the methods of analysis. To manage the historical analysis, I define four time periods, each of which has different contextual elements with different implications for the following case studies. The first time period (t0) covers the years between 1880 and 1918, when health care and public health emerged as two different policy sectors. The second time period (t1) focuses on the time frame between 1918 and 1945. In the interwar period, the main theme was the competition between health care and public health. A third time period (t2) covers the years between 1945 and 1980, which entail the establishment of individual health care. Along with the increase of the welfare state services and economic development, facilities of individual health care expanded enormously. Time period four (t3) spans the years 1980 to 2010, during which new policy challenges, such as new infections and noncommunicable diseases, returned to the agenda of health policy and created a demand for more integrated solutions of health care and public health. In the second part of this chapter, I justify why I focus on five countries, namely Australia, Germany, Switzerland, the United Kingdom, and the United States. The main criteria for selecting these nations is that the countries differ regarding their condition of unified government and professionalization of health professions. Then, I present briefly the operationalization and the sources – secondary literature, documents, and interviews – as well as the method of data analysis for the comparative case studies.

4.1 Emergence of Health Care and Public Health as Two Policy Sectors (1880–1918)

In order to understand the economic, social, and technological context of the coevolution of the health care and the public health sectors,

59

I start my analysis in the second half of the nineteenth century. This is the time when modern states began to take concrete forms and to differentiate policy sectors, such as the health care and the public health sectors.[1] During this time, public health policy instruments were very important to respond to the most pressing health problems. Thus, public health legislation entailed the creation of boards – and later on departments – of health, in the beginning mostly at the local and state or regional level. These institutions were responsible for the implementation of sanitary reforms, such as laws concerning food safety, building of sewages, provision of clean water, regulation of medical degrees, planning of hospitals, bacteriological interventions, programs to improve the physical condition of the entire nation, medical inspection of children, and hygiene education for the general population. In addition, infrastructure for the provision of individual health care was developed and improved (Tulchinsky and Varavikova, 2009, 40; Baum, 2008; Leeder, 2007).

Many of the public policy interventions that occurred at this time entailed preventive measures in order to stop rampant epidemics and infectious diseases. The idea of community health, which reappeared in the 1970s in order to integrate health care and public health policies, had emerged around the turn of the twentieth century and included health care and public health measures. It referred to emergency treatment by doctors as well as health counseling, but centered on a doctor and a patient in a more hierarchical way. However, it included preventive work of nonmedical personnel as well. Yet, most of the curative services were provided by doctors on a fee for service basis (M. Lewis, 2003a). At the time, state- run public health services were a good option for doctors to find paid work, because in most cases there was no health insurance paying for individuals' treatment and thereby ensuring payment of physicians (Alber and Bernardi Schenkluhn, 1992). The long economic crisis in the late nineteenth century made this effect even stronger (Capie and Wood, 1997). Public health services provided health counseling and planned population health programs, but they also registered and isolated cases of dangerous infectious diseases and they became the origin for the development of public health professionals with different interests from the medical profession (Porter, 1999).

As this book will discuss in the following case studies, professional politics and health policymaking differed among countries. At this stage it is important to consider the contextual factors to which these policies responded during the first time period:

1. Infectious diseases and sanitary issues were urgent *health problems* in the second half of the nineteenth century and thus a key challenge for health policymakers. For instance, from 1817 to 1912 eight global pandemics of cholera hit the world and inspired public health legislation in many countries (M. Lewis, 2003a).

2. *Technological development* is an important factor, such as in this case, the availability of new and effective drugs and medical equipment. For instance, antibiotics were not yet available, which made finding a cure for some infectious diseases, such as tuberculosis, rather difficult. Advances in research occurred in the area of disease prevention and provided information for public health policies. Progress happened, for instance, in the field of epidemiology. Between 1881 and 1898 many significant pathogenous organisms were detected and isolated, which made it possible to counteract them with public health measures, such as typhus, lepta, malaria, tuberculosis, plague, and many others (Rosen, 1993 [1959]; Gottweis et al., 2004).Yet, research did also advance in areas that are important for health care. For instance, research on antiseptic products and methods improved the efficiency of surgical interventions (Tulchinsky and Varavikova, 2009, 41–42).

3. As a consequence, *ideas* regarding health policy emphasized the importance of prevention as well as the integration of health care and public health. That this time period was also one of nation building enhanced the focus on population health even more. Emerging modern states wanted to improve the health of their fast growing population in order that it would be was fit for modernization and economization as well as competition with other nations. Ideas such as vitality, efficiency, purity, and virtue of the nation – rather than the individual – were important and needed well-organized public health policies, whereas health care for the individual was not yet the most important concern (Baum, 2008). The focus of health policies on the health of the nation and its fitness for the competition with other countries pointed to the importance of the collective rather than the individual in health policy.

The implications of these contextual conditions on the expected relationship of health care and public health is as follows. Due to the pressing problem of infectious diseases and the lack of medical and pharmaceutical technology, the context is favorable to public health policies, but also to responsiveness and unification of health care and public health policies. What is more, the importance of nationalistic ideas should enhance the contextual demand in a way that was favorable to the integration of both sectors.

Contextual condition t0: During t0, the context is favorable for responsiveness and unification of health care and public health, due to the prevalence of infectious diseases and limited medical and pharmaceutical development.

4.2 The Turn Toward Individual Health Care (1918–1945)

The second contextual sequence concerning the coevolution of health care and public health can be dated to the end of the First World War. This makes sense for two reasons: First, the end of the war marked a turn in the demands for health policies, as the war showed that it is important to pursue population health policies in a directed, more individual-based manner. What is more, at the time, some countries had already established comprehensive health insurance programs, which set the stage for interactions and possible conflicts and cooperation between the two sectors.

The turn toward individual health policy began with the establishment of national health insurance programs that were created in many countries, beginning in Germany in 1883; followed by England in 1911 (Porter, 1999), and France in 1930 (Alber and Bernardi Schenkluhn, 1992), for example In Switzerland, a very limited national health insurance law was put into place, in 1911, after a legislative proposal that followed the German model had failed in a popular vote (Uhlmann and Braun 2011) (cf. Chapter 8). The introduction of comprehensive health policies failed in other countries and was postponed to later periods in time, such as in Australia (M. Lewis, 2003b) and the United States (Schild, 2003).[2] National health insurance plans signal the increasing importance of health care policy as they institutionalize financial support for individual health care and a shift of attention from population-based and preventive policies to more curative health policies. Consequently, this bore the potential for significant conflicts between the two sectors, respectively administrators and professional actors.

Yet, public health remained an important part of health policies in many respects during that time. For instance, preventive care for women and children emerged in the late nineteenth century and expanded during the early twentieth century. Public health officials discovered the necessity to expand preventive services to needy and poor groups, which were often women and children, in order to respond to the negative health effects of poor living conditions, bad general hygiene, lack of prenatal care, and scarce nutrition (Tulchinsky and Varavikova, 2009, 44). Public health policies began to change though, as policymakers adapted results of health research, especially bacteriology. Disease specific and restricted interventions were already carried out in the early twentieth century to reduce the prevalence of infections. Some members of the public health profession opposed these policies, for instance, representatives of the Progressive Movement in the United States, who preferred structural interventions to improve public health, such as the improvement of housing and schooling (Porter, 1999).

During the interwar period, governments increased health care as well as public health policies at the national level. With the establishment of the League of Nations, founders also created a League of Nations Health Organization, which attempted to help with the implementation of population health measures in the participating countries (Weindling, 2002, 2006).[3] In addition, the organization carried out and supported cross-national studies concerning population health (Rosen, 1993 [1959]).

With regard to contextual elements that led to the mentioned political situation, specifically the following points are important to keep in mind in order to understand the interwar period.

1. *Health problems:* As in the previous period, between 1918 and 1945, infectious diseases still were amongst the most urgent health problems. Tuberculosis especially was a major issue for health policies in the first half of the twentieth century. The sickness had been present since the early nineteenth century; however, it had been less visible because of infant mortality from gut infections, smallpox, and other pandemics. Once these diseases were under control in the late nineteenth century, tuberculosis became more visible and subject to health policies. Finding a cure was difficult and, consequently, health policymakers focused mainly on pre-

venting tuberculosis infections using instruments of public health policies (Porter, 1999, 282; Dubos, 1987; Rosenkrantz, 1994).

2. *Technological development:* The development of new anti-bacteriological technologies continued to advance during the interwar period. Major breakthroughs that helped to control some of the most important public health problems had already been in effect before the First World War. However, a cure for other diseases, such as tuberculosis, was not yet possible. Therefore, infectious diseases remained at the top of the health policy agenda at the time. The development of antibiotics, such as penicillin, did not occur prior to the mid-1940s (Tulchinsky and Varavikova, 1996, 44). The continuing, but slow, improvement of pharmaceutical technologies improved the curability of diseases and enhanced the arguments of those who were in favor of more health care policies. Nevertheless, the demand for more public health policies remained important, due to the obvious shortcomings concerning the curability of certain infectious diseases.

3. *Ideas:* Ideas regarding health policies still focused on the fitness of the nation and the popular body. Especially after the First World War, many European governments sought to regain their strength as a nation. Therefore, it remained an important goal of health policy to improve the health of the entire population in order to keep it fit for competition with other European nations. Such policy ideas included racist policy ideas derived from eugenics (Weindling, 1989; Bashford and Levine, 2010). Subsequently, population-based measures, including medical inspection of children and hygiene education of the population had a high priority in health policy (Baum, 2008). At the same time, however, individual health care became more important and the voices of those who argued in favor of more services of this kind became louder. Consequently, in many countries there was a general conflict regarding the institutionalization of health policy between health care professionals supporting suggestions to establish national health services that would combine population- and individual-based measures and those supporting health insurance schemes, e.g., corporatist, market-based, or more state-centered health care plans (Porter, 1994).

4. *Economic crisis and the Second World War:* Apart from specific health problems, technological development, and ideas, crisis events played an important role for the relationship between the

two sectors. During t1, there were two events that potentially had an important impact on the relationship of policy sectors in general. First, the economic crisis of the 1930s had a significant impact on health policy. Demands for public health policies consequently increased and so did the demand of doctors to find employment in public health services because private practice became more difficult. However, in such times of economic hardship we can also expect to find politicized distributional conflicts between professions and other interest groups of both sectors, since some governments responded to the crisis with austerity policies (Eichengreen, 1992). Second, the war between 1939 and 1945 increased the demand for public health policies, above all to support military operations, but also to protect the population at home (Levy and Sidel, 1997). This implies, for the context of coupling of health care and public health, that war and economic crisis should decelerate the development toward more individual health care and keep public health on the political agenda of national governments.

The factors discussed show that the contextual conditions regarding the coupling of the health care and the public health sectors matter in two ways. First, due to the continuing importance of infectious diseases, the limited technological possibilities of curative medicine, and the public health situation in times of war, context should remain favorable to the demands of public health. On the other hand, the tight economic and fiscal situation, especially after the financial and economic crises in the 1920 and 1930s, is likely to create distributional conflicts among the actors of the two sectors.

Contextual condition t1a: During t1, infectious diseases, limited medical technology, and the war situation should create a demand for sectorial responsiveness and unification.

Contextual condition t1b: During t1, the difficult economic and fiscal situation should lead to conflicts between actors of the two policy sectors.

4.3 Dominance of Medical Care and Marginalization of Public Health (1945–1975)

After the Second World War, the relationship between health care and public health changed. In many countries, health policymakers began to focus on individual cure of sick patients, leaving population-based measures to the side, or only employing them in an ad hoc and secondary manner. As a consequence of the medical turn in health policy, preventive health policies often occurred in the form of individual counseling, for instance, by doctors.

Thus, in the aftermath of the Second World War, health care entailed the development of more and more sophisticated medical services, for instance, an increase in the numbers of hospital beds as well as pharmaceutical services, clinical care, and the transplantation of organs. The rationale behind these policies has been labeled the biomedical paradigm, which understands health policy as the need to cure sick bodies of individual patients (J. Lewis, 1999, 154). On the contrary, public health played a marginal role compared to health care (Baum, 1998). The evolution of health expenditures into individual care and prevention illustrates this point. In comparing OECD average numbers from 1970 to 2015, we see that there is a large difference in what has been spent for policies focused on sickness compared to expenditure dealing with health hazards (Figure 4.1) or, to put

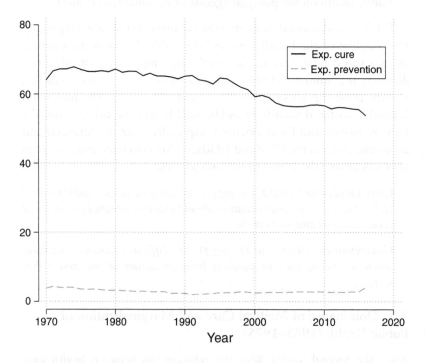

Figure 4.1 Expenditure on prevention and cure I (percentage of health expenditure, OECD average).

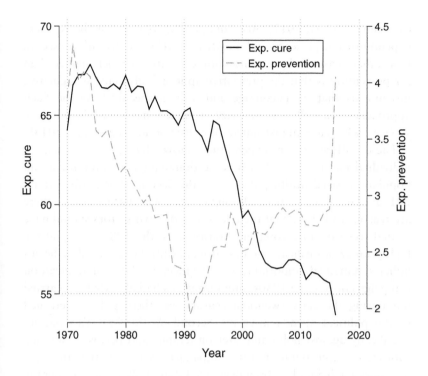

Figure 4.2 Expenditure on prevention and cure II (percentage of health expenditure).

it differently, a large discrepancy between expenditure for curative medicine and for prevention.[4]

The graphs in Figures 4.1 and 4.2 show that from 1970 to 2015, the expenditure share for curative care decreased constantly. However, this was only partially at the expense of more preventive care. Expenditures for public health (preventive care in terms of the OECD) peaked in the 1970s, declined during the 1980s and began to increase again since then. This shows that public health expenditures are very sensitive to budgetary cycles and were cut first when the period of budgetary austerity began in the 1980s. Similarly, in the post-2007 recession, governments in many OECD countries reduced expenses for preventive care again (Morgan and Astolfi, 2015), and increased them again thereafter. Other expenses related to health are those for pharmaceutical products and long-term care, which are not shown here. Both – especially expenditure for long-term care – have increased over time (OECD, 2017). According to the logic of this book, these expenditure categories would mostly be part of the health care sector. One other reason why expenses for care are so much higher than for prevention is that the preventive approach also entails regulative instruments that try encourage and force a specific behavior. Such approaches naturally do not cost as much money as health care services, which are an instrument of redistribution (Levi-Faur, 2014).

These differences in expenditure show that the approach of individual curative care has become dominant over preventive and population-based health policy since the Second World War (Trein, 2017a). This remains true, although – as I will discuss later – there are reasons to believe that the relation of the two sectors should have shifted toward more complementarity since the 1980s. Despite the high priority of medical care in national health policies, public health policies remained important, for instance, by large immunization campaigns during the 1950s. Immunizations had already been carried out during the early twentieth century, yet these policies returned to the political agenda after the Second World War. Vaccination, specifically against polio and later on tetanus and pertussis, was the subjects of large public health campaigns because at that time the necessary medicines had been developed (Baum, 2008, 27). Generally speaking, the dominance of health care over public health is related to the following contextual elements:

1. During and immediately after the Second World War, there were important *technological developments* regarding health policy, namely pharmaceutical technologies. Researchers developed more effective drugs, particularly antibiotics, penicillin and streptomycin, which later on became powerful tools to treat infectious diseases. As a consequence, many communicable diseases, such as tuberculosis, could be cured (Shield et al., 2009; Eckart, 2011). Another result of the progress in technological development was the development of vaccinations for dangerous infections, such as immunization against polio (Tulchinsky and Varavikova, 2009). These pharmaceutical innovations allowed for the curing of more diseases, but also shifted public health even further toward individualist approaches and therefore under the umbrella of individual health care. At the same time, new options became available for public health itself, such as fluoridation of drinking water.

2. *Health problems:* Due to 100 years of public health policymaking (approximately 1850–1950) and new medication, infectious diseases, which had been the most pressing health problem for centuries, suddenly no longer posed a major problem because they could, in many cases, be cured (Rosen, 1993 [1959]; McKeown, 1979; Haines, 2001; Tulchinsky and Varavikova, 2009; Nathanson, 2007). Longer lives, however, came along with higher prevalence of other diseases related to longevity, notably cancer, stroke, and diabetes. These diseases were known before, but had been less important since the risk of dying from an infection was much greater. Once infections could be cured, the importance of the classical "preventive approach" lost in importance compared to curative medicine (Baum, 2008).

3. *Economic development:* The economic development is another quite important factor regarding the relationship of health care and public health in the postwar period that boosted the dominance of individual health care. This was a time of unprecedented economic growth, especially in Western democracies. Consequently, governments had the option to increasingly invest in individual health services and hospitals, which institutionalized the more prominent position of health care compared to public health, and made medical practice attractive to many individuals (Fee, 1994; Baum, 2008).

4. In this period, *ideas* about social policy changed profoundly, which also had an impact on the relation of health care and public health. Along with unprecedented economic growth, the postwar era was a time of welfare state enlargement and in many countries the range of social policies increased greatly in terms of benefits and recipients. Furthermore, the stronger focus on individualism in many policies opposed to communitarian ideas favored the dominance of the health care sector, particularly in "Western liberal democracies" (Castles et al., 2010). "Communist autocracies," on the other hand, created huge national health services, which unified individual health care and public health policies institutionally, although they also evolved toward a greater focus on medicine opposed to nonmedical health policies, for instance, in the Soviet Union or the GDR (Tulchinsky and Varavikova, 1996; M. Schmidt, 2004). This development of health policy in the former Soviet states led to opposition against public health policies, notably

population-based measures, in some Western countries (Fee, 1994). Nevertheless, public health gained importance at the international level. The foundation of the WHO in 1948 was the starting point to lift prevention, control of communicable diseases, and social medicine to the international level (WHO, 1953). Although national health policies in Western democracies focused on health care development and the improvement of individuals' quality of life, the WHO continued to keep the focus on public health measures, which were still very important for less developed countries.

Contextual condition t2: During t2, new medical technology, the success of prior public health policies, and the cold war competition between political systems reduced the demand for sectorial unification, including policy integration.

4.4   The Long Return of Public Health (1974–2010)

In the postwar period, health care and public health diverged. However, the landscape of health policies began to change again in the mid-1970s. Prevention and population-based interventions returned to the focus of health policy because the focus on individual health care was not able to cope with the problems that "diseases of affluence" posed for health care. These typically included noncommunicable illnesses that occurred due to behavioral factors such as smoking, drinking, and unhealthy diets (M. Lewis, 2003b).

Public health returned to the political agenda in 1974. One of the most influential documents in this regard was the Lalonde Report for the Canadian government in 1974, where the minister for health demanded the inclusion of individual and population-based policies in national health policymaking and that individual health care should only be one element among others to influence good health (Lalonde, 1974; T. Hancock, 1986). Other countries, especially in the Anglo-Saxon world, published similar documents, such as the "Life: Be in it" (1975) campaign in Australia. Other countries, such as the United States and the United Kingdom, followed (Baum, 2008). Concerning the provision of health, the first new public health efforts, especially community health programs, were put into place. Consequently, in the 1980s and 1990s, health policymakers began to pass public health policies concerning lifestyle factors, such as tobacco, alcohol, and later on obesity, and the focus of health policy shifted from the individual to the collective level (healthy cities, schools, worksites, hospitals) (Hunter, Marks, and Smith, 2010). In the 1980s, disease-focused programs increased with the return of infectious diseases, especially the AIDS epidemic, and gave rise to public health in the domain of infectious diseases (Baum, 2008).

The renewed focus on public health has also been labeled *new public health*. It denotes the renewed focus on population health policies, which included lifestyle-related risk factors, such as tobacco and excessive drinking, as health problems along with the response to new epidemiological problems, such as AIDS. The term *new public health* was formulated in the 1980s in order to distinguish the "new" public health policies at the time from old public health, which mostly focused on quarantine regulations, programs for immunization, clean water, and safe food legislation (Baum, 2008). New public health added elements such as environmental health and health promotion. One of the main proponents of this new paradigm in public health was the World Health Organization (WHO) that evaluated its member states and demanded more preventive health policies (WHO, 2000, 2002). Since the 1970s, there was a series of milestones of reports, international activities, strategies, and treatments with regard to encompassing health policies that included prevention and disease treatment. In the 1970s, it was the abovementioned Lalonde Report and the WHO Alma Ata Declaration of 1978. In the 1980s, goals and targets concerning "health for all" were established in Europe and North America, including behavioral risk factor programs. In the 1980s, the milestone was the Ottawa Charter for Health Promotion, the launch of the European Healthy Cities Programs and the Adelaide Statement on Healthy Public Policy. In the 1990s, there was the 1991 Sundsvall Health Promotion Conference (1991), the UN's Rio Earth Summit Agenda 21, the Global Health Cities Program, and the Jakarta Conference on Health Promotion, in 1997. In 2004, the FCTC (Framework Convention on Tobacco Control) treaty passed, which commits signing members to increase tobacco control policy (Orme et al., 2003; Baum, 2008). In 2013, a global action plan against noncommunicable diseases was passed (WHO, 2013a).

Consequently, the context for health policy changed again. Disease pressures, health policy ideas, and the economic and fiscal context

changed in a way that created a more favorable context for the
coordination and integration of health care and public health.

1. *Health problems:* There are two important factors with health
   problems that help us to understand the shift in the health policy
   agenda. First, there is the increasing importance of noncommunicable diseases that are caused by lifestyle and the return of infectious
   diseases. Beginning in the 1970s, the prevalence of noncommunicable diseases became increasingly clear. Cancer rates that are related
   to lifestyle causes peaked in the 1970s, especially lung cancer, which
   could easily be addressed by tobacco control policies. The development of other kinds of cancer and different noncommunicable
   diseases, has, however, been an increasing problem since the 1970s
   (OECD, 2017). Second, with the advent of AIDS, epidemic diseases
   returned to the agenda of health policies and shifted the focus
   back to public health. New forms of infectious diseases, such as
   SARS and HNV1, but also fears of bioterrorism and the increasing
   occurrence of bacteria that are resistant to antibiotics, such as new
   tuberculosis bacteria, are part of this development that put the
   focus back on communicable diseases (Tulchinsky and Varavikova,
   2009; WHO, 2013b).
2. *Ideas:* Ideas have been another important element concerning
   changing relations of health care and public health in the last
   thirty years. This concerns two levels of the analysis. First, since
   the 1980s, there has been a time of retrenchment in welfare state
   policies, which came along with at least a stagnation of social
   expenditure and budget consolidation in the 1990s. However, most
   countries did not significantly reduce their health expenditures,
   certainly not in the sense of investing less in clinical care and at
   the same time more in preventive and collective services (Wagschal
   and Wenzelburger, 2008; OECD, 2017); however, the cost of health
   policy, especially health care, became a topic of public discourses
   (Baum, 2008, 29). Second, critical voices about the role of medicine
   became louder. Several authors, most of them doctors, suggested,
   already since the 1970s, that it is necessary to develop a new
   medical model, which not only encompasses the aspect of treating
   existing diseases in a clinical face-to-face intervention, but also
   includes psychological and social factors in relation to patient,

doctor, and disease (Adler, 2009; Fava and Sonino, 2008; McLaren, 1998; Herman, 1989; Schwartz, 1977, 1982; Engel, 1977, 1978, 1980). At this time, these authors demanded the inclusion of the behavioral and social dimension into the education of doctors and nurses, the research of medical systems, and modes and types of treatment (Engel, 1980; Kleinman, 1978).

3. *Economic and fiscal development:* From an economic and fiscal perspective, the context also changed for health policymakers. Beginning in the 1970s, when the oil crises brought constant economic growth to an end and public budgets began to become tighter, there was also an impact on health policy (Pierson, 2001; Korpi and Palme, 2003). Also in the early 1970s, many governments sought to reform the health care sector in order to contain costs, especially for medical treatment. One element of these reforms was the reduction in hospital capacities, but also reforms of hospital financing. As of the 1980s, governments began to reduce capacities in hospitals (OECD, 2017), but tried also to rationalize treatment by introducing DRG programs that aimed to reduce the costs of individual care (Rothgang, 2010), especially in countries where health expenditure continued to rise (Weisbrod, 1991; Braun and Uhlmann, 2009; Gilardi, Füglister, and Luyet, 2009).

As a consequence, the contextual condition changed to be more favorable for public health policymaking as well as the responsiveness, coordination, and integration of both sectors.

Contextual condition t3: During t3, pressure of health problems, experiences with health policy, and the fiscal and economic development made the context more favorable for responsiveness and integration of health care and public health.

4.5 Implications for the Country Studies

The discussed theoretical conditions lead to expectations regarding the responsiveness and distinctiveness of the health care and public health sectors in various countries. The basic assumption is that – overall – context is more or less similar for all developed democracies, in each time period, and thus we can propose a condition regarding how favorable context is for responsiveness and integration for each time period, which can be applied to all five countries in the sample.

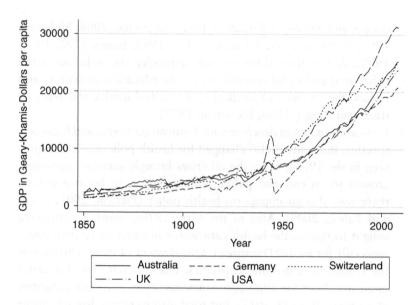

Figure 4.3 Development of GDP in selected countries.

It is reasonable to assume that in the long run, disease pressure adapts similarly across countries, for example, tuberculosis cases, as long as the absolute economic development is similar, which is the case for the countries selected for this study (Colgrove, 2002; McKeown, 1979) (see Figure 4.3).

During the first sequence, t0, health care and public health emerged as two different policy sectors. The contextual condition at that time was favorable to public health and the unification of both sectors. The reason for this was that infectious diseases were the most pressing health problem. At the same time, the possibilities that medical care provided to cure infections were limited. Eventually, this was a time period in which policymakers conceptualized policy interventions aiming at preparing the population for competition with other nations. During the second sequence, t1, the contextual condition regarding the relation of health care and public health changed slightly. Overall, context was still favorable for public health policymaking and the unification of both sectors; however, the economic situation worsened in the interwar period. Due to the long economic and fiscal crisis, we can expect distributional conflicts between the two sectors (Table 4.1).

Table 4.1. *Summary of contextual conditions of health care and public health.*

Sequence	Contextual elements	Contextual condition
t0 1850–1918	Infectious diseases very problematic, limited medical possibilities, competition of nations	Favorable to responsiveness and unification
t1 1918–1945	Infectious diseases still important, improved medical possibilities (immunization), competition of nations, economic crisis	Favorable and not favorable to responsiveness and unification
t2 1945–1970	Success of prior public health policies: infections under control, economic prosperity, public health associated with autocratic and Communist governments	Not favorable to responsiveness and unification
t3 1970–2010	Noncommunicable diseases, criticism of medical focus in health policy, end of economic growth and begin of budgetary austerity (especially in 1990s)	Favorable to responsiveness and unification

In the postwar period (t2), the contextual condition changed and became less favorable to policy integration. The main reason for this was the success of the public health policies that had been put into place as well as the milestones in medical development, especially during the 1940s. The latter permitted the development of cures for infections and immunization of the population. Another reason was the change in the ideational context during the postwar period in which some governments in Western Europe, North America, and Australasia associated public health policy with Communist ideas, because this had encompassing state governed health systems. Yet, the contextual condition changed again during the fourth sequence (t3) and became more favorable to public health policies and policy coordination and integration of the two sectors. One reason for this is that the pattern of disease changed toward more noncommunicable diseases, which are difficult to cure and need to be prevented, such as promoting nonsmoking. Another element that shifted the context for health policymaking was that many scholars criticized the prevalent medical model as focusing too much on individual medical care while neglecting sociological elements.

With these contextual premises in mind, the next sections will discuss the research design of the country studies, which form the main part of the empirical analysis in this book.

4.6 Case Selection for Country Studies

With the case studies, the research design of this book follows prominent authors in political science who pursue comparative historical analyses. According to Mahoney and Rueschemeyer (Mahoney and Rueschemeyer, 2003), comparative historical analyses have a long tradition in the social sciences. Works in the field focus on the evolution of welfare states (Esping-Andersen, 1990; Immergut, 1992; Huber and Stephens, 2001; Pierson, 2004), political economies (Thelen, 2004; Steinmo, 2010), state formation, and the emergence of democratic and authoritarian regimes, among other topics (Linz, 1996; Mahoney, 2001). Some of these authors have argued that comparative historical analyses are often used to tackle big questions in political science through comparative analyses of historical sequences (Tilly, 1984; Pierson, 2000, 2003), which allows for a careful tracing of causal mechanisms by analyzing a small number of cases in a contextualized manner (Mahoney and Rueschemeyer, 2003). This is a suitable approach since it is the goal of this book to improve our understanding of the historical development of sectorial coupling and coevolution.

This book combines historical analysis with concepts rooted in comparative public policy analysis. Public policy analysis often focuses on one specific policy, in a certain time period, or an important reform in a policy field (Fischer, Miller, and Sidney, 2006; Howlett, Ramesh, and Pearl, 2009; Knoepfel et al., 2011; Weimer and Vining, 2005). Thereby, agenda setting and decision-making processes are at the center of attention, including partisan influence (M. Schmidt, 1996) or broader actor constellations, such as advocacy coalitions (Sabatier, 1993). Oftentimes public policy analysis takes a comparative approach, such as a comparison of one or several policies in different countries or different policies in the same country (Dodds, 2012), frequently with the goal to promote learning between policymakers (Rose, 2004). The following analysis combines some of the actor-centered concepts of comparative public policy with a comparative historical analysis. This allows to forge a connection between professionalism, unified government, context, and the coupling of policy sectors at different analytical levels, namely actors, policies, and institutions over a long time period (Pontusson, 1995).

To carry out the country level analysis, this book proceeds with a comparative analysis of the coevolution of the health care and the public health sectors in Australia, Germany, Switzerland, the United States, and the United Kingdom. The selection of these countries follows a similar systems design (George and Bennett, 2005; Gerring, 2007). From the outset the comparative case study approach follows what Blatter has called a covariational approach. Ideally, this approach explains the variance in the outcome y based on the variation in the independent variable x, whereas some control variables are kept constant (Blatter and Blume, 2008; Blatter and Haverland, 2012). The selected countries are similar in the sense that they are developed democracies, OECD members, and followed similar paths in their evolution into modern states. They vary, however, in professionalism, institutions of interest intermediation, and unified government. Therefore, we can expect to find differences in the coupling of the health care and the public health sectors (Geddes, 2003).

According to the configurations of professionalism, interest group inclusion, and unification (strength) of government, we should find differences regarding the coupling of the health care and the public health sectors (see Table 1.1). The United States is a case of politicized health professions and pluralist interest intermediation on the one hand and fragmented government on the other (Henisz, 2000; Hall and Soskice, 2001; Macdonald, 1995, 66–99). Consequently, we can expect that there is loose coupling of the health care and the public health sectors. Switzerland has politically weak health professions and a corporatist form of interest group inclusion. In addition, government is fragmented and has many veto points (Vatter, 2014; Macdonald, 1995, 66–99; Hall and Soskice, 2001). Therefore, both sectors should be decoupled. To analyze a case of tight coupling, this book examines

Australia, because it displays a combination of unified government, i.e., a centralized federation (Painter, 2009), and high professionalism (Macdonald, 1995, 66–99) as well as pluralist interest intermediation (Hall and Soskice, 2001). To account for the fact that federalism is important, and there might be a difference between centralized federations and unitary countries (Hueglin and Fenna, 2006), we also include the United Kingdom in the analysis, which is a case of unified government, but also strong professionalism (Macdonald, 1995, 66–99) and pluralist interest intermediation (Hall and Soskice, 2001). I expect to find decoupling in both Australia and the United Kingdom. Finally, Germany combines low professionalism (Macdonald, 1995, 66–99) and corporatism with unified government (M. Schmidt, 2005a), because it is a centralized federation. Accordingly, there should be noncoupling of health care and public health.

I assume that contextual factors are similar for all countries. In other words, these countries became rich democracies during the twentieth century in contrast to non-OECD countries (Figure 4.3).[5]

The selected countries are also similar regarding the evolution of diseases. In a nutshell, along with these nations' economic development, infectious diseases became less visible in all five countries. At the same time, noncommunicable diseases increased, especially different forms of cancer. This chapter does not present the exact figures for each country regarding the evolution of diseases because the available statistics are not really comparable. Nevertheless, the trends are similar in all the countries under consideration in this book.[6]

4.7 Data, Operationalization, and Method

To examine the coevolution of the health care and the public health sectors, this book analyzes the institutional and organizational development of health policy, actor constellations, relationships between private actors of both sectors regarding the politicization of the other sector, and the coordinated and integrated policy output of both sectors over time. This allows me to trace the distinctiveness and responsiveness of the two policy sectors at the level of actors and institutions. This book examines the actor groups that are important to put the main issues of the policy sector on the political agenda and whether they belong to one of the two sectors. Furthermore, the analysis examines whether the actors of the two sectors are responsive to one another, for instance, if they support the other sector with regard to agenda setting or lobbying for specific issues or if they form a discourse coalition. Concerning the institutional level, I research if the main laws, jurisdictions and public sector organizations for health policy create distinctive institutional arenas. In addition, this book examines if the sectors are connected by common policies and policy programs that entail prevention and care in health policy or individual and population level approaches against certain diseases.

Table 4.1 shows the operationalization of distinctiveness and responsiveness more precisely and the specific indications used to understand the coupling of the health care and the public health sector, which were discussed in the previous chapters. This book examines distinctiveness and responsiveness of coupling in policy sectors. Distinctiveness is at issue if the health care and the public health sectors are located in different institutions, such as ministries or administrative units. Another indication of sectorial distinctiveness is if the sectors are located on different levels of government. Responsiveness analysis relies on qualitative information, more specifically, this book looks at whether private actors, such as professional organizations of both sectors are politically active and visible in the political process. If this is the case, and they are supportive of the problems of the other sector (especially if the medical profession supports public health policies), responsiveness is present. In contrast, if there are conflicts between both sectors' actor groups, responsiveness is absent. As far as policy integration is concerned, this analysis researches whether there are specific policies integrating both policy sectors, such as health strategies combining prevention and cure for cancer patients.

Despite the logically covariational approach to the case studies, the analysis focuses on the dependent variable, i.e., distinctiveness and responsiveness of health care and public health. The observation of the independent variables remains in the background of the analysis. To put it differently, the narrative accounts for changes in unified government, i.e., the de/centralization of legislative competences and veto points at the national level, conditions for health professions' and interest groups' political activity, and contextual changes are in the background of the analysis.

The main sources of information for this book are secondary literature and some documents that contain information concerning the relation of the two policy sectors to each other. Most important are, however, books and articles in scholarly journals. These are mostly works by historians, but also political scientists and public health scholars. In order to find these works, I conducted searches in catalogues of libraries and Internet search engines, using a series of keywords. Among these keywords were "public health," "public health policy," "health policy," "public health care," and "prevention" mostly in combination with one of the five country names (Australia, Germany, Switzerland, UK/England/Great Britain, US/United States). Respective equivalents were used in German such as "Gesundheitspolitik," "Öffentliche Gesundheit," and "Prävention" in order to find the essential books and articles for Germany and Switzerland. To select among the numerous articles and books retrieved by the search, the analysis focuses on those that mention public health policy in general and/or with regard to the historical development of public health or health care policies. Furthermore, articles on specific public health issues, such as tobacco control, were added to the analysis if they made a general contribution to public health policymaking in one of the countries or examined public health policymaking from a comparative perspective. Most of the journal articles could be accessed online and the necessary books for Europe and North America through interlibrary loan. I had the opportunity to access some additional books on Australia, that were not available in Europe, during a research stay at the National Library of Australia in Canberra.

The second source of information are semistructured expert interviews, which were conducted in the context of a research project by the Swiss National Science Foundation.[7] We conducted interviews with experts, interest groups, members of the administration, and policymakers. A detailed (anonymous) list of all interview partners and an example of the interview guidelines can be found in the appendix to this book. The interviews were thematically structured around two topics: public health and health care policy in general, and tobacco control policy.[8] The interviews were conducted on the basis of a guide with some basic questions/topics, which we shared beforehand with the interview partners when needed. We recorded the interviews and made a summary of the results with regard to the most important variables of this research project, namely distinctiveness and responsiveness of health care and public health as well as the importance of unified government and professionalism (Table 4.2).

Table 4.2. *Operationalization of key variables and sources.*

	Measures	Sources
Dependent variable (coupling of policy sectors; main focus of analysis)	*Distinctiveness:* events institutionalizing health care and public health (appendix). i.e., public health legislation, such as public health acts regarding food safety or quarantine, but also protection against risk factors. Health care legislation, for example, the establishment of a national health insurance or a national health service. *Presence of distinctiveness:* location of sectorial institutions in different ministries and administrative units and/or different levels of government. *Absence of distinctiveness:* sectorial institutions in the same ministry/administrative units/levels of government.	Secondary literature, interviews
	Responsiveness: behavior of private and public actors. Support of health professions and interest groups for the other sector. Interaction of public actors from both sectors. *Presence of responsiveness:* private actors of sectors publicly support policies of the other sector (mutual support for agenda setting) – discourse coalition; e.g., doctors and medical organizations are politically active regarding public health policies, such as tobacco control policies. *Absence of responsiveness:* private actors are not politically active regarding the policies of the other sector, i.e., doctors are only interested in health care governance; conflicts between actors from both fields, for example, conflicts regarding expenditure for health care vs. public health policies or about research funds.	Secondary literature, interviews

Table 4.2. (*cont.*)

	Measures	Sources
Independent variables (back-ground of analysis)	*Policy integration*: common policies that combine health care and public health principles. For example, tobacco strategy, noncommunicable disease strategy, cancer strategy.	Secondary literature, interviews, official homepages (e.g., ministry of health)
	Unified government: development of the distribution of competences between the national and the subnational governments; i.e., is there increasing centralization of legislative competences, in general? Changes in veto structure or type of government over time	Secondary literature, interviews
	Professionalization/Institutions of interest intermediation: Political activity of health professions in general. How visible are they in the political process independently from the relationship between sectorial actors	Secondary literature, interviews
	Context: Information presented in chapter three. In addition, this book uses some of the information that came out of the case studies, but no directed search for contextual elements in the countries	Secondary literature, interviews

82

This book relies mostly on qualitative data analysis, which entails on the one hand the recording of events (Braun and Trein, 2014), such as in the case of legislation/institutionalization of the health care and the public health sectors. On the other hand, this book looks at actor coalitions to understand who are the actors, interest groups, and members of public administration that support public health issues and bring them to the political agenda and keep them on it. The strategy for the presentation of the results comprises qualitative historical case studies that discuss distinctiveness and responsiveness of the two policy sectors (Chapters 5–9). In Chapter 10, I also demonstrate the coevolution of the health care and the public health sectors based on a quantitative description reform activity over time.

4.8 Discussion and Summary of the Approach

The research design and method used in this book is in some ways unusual for comparative public policy analysis. Notably, this book approaches its topic with a historical analysis of institutions providing interesting and unique insights on the development of two related policies. This analysis shows how the health care and the public health sectors evolved over time by taking into consideration the relation of both fields to each other. Such an analysis could also be used to examine the relation of other policy sectors to one another.

However, the long time period and the many countries under consideration necessarily come at a cost. In particular, it is not possible to assess the relationship between the two policy sectors at the same level as it is usually done in comparative public policy analyses that are based on qualitative case studies focusing on single or very short time periods. This is less of a problem with institutional distinctiveness, since institutions evolve slowly and if there are important changes they are hard to miss. Concerning responsiveness between policy sectors, it is difficult to get an entire picture of all the important events in which private actors have supported the issues of another sector, especially because this research is primarily based on the reading of secondary literature. Therefore, this book cannot give the same granular account of sectorial responsiveness compared to analyses that focus on one or two specific policies.

Nonetheless, the long time period and broad definition of policy sectors provide an historical overview and connect the emergence of the health care and public health sectors to their context. Although this approach forgoes a more formal analysis of actor relations, the case studies presented in the following provide an impression for the actor coalitions that connect the two sectors in these five countries. What is more, the interview material for three of the five countries helps to fill this information gap.

Another caveat that needs to be addressed is that the information acquired through the sources presented before is not the same for every time period. Since the interviews cover only the more recent periods, there is a considerable asymmetry in the available information. This can be an advantage as well as disadvantage, because on the one hand the analysis is more fine-grained, at least for the last time period, which is a good thing. Though, on the other hand, this is a shortcoming, because the interviews do not cover the coupling of health care and public health in the other time periods. Nevertheless, there is no satisfying solution for this problem because interview information for earlier time periods cannot be generated. To account for this shortcoming, this book relies on extensive and encompassing research of secondary literature.

To sum up, the research design of this book combines a covariational approach to case studies with a comparative historical analysis of five different countries, namely Australia, Germany, Switzerland, the United Kingdom, and the United States. Using a comparative historical design permits me to trace the historical origins and the relation of the health care and the public health sectors, including public health policymaking. The countries were selected based on their configuration of the main independent variables, namely unified government and professionalism as well as institutions of interest intermediation. Starting from secondary literature and expert interviews, this book will now examine institutional distinctiveness as well as responsiveness between policy sectors on the actor level from a historical perspective. This allows to demonstrate how the health care and the public health sectors are coupled and how the coupling evolved over time, but by including a focus on the interaction of actors and the integration of policies between the sectors.

5 | United Kingdom: Institutional Unification and Tight Coupling of Health Care and Public Health

The first case study in this book discusses the United Kingdom. The reason to start the analysis with this country is because it is the only unitary state in the sample and is therefore different from the other four countries. It allows to extend the test of the argument beyond federal states. As discussed in the previous section, the empirical expectations that follow from the argument for the United Kingdom regarding the coupling of the health care and public health sectors are the following: on the one hand, professionalism is high and institutions of interest intermediation are pluralist, which means that there should be responsiveness between the two sectors. On the other hand, due to the unitary government and few veto points, both sectors should be institutionally integrated. This chapter analyzes the coevolution of health care and public health in the United Kingdom by discussing the historical development of both sectors' relationships in the four defined time spans. The results show that health care and public health coevolved from noncoupling to tight coupling. The analysis shows that unified government was the driving force behind these reforms whereas interactions between health professions was less important – although the theoretical priors led me to expect professional discourse coalitions to be important.

5.1 Origins of Public Health Policy (1850–1918)

During the second half of the nineteenth century, the United Kingdom was among the countries that were considered as forerunners of public health legislation, especially among other English-speaking countries, notably its former, or at the time still current, colonies (Baldwin, 1999; M. Lewis, 2003a). Demand for public health policies was high during this time, due to the limited possibilities to cure contagious sicknesses.

5.1.1   Unification of Both Sectors in National Public Health Legislation

The United Kingdom already had encompassing health legislation during the nineteenth century. During this period, the country experienced a comprehensive sanitary reform. Specifically, a series of public health acts was passed, most of which entailed public health regulations for England and Wales. These acts governed, for instance, waste removal and disease prevention, sewers, housing management, vaccination, and established general boards of public health (Porter, 1999, 127). Based on these laws, the national government pursued a restrictive and interventionist policy with compulsory vaccinations, such as against smallpox and other transmittable diseases. Noncompliance was subject to fines. The interventions were based on the arguments of advocates for state medicine. The basic idea behind these laws was that the individual's right to die and to be sick needs to be suspended in favor of the community. Nevertheless, these laws helped to prevent but could not cure infectious diseases; for instance, a number of syphilis cases were transmitted during an epidemic in 1871 (Porter, 1999, 128–129).

Doctoral organizations and popular movements, for example, the National Anti-Vaccination League, protested against this legislation and demanded to repeal restrictive public health legislation, such as the Contagious Disease Act. The opponents succeeded in the repletion of compulsory legislation on vaccination of infants as well as the legislation permitting the arrest and detention of prostitutes (Porter, 1999, 130). Yet, many of the interventionist public health policies in the United Kingdom went unopposed, because the government introduced most of these policies at the end of the nineteenth century based on the findings of bacteriological research. Therefore, the discretion of the national government to regulate individual lives augmented during this period. For example, the Local Government Act of 1875 allowed public health officers to remove sick individuals from the community and place them in homes (Porter, 1999, 134–135).

Around the end of the nineteenth century, the United Kingdom's public health sector was a very important part of health policymaking. MOsH (medical officers of health) were appointed throughout the country. They were part of the public health system and essentially responsible for a population-oriented health system. MOsH were hired by the local and municipal public health services, which the national government coordinated. In that period, the power of the medical profession declined with respect to preventive health and administrators' roles became more important (Porter, 1999, 137). According to Dorothy Porter, "[the public health movement] was a movement much broader than state medicine, outside the central corridors of power and beyond the elite province of the medical and scientific communities. It was not, however, a 'lay' organization, but was associated with the growth of prevention as a professional practice distinct from cure" (Porter, 1999, 138). Prevention efforts involved a group of doctors focusing on community health issues supported by a "community" of interests surrounding preventive medicine, communicated through journal literature and high-profile conferences, and embodied in a variety of institutions set up for educational and research purposes (Watkins, 1984; Porter, 1999, 138).

The development of this preventive sector replaced the technical philosophy of environmentalism, which attributed health problems to broader environmental factors, with a more technical imperative. In 1872, the British government created a national service of doctors responsible for prevention rather than treatment who were employed by local authorities. The main goal was the implementation of sanitary legislation in lodging houses, bakeries, and other public facilities or areas that involved working with food or dairy products (Porter, 1999, 281).

At the time, health policy clearly focused on public health policies. However, following the 1904 report on physical deterioration in the British population, the national government decided to focus British public health policy more on the development of personal health services, which is a development that is similar to those in other countries (Porter, 1999). Of course, facilities and structures providing treatment for diseases had already existed during the nineteenth century, yet they were not the first priority of health policy (Porter, 1999, 283). Furthermore, treatment facilities were very different from today's hospitals. Sanatoriums were built with open windows and no heating to constantly expose the patients to nature. Yet cure rates did not match expectations of policymakers and mortality rates remained very high despite treatment in the institutions (Bryder, 1988; Porter, 1999, 284). The lack of knowledge and technology regarding curative approaches increased the demand for prevention.

The National Health Insurance (NHI) Act of 1911 established the reimbursement of medical services and indicates that the health policy agenda moved toward individual health care. According to the law, hospitalization became mandatory for all those who were chosen by the local health officer. In addition, throughout the first twenty years of the twentieth century, a series of new health services emerged. Most of these services were welfare oriented, e.g., local authorities and voluntary organizations began to provide milk supplies and infant welfare. What is more, the community health services provided district nursing and health visits. At the same time, there was close coordination among local authorities, voluntary organizations, and self-employed individuals to provide a dense web of health services. Beginning in 1912, schools began to develop medical services, such as school nursing and dental clinics (Baggott, 2011). However, at the same time, the treatment of many diseases remained difficult, simply due to the lack of medication. One pertinent example in that regard is TB, which, despite the discovery of the disease's bacteriological origins, was only possible to treat successfully after the invention of a vaccine and antibiotic cures, such as streptomycin, in 1946 (Porter, 1999, 284).

What does this tell us regarding the institutional distinctiveness of the United Kingdom's health care and public health sector? Public health services were introduced all over the country under the responsibility of the municipal governments. A formal national institutionalization of the health care sector came later, namely with the establishment of national health insurance. Strictly speaking, health care and public health were distinct from one another in the sense that both sectors were not unified at the national level in the same department, although this occurred in 1919. However, health care and public health were unified at the local level, because the MOsH were responsible for the provision of health services, together with voluntary organizations, and were in charge of preventive health. Yet, the analysis also shows that public health was professionalized separated from the health care sector, a process that already began during the late nineteenth century.

5.1.2 Responsiveness of Actors from Both Sectors

During t0 there was interaction between private actors from both sectors; however, there were both conflicts and mutual support. This can be demonstrated with a look at the development of the medical profession and the public health professions. Beginning in the early twentieth century, public health had been run by doctors who saw it as "state medicine" and "preventive medicine." Public health diplomas certified a specialization that was only possible for doctors, but not for engineers (Porter, 1991). In 1872, there were conflicts with private practitioners from the moment when the first medical officers were appointed. The obligation to report infectious diseases put an additional administrative burden on GPs for which they were neither qualified nor reimbursed. This oftentimes caused hostilities within the same administrative district, as public health organizations identified more and more groups as needy and targets for state funded services, thereby increasingly threatening the territory of GPs (Porter, 1999, 289). In Victorian times, public health developed from a social reform movement to a civil service and the system was bureaucratized and medicalized. At the same time, primary medicine and hospitalized medicine became increasingly separated in the country. Clinical care became medical science; at the same time, primary medicine was deflected to the GPs who were no longer permitted to treat patients in hospitals (Gottweis, Prainsack, and Doris, 2004, 72).

Overall, however, little resistance came from the medical profession regarding the creation of the aforementioned public health acts as well as the nationalization of medicine and health services. First of all, there was a strong public health "profession" and bureaucracy that was different from the medical profession, which in turn defended public health against the influence of other professional groups, such as engineers. At the same time, doctors participated in the establishment of state medicine, which entailed prevention and cure, and accepted to a large extent the reduction of doctoral freedom concerning private practice (Baggott, 2011).

In 1909, a royal commission produced two reports that evaluated the relationship between health and welfare. The commission was divided between reformists and abolitionists with regard to the relationship between welfare and public health. The majority report favored a system that would increase health care services for the poor, but integrated into a national health service. The minority report suggested pursuing labor market policies, rather than providing health care for the poor (Baggott, 2011). Consequently, a strong public health coalition supported comprehensive public health legislation. In 1910, the chief medical officer of the Local Government Board, Arthur Newsholme, argued that public health required combining measures to change domestic hygiene as well as public hygiene education and the identification of at-risk groups. The main problem at the time was childhood mortality, which led to the demand of integrating health care and public health (Porter, 1999, 177). However, the National Health Insurance Act of 1911 failed to achieve a unified comprehensive system of public health and health care. The national health insurance included some reimbursements, such as a benefit for stays in sanatoriums. Although The public health profession, above all the MOsH, was a professional group that clearly viewed health as determined by historical and sociological determinants, more than the biological dispositions of humans including social behavior, they did not succeed in bringing their ideas into the creation of a national public health service and the MOsH regarded the 1911 act as a major defeat with respect to the building of a universal health service (Porter, 1999, 145).

Regarding the responsiveness between both sectors, this analysis shows that there was, above all, policy responsiveness. This conclusion derives from the fact that health care – which at the time was mostly primary care – and public health had been carried out by the municipal public health services, which implemented the majority of public health acts. Between private actors, namely those from within the medical and public health professions, there were conflicts regarding public health duties and the de facto "conscription" of doctors into the service of public health. GPs opposed the idea that they had to participate in public health services. However, at the same time they received the monopoly on public health degrees, because it was only allowed for doctors, but not for engineers to receive a higher degree in public health. This is an indication of interest and support for the public health sector by the medical profession in the United Kingdom. Nevertheless, there are no strong indications of collaboration and common policy advocacy between the two sectors.

To summarize, this analysis shows that both sectors were institutionally unified and not separate from one another, during the second half of the nineteenth century. At the time, health legislation mostly entailed public health acts regarding food safety, infections, and quarantine. On the other hand, an important legislation in the area of health care, namely health insurance, was introduced in 1911.

Before that, care for the sick, such as by hospitals, was closely connected to public health legislation. Regarding responsiveness, both sectors were connected by common policies, but not so much by cooperation between the professions or other private actors between the two fields; rather, they were connected by a continuing struggle over the rights and duties of the medical profession in the public health sector.

What do these findings imply for this book's argument, i.e., the hypothesis that health care and public health should be tightly coupled due to the United Kingdom's unified government and high professionalism, especially when the context is favorable to responsiveness, due to the problem's pressure? The results show that the argument is correct with regard to unified government. Health legislation in the United Kingdom has been unified, and there was no long lasting institutional separation between the health care and public health sectors. This occurred against a background where the municipal governments were responsible for both public health and primary care under the influence of the national government.

The results for professionalism and interest intermediation were different than expected. Competitive interest group inclusion and free professions indeed led to politically active professional organizations in the health care and public health sectors. Yet, their relationship was above all conflictive, especially with regard to the distribution of the roles for GPs on the one hand, and MOsH on the other hand. Their relationship was not very cooperative, despite a context that was favorable to public health and that should have led to responsiveness. Admittedly, at the time, the medical profession was not as powerful as the public health sector is today. Nonetheless, the politicization of health policy issues and the involvement of health professions played out as expected.

5.2 Cooperation and Conflict in the Interwar Period (1918–1945)

During the interwar period, the context for the relationship between health care and public health remained in demand for public health policy. Although the aforementioned public health policies showed some success, the most pressing health problems were still infections. At the same time, however, medical technology and pharmaceutical drugs became more fully developed, although states still operated in a context of competition between nations. Therefore, overall I expect to find a demand for public health and that there should be responsiveness between both sectors' actor groups.

5.2.1 Toward more Institutional Unification

In the United Kingdom, health care policy had been nationalized via the establishment of the 1911 national health insurance legislation, which created a compulsory social insurance program based on contributions and provided financing for private medical care as well as sickness benefits to salaried employees. Yet, the program did not cover hospital care or services for specialists; the coverage was mostly extended to manual laborers and did not include low-income, white-collar workers and their dependents. The law of 1911 was not the result of a large consensus, but the fact that many members of the medical profession favored employment by the state since most patients were members in friendly societies that paid doctors an annual fee per capita only (Day and Klein, 1992; Hacker, 1998).

The Health Policy Act of 1911 was a defining element for the national health care legislation in England until the introduction of the NHS in 1946. During the interwar and Second World War periods, the system was complemented by some laws, such as in 1929 when a national assistance scheme in the form of a medical-tested welfare scheme had been created (Porter, 1999, 289). However, during the 1940s the Beveridge Report created the basis for the establishment of the NHS, by demanding the creation of a tax-financed welfare state in England, contrary to the German model, which entailed the delegation of tasks to social health insurances (Abel-Smith, 1992).

In the post-World War I period, public health policies advanced due to the detrimental impact of the First World War on public health in all countries (M. Lewis, 2003a). Aside from the medical policies discussed before, the national government invested massively in the creation of public housing in order to provide better working conditions, especially for the poor. Under the leadership of the Ministry of Health (established in 1919), new legislation in 1923 and 1924 permitted the use of subsidies to improve public housing, and the state became the main provider of housing during the interwar period. A series of laws had already been passed during the First World War in order to create better housing conditions, for example, the Rent and Mortgage Restriction Act 1915 (Stewart, 2005).

What is more, poor laws continued until 1929 to be the major form of public health legislation to assist needy population groups. They were replaced by public assistance committees only in 1929. The reform of 1929 strengthened the powers of local health authorities with regard to public health. The Local Government Act allowed local authorities to bring poor law hospitals under the control of local governments. In addition, local governments could interfere in maternity and child welfare and tuberculosis (TB), immunization, and develop a more comprehensive public health approach with regard to blind people and mental deficiency (Baggott, 2011).

This brief discussion on health care and public health reforms in the interwar period shows the increasing unification of both fields, rather than the increasing distinctiveness of the two sectors at the local level and against the background of a national framework law. In particular, the creation of a national ministry of health that connected health insurance as well as public health problems is a strong indicator for this. As in the previous time period, the national government passed a series of public health acts; this time, however, they were more related to housing. This trend of institutionally unifying health care and public health continued with the Beveridge Report, which demanded the creation of an encompassing national health service.

5.2.2 Professional Conflicts but Unification of Public Services

As far as responsiveness between the two policy sectors was concerned, the interwar period shows the responsiveness of public health and health care profession in the sense that doctors were favorable to the idea of public health policy although it was not their primary domain. However, there were also conflicts between the actors in both sectors, notably among GPs and MOsH.

In 1919, the government created the Ministry of Health, which was responsible for health care and public health. Its task was to prepare, carry out, and coordinate measures that might be conducive to the health of the people. Specifically, it was responsible for environmental health, child and maternal welfare, the water supply and sanitation, housing, local government, the NHI scheme, and poor laws. Other health-related functions were in the hands of the Home Office (industrial hygiene), Board of Trade (health and safety at work), and the Board of Education (school health services). However, the Ministry of Health was responsible for coordinating all of these agencies. What is more, the law also coordinated the Education Act of 1918, which made the treatment of certain diseases, such as skin problems and dental disease, in schoolchildren mandatory (Stewart, 2005; Baggott, 2011).

In 1920, the Dawson Report, which was issued by the Central Council on Medical and Allied Services under the leadership of the Ministry of Health, suggested the creation of health centers that would bring together independent GPs, nursing staff, and technicians and provide access to diagnostic and treatment facilities. Although the report was never fully implemented, it had some impact as it signaled to GPs that it was worth claiming their position in this area. Yet, conflicts between the medical profession and medical officers of public health increased during the 1920s and 1930s (Porter, 1990). Both lacked prestige, but after the introduction of the NHI the status of the medical profession increased in comparison to the public health profession. During the political process resulting in the creation of the NHS, doctors secured their position even more (Baggott, 2011, 46–47).

What happened regarding the responsiveness of the United Kingdom's health care and public health sectors during the interwar period? From the discussion in this section, we found that, along with the institutional unification of both fields, the coordination activities between the two sectors increased because the Ministry of Health Report was in charge of many health care and public health related activities. Yet, this is not as evident for private actors. On the one hand, GPs were favorable to increased activity by the state in public health and health care; however, there were also conflicts with the MOsH about the direction of the national health policy as well as struggles for influence among the professions.

What are the implications of these findings concerning my expectation that the United Kingdom is a case of tight coupling of the health care and the public health sectors? The establishment of a national ministry of health and the coordination of various health policies under its leadership support the argument that the national government was favorable to sectorial integration. Alternatively, there is little evidence for professional responsiveness at the time, but rather the impression that conflicts prevailed between the two fields. Therefore, the analysis shows that during this period of institutional formation in which the main policies and public sector organizations emerged for the two policy sectors, there was mainly a struggle between the professions regarding their place in the new order of health policymaking. The presence of high professionalism and institutions of pluralist interest intermediation did not redound to a discourse and pressure group corporation between actors of the two fields, such as professional organizations.

5.3 Toward Responsiveness in the Shadow of the NHS (1945–1980)

After the Second World War, the context of the relationship between the health care and public health sectors changed. Medical technology had advanced considerably and more infections could be cured. This was already the case during the war, but public health remained important as long as fighting and destroying went on. Nevertheless, in 1945, a century had passed, since the first public health policies had been put into place; therefore, I expect that those policies had an effect on the outcome of public health and important feedback implications for further public health policies.

5.3.1 *Institutional Unification through the NHS*

The United Kingdom experienced a landmark change in health policy after the Second World War, namely the establishment of the NHS, which became the most important institution of health governance ever since then. The NHS implements the Beveridge Plan of 1942, which proposed to create a new system of social security and comprehensive and universal medical care to improve the health of the population as a whole in the long run (Gottweis, Prainsack, and Doris, 2004). In principle, the NHS is a system of free health care services paid by tax-like contributions. This was a critical juncture in English health care policy (Hacker, 1998). The NHS combined individual health care services with a population approach that would – in principle – also allow for preventive health policies (Webster, 2002; Baggott, 2011).

The implementation of the NHS began when the Labour Party came into government in 1945 (Day and Klein, 1992). Its large majority in the national parliament opened the pathway for encompassing political reform as well as in the field of social policy (Hacker, 1998). The establishment of the NHS is often explained as an inevitable consequence of the National Insurance Act of 1911. However, the establishment of the NHS was rather the effect of a much more consensual reply to policy formation by interest groups and policy-makers, for example, between the medical profession and the Labour Party. To transform the existing national health insurance into the NHS required major reform efforts. The system was founded upon an implicit bargain between the state and the medical profession which secured clinical autonomy for the profession and the ability to allocate resources in the state's budgetary framework (Tuohy, 1999, 118).

The NHS became the defining element of health policy in England after the Second World War. It underwent major reforms in 1974 and 1982, which aimed at reorganizing the service, but that did not change the core principle of the health care system at all (Tuohy, 1999).

Parallel to the transfer of health care into the hands of the public, public health policy remained important on the agenda of health policy, but with changed priorities. As discussed before, the invention and introduction of better antibiotics increased the possibility of curing diseases, especially infectious diseases. This development also shifted the agenda of public health policy. The prevention of infections, especially genital diseases and TB, remained an important priority for public health policy, as did immunization, such as against polio. The NHS in the United Kingdom made the organization of these policies easier than, for instance, in Germany, where such structures were lacking (Lindner, 2004a, 2004b).

Apart from infectious diseases, chronic health problems and risk factors also became more important in public health policy agendas, such as tobacco control policy. The United Kingdom was among the countries that produced the first scientific evidence on the danger of smoking for health. After some preliminary studies in the 1950s (Berridge, 2003), the Royal College of Physicians published a report in 1962 that established the connection between smoking and lung cancer (RCP, 1962). In the 1970s, these ideas began to be transferred into more tobacco control policies, based on the premise of reducing the harm and risk from smoking. Tobacco control policies largely comprised of health education campaigns and voluntary agreements between the government and the tobacco industry as well as the scientific development of safer smoking, a strategy that also won support in public health circles. These new policies were based on a new report by the Royal College of Physicians on the dangers of cigarettes. Another reason for the change in tobacco control policy was the creation of ASH (Action on Smoking and Health), a voluntary movement pressing for stronger tobacco control policy. It was based on the US Interagency Council that was formed after some civil servants had mentioned that tobacco control policy would become stronger if some pressure groups advocated for it (Berridge, 2003).

Other preventive health policies remained in the hands of local health authorities, which were part of the NHS but operated as a team of public health workers, including mental health officers, health visitors, and welfare officers, who dealt with population health issues. The reform of the NHS in 1974 shifted medical officers and mental health officers into the NHS. At the same time, public health medicine was recognized by the medical profession because the first faculty of public health was established (Orme et al., 2003). Yet, this reorganization pushed public health to the margins because public health services came under the auspices of the NHS's managers who often set priorities in the service according to budgetary interests (Hunter, 2003).

In conclusion, the institutional, and organizational unification of health care and public health tightened even further during the postwar period. After the First World War, both sectors were already organized under the umbrella of a national ministry of health, but they moved even closer together after the Second World War as a result of the introduction of the NHS. The main reason behind this institutional and organizational unification was the national government's attempt to provide a more encompassing health service. Although the GPs and the focus on curing sick individuals dominated the service and the system evolved into a national health care service, the focus on the population was an important element indeed. Prevention played a similar role, but not as implicit as health care. What is more, the NHS shows the effects of a unified government. Although there was wide support for more social policy action in the United Kingdom, it is questionable whether the creation of the service in this way would have been possible without the Labour Party's vast majority in Parliament.

5.3.2 Conflicts and Cooperation between Actors from Both Sectors

After the war, public health professions lacked an encompassing theory for the prevention of diseases to deal with the changing context for health policy discussed in the previous chapter, namely the success of prior public health policies as well as the possibilities of pharmaceutical technology. The medical profession thus superseded the public health professionals and claimed to be better at the management of chronic disease and clinical medicine (Porter, 1999, 145). Consequently, health care policy became dominant with the creation of the NHS (Baggott, 2011).

By the time the NHS was created, deep divisions existed between the professions of the two sectors. The local public health services were part of an organizational quagmire and suffered from fragmentation and coordination problems. Although rationalization was needed, it did not successfully occur during this reform period because public health officials were lost in the problems of epidemiological transition during the postwar period and lost the opportunity to develop their professional specializations. After the establishment of the NHS, public health officers' managerial roles increased steeply. Local health officers worked to coordinate an increasing range of community services, such as environmental and social work administration (Porter, 1999, 289).

Although public health remained unified with the NHS, individual health care became dominant in the shadow of a relative institutional unification of health care and public health. Nonetheless, with regard to certain ilnesses, such as tuberculosis and genital disease, the NHS allowed for a better coordination of prevention and individual care (Lindner, 2004b). Yet, the institutional integration and "statization" of health care in the NHS put pressure on the actors in the public health sector. In the early 1970s, an NHS reform integrated the local MOsH into the NHS and increased the administrative charges of the public health sector. Although the reform was intended to provide better integration between the two sectors, it led to burden shifting from the "stronger" health care sector to the "weaker" public health sector (Hunter, Marks, and Smith, 2010).

Whereas the aforementioned administrative coordination between both fields was not free of conflicts, there was responsiveness between professions from both sectors in another domain, namely health research. The most prominent example for this is smoking and health. As mentioned before, the Royal College of Physicians published a report in 1962 that showed the connection between smoking and lung cancer. In the report, doctors and public health doctors pushed the government to make more public health policies, mainly against tobacco, but also in other areas of public health (Berridge, 2003).

To sum up, the postwar period featured conflicts and cooperation, respectively, as well as communication between the actors, especially among the professions of both sectors. There were conflicts between the professions concerning the creation of the NHS during the postwar period, but GPs remained the more powerful group in the end. Yet, there was cooperation between both fields concerning newly emerging public health issues, such as smoking. Notably, the medical profession supported and advanced health research regarding the negative effects of smoking and advocated for policymakers to account for this problem.

What are the impacts of these findings for this book's argument? As argued before, there should be noncoupling between health care and public health in t2 because of the unfavorable context. Yet, independent of the context, health care and public health could be tightly coupled because of the United Kingdom's high professionalism and unified government. My results partly confirm this argument. Notably, there was an absence of responsiveness regarding the creation of the NHS, because conflicts between the medical and public health professions about the right approach to health policy prevailed at the time. Although the NHS clearly states a population health related mission, it essentially dealt with curing sick patients rather than implementing large prevention campaigns. The English NHS was no copy of the Soviet public health service, although it resembles the general idea behind it to combine population health and individual health care (Tulchinsky and Varavikova, 1996).

Nevertheless, there was also responsiveness between the health care and public health sectors, notably regarding tobacco control policy. Here, doctors and public health professionals not only advanced research and established scientific knowledge that smoking is bad for health, but actors from both policy sectors also openly advocated for the government to enact more preventive health policies, notably in the area of a tobacco control policy. In that sense, the responsiveness between both sectors had been established regarding public health policy, whereas there had been conflicts regarding the NHS. Interestingly, the context plays out differently than expected in theory. As previously argued, there should have been no incentives for health care and public health to cooperate after the Second World War, because the context for public health had changed significantly. The analysis of the United Kingdom shows that there were indeed conflicts regarding the NHS, not regarding public health policy, but rather about health care issues such as the NHS. This indicates that during the formative period of the NHS, conflicts appeared about basic and economically important problems from the points of view of interest groups and professions, such as who would receive the most pay and say in the NHS. Yet, the situation changed regarding risk factor-related public health problems and the strong health professions played an important role in politicizing important public health problems, including those in the medical profession. Nonetheless, this process within the United Kingdom occurred in the shadow of a strong, unified national government.

5.4   Toward Further Unification between Health Care and Public Health (1980–2010)

The last time period in the analysis of the health care and public health sectors' coevolution spans 1980 to 2010. During that period, the context was favorable to the responsiveness and policy integration of health care and public health because public health problems returned to the political agenda at the time. Nevertheless, budgetary problems also existed, which had the potential to cause disturbances between stakeholders from both policy sectors.

5.4.1   Remaining Institutional Unification Despite Delegation and Liberalization

The NHS remained the defining institutional scheme for health policy in the United Kingdom during this time period. Some attempts were made to introduce private practice and health care services in the sector during the early 1980s and some elements of competition were introduced. There were also some debates in which the Tories underlined that the NHS should be abolished entirely. Despite these debates and the many suggestions to introduce private and corporative elements in the provision of health, the NHS was still intact when Thatcher left office (Porter, 1999, 252–253). One of the main reform suggestions had been to introduce co-payments for health care, especially from those with higher incomes. However, such a strategy would have put the most financial burden on the middle class. Policymakers dropped the idea and suggested creating an internal market for health care measures (Porter, 1999, 255).

In the NHS reform of 1982, district health authorities (DHAs) replaced area health authorities (AHAs) (Hunter, Marks, and Smith, 2010). In the reform of 1988, there was a split between the Department of Health and the Department of Social Security (Acheson, 1988). The report by Acheson also recommended that each DHA appoint a director for public health, replace the term "community medicine" with public health medicine, and resurrect the tradition of the annual reports of the MOsH (Hunter, Marks, and Smith, 2010).

In the organization of the NHS in Britain, the medical profession had a privileged role regarding the formulation and implementation of policies together with ministerial bureaucrats and NHS managers. The governance form of the NHS was a mixture of statism and corporatism. In addition, employers in Britain played a less important role than in the United States and Germany because the NHS was financing health care throughout the state rather than employers. In the reform debate at the end of the 1980s, Thatcher argued that the system needed to change due to its inefficiencies and the very long hospital waiting lists. Consequently, market reforms – a split between purchasers and providers – were at the heart of her white paper for a reform of the health system in the late 1980s. In the end, the reforms entailed more centralization of powers into the NHS but limited market reforms. Thatcher used the majoritarian system of decision making in the United Kingdom to centralize health policy even further in order to break the corporatist power of the doctors. However, solidarity and equity had significant public support. As a consequence, far-reaching reforms to introduce market elements were not possible (Giaimo and Manow, 1999, 971–974).

Nonetheless, the idea of internal markets remained important and continued to be part of the debate concerning NHS reforms (Gottweis et al., 2004; Hunter, Marks, and Smith, 2010). In April 1990, the British government created, for the first time since the establishment of the NHS, a contract for practitioners working in the NHS (Day and

Klein, 1992). The NHS and Community Care Act of 1990 established an internal market with contracts between independent purchasers and providers (Tuohy, 1999). Apart from keeping costs under control, one of the most important issues in health policy for the governments – Tories and Labour alike – at the time was tackling health inequalities. The Treasury supported the Ministry of Health in reaching this goal (Hunter, 2003).

In the period since the 1980s, public health remained institutionally closely linked to health care in the United Kingdom. The British government had already published a report on prevention and health in 1976 and the Black Report on Economic Inequalities in 1980 (Marmor and Klein, 2012; Smith, Bartley, and Blane, 1990). Although policymakers largely ignored the specific recommendations of these reports – such as those from the Black Report (Marmor and Klein, 2012) – public health policies returned to the political agenda. A new public health movement, created in Great Britain during the mid-1980s, aimed at combining environmental health and public health medicine. "New Public Health" issues became part of the political discussion, yet it took some time before these matters were implemented (Hunter, Marks, and Smith, 2010)

The appearance of the AIDS epidemic in the 1980s was another major issue that helped to re-shift public health issues to the political agenda. It was after 1986 when the national government became aware of the problem and took action by launching a public education campaign and investing into research on the disease (Fox, Day, and Klein, 2012). AIDS was not a return of the plague, but it was regarded as a plague itself and came along with health-policing interventions (Porter, 1999; Porter and Porter, 1989; Gottweis et al. 2004, 302–303).

Public health policy changed in many ways when New Labour took over power and entered government in 1997. First, the required qualifications for obtaining a post in the public health sector changed. Prior to 1997, a medical qualification had been required to occupy a senior post in public health within the NHS. After 1997, the Labour government announced its intention to strengthen public health and open positions in the field to individuals with a variety of different professional backgrounds (Evans, 2003). Second, the Labour government published a series of public health strategies, for example, the 1998 Acheson "Independent Inquiry into Inequalities in Health."

In 2000, the new Health Development Agency had been set up with the goal of strengthening the evidence base of public health, as was a new NHS plan that criticized the limited focus on public health within the NHS. The Wanless Report on future health trends and inequalities was published in 2002, stressing the connection between health and economic benefits (Hunter, 2003). What followed was a number of policy reforms toward integration of health care and public health, such as the NHS Health Checks Program and the Health and Social Care Act of 2012, which shifted the public health back to municipal governments. These reports and reforms exemplify the renewed focus on public health policy and new dynamics of policy sectors regarding sectorial integration, such as emphasized in the joined-up government and whole of government literature (Hunter, 2003; Bogdanor, 2005; Christensen and Lægreid, 2007; Baggott, 2013).

5.4.2 Policy Instead of Professional Responsiveness

In the United Kingdom, responsiveness of both sectors has increased since the 1980s compared to the previous period. This occurred with respect to the interactions among actors when occupations other than doctors were also involved in the public health sector, as discussed before. For instance, doctors supported research in public health and the government invested into public health research from a general perspective, including in health care and public health. One example of this is the research by the Marmot Commission, which had produced large reports on broader sociological causes of public health problems (Int-Ger-7) as well as the increasing importance of the Faculty of Public Health in the United Kingdom (Holland and Stewart, 1998).

However, judging from the secondary literature reviewed, there was responsiveness between health care and public health, but mostly on behalf of political and administrative activities. The inclusion of public health and especially health inequalities into the NHS increased the policy integration of health care and public health. This development had already begun with the Health of the Nation Strategy (1992–1997). With the election of the Labour government in 1997, the turn toward a new public health increased even more. It replaced the Health of the Nation Strategy by a new public health strategy involving new public health activities focused on inequality. Led by Donald Acheson, a new inquiry into health inequalities made a new

plan to reduce inequalities in public health (Hunter, 2003). The 1997
white paper entitled "The New NHS" demanded the establishment of
481 primary care groups and local authorities with the statute of local
authorities (which later became primary care trusts) and a minister of
public health to be appointed (Hunter, Marks, and Smith, 2010). (See
the Appendix for further examples.)

Although the institutional connection between health care and
public health in the NHS created some problems between community
physicians, who were concerned with the health of the population as a whole, and medical practitioners, who were interested in
individual health care, this approach allowed for a health policy
where health care and public health were much more integrated
than in other countries. Some of the main criticisms were that
the NHS was mostly concerned with health care services and that
community physicians were relegated to managers in the public
health service (Hunter, Marks, and Smith, 2010). Nonetheless, this
close connection between both sectors had a positive effect on the
adoption of public health policies, such as on tobacco control, which
profited from the centralized authority in health policy as well as the
powerful public health coalition (Berridge, 2003; Joossens and Raw,
2014).

In conclusion, the responsiveness between health care and public
health became visible in policy integration, namely that the government pursued more encompassing public health policies, notably
those that targeted health inequalities. The evidence for responsiveness
between actors and professions from both policy sectors is rather
indicative. Public health activities like the Acheson report and the
establishment of a minister for public health did not cause opposition
from the medical profession. Yet, this analysis did not reveal strong
evidence that these political actions overtly supported the "public
health turn" in British health policy, and needs further research.

What are the implications of these results for the argument concerning the relationship between health care and public health in
the United Kingdom? We expected to find tight coupling as a result
of the country's unified government and high professionalism as
well as pluralistic institutions of interest intermediation along with
a favorable contextual situation. There had been tight coupling in
this time period between health care and public health. On the one
hand, both sectors remained institutionally unified. On the other

hand, concerning research and development, both sectors responded to each other, especially regarding the renewed interest in public health issues that also extended to the medical profession. The findings of the last section confirm to a certain extent the hypothesis for the United Kingdom. A particularly interesting finding concerns the role of professions. Although I expected professional actors to be politically active and to form a cross-sectoral discourse coalition, the "state" – notably, a unified government – showed to be most important for understanding the members' limited role. Although t3 clearly entailed a shift toward a favorable context for public health policy, responsiveness between professions did not play an outstanding role; rather, the stronger demand by policymakers for more public health research and more integration of health care and public health policies played a larger role despite the fact that the United Kingdom had a strong and politically active medical profession.

5.5 Discussion

This chapter examined the coevolution of health care and public health in the United Kingdom. Taken together, the results show how the relationship between both policy sectors changed and coevolved over time from the dominance of noncoupling to tight coupling (Table 5.1). Both sectors were rather noncoupled during the first time period because unified government led to the institutional unification of both sectors, as expected. Yet, despite the favorable context, there were mostly conflicts between the professions of both sectors. During the second time period, both policy sectors remained mostly noncoupled. In 1911, a national health insurance had been created and in 1919, the government established the National Ministry of Health, which was responsible for public health services and the national health insurance. This structure remained intact until the creation of the NHS in 1945. Regarding responsiveness, there was a consensus concerning the establishment of the public health acts and the national health insurance. Yet, conflicts remained between the public health and medical profession regarding the role of each profession and health policy in general as well as particular reforms in national health policy, e.g., the creation of the NHS.

The conflicts between the health professions during the interwar and Second World War periods ended with the establishment of the

Table 5.1. *Coevolution of health care and public health in the United Kingdom.*

1880–1918 (t0)	1918–1945 (t1)	1945–1980 (t2)	1980–2010 (t3)
Noncoupling (Tight coupling): Unification of both sectors through national public health acts; national health insurance legislation; conflicts between the medical profession and MOsH regarding their respective roles in health policy; policy integration in public health	*Noncoupling (Tight coupling)*: Further institutional unification in a national Ministry of Health; conflicts between actors of both sectors continued; agreement in the refusal of eugenics	*Tight coupling (Noncoupling)*: Continuing unification in NHS; dominance of individualized medicine; responsiveness among professions between both sectors	*Tight coupling*: Unification of both sectors; Public health focused on social inequalities; professional responsiveness, but mainly on policy integration of both sectors

106

NHS, which also enshrined the dominance of the medical profession over national hygienists. However, the service took a distinctive public health perspective, as it focused on the provision of population health, yet primarily by means of individual treatment. The presence of such an institutional framework nevertheless made it easier to organize public health campaigns and to support municipal public health services. Since 1945, the NHS remained the most important health policy institution in the United Kingdom. Although the coordination between health care and public health came along with conflicts between the professions at times, overall the coordination between health care and public health functioned rather well. What is more, concerning new public health policies, such as for tobacco control, the medical profession had an active role in providing research on tobacco control, but also for publicizing its findings and demanding more tobacco control policies along with public health groups.

During the fourth time period, health care and public health remained tightly coupled. Public health was again reinforced after New Labour came into power in 1997, but with a distinctive focus on social inequalities. Aside from the institutional unification of both policy sectors, there was responsiveness among the actors, in the sense that the medical and public health professions were both interested in and occupied with public health issues. However, the national government took the most visible role in pushing public health problems back to the political agenda, which we can see from the frequent reporting on public health, such as the results of the Marmor Commission. This clearly had a visible impact on health policymaking, which shifted back to public health policy and integrated prevention and cures in health policymaking. However, in this last time period, the responsiveness between both sectors was mainly visible at policy integration and administrative coordination and less so at the interaction between professional actors.

5.5.1 Unified Government and Professionalism in the United Kingdom

What are the implications of these findings for this book's argument? The theoretical chapter hypothesized that health care and public health are either tightly coupled or noncoupled in the United Kingdom. Generally, the chance for tight coupling between sectors is high in the United Kingdom because of the politically important role for professions and unified government. In combination with a favorable context for sectorial integration, there should be tight coupling between both sectors. To what extent do these expectations hold in light of the results?

Concerning unified government, the findings are clear and support the prior argument. Specifically, the results show that health policy was in the hands of the national government. The United Kingdom's strong central government was a constant element, from the public health acts in the nineteenth century, the national health insurance law in 1911, and the creation of the NHS, as well as the 1980s, which was a period of delegation and liberalization of public health services. There were very few serious discussions to disintegrate (i.e., to create more distinctiveness) health care and public health entirely, for example due to a privatization of health care services or because of a delegation of public health services. These results confirm the findings of other research on health care institutions. Especially during the second part of the twentieth century, health care institutions evolved by institutional drift (Hacker, 1998, 2004b). My results show that this was also true for the institutional relationship between health care and public health. Although public health policies were added as layers of new legislation, depending on the most pressing public health problems, they remained closely linked institutionally with the NHS and the national ministry of health (although there were, of course, slight changes, there were no fundamental reforms). Similarly, the fact that a strong national government leads to more unified and comprehensive public health policies is a finding that confirms prior research on public health (Albaek, Green-Pedersen, and Nielsen, 2007; Mayes and Oliver, 2012; Oliver, 2006; Nathanson, 2007).

Nevertheless, this research provides new insights on the role of the health professions. I hypothesized that strong professionalism and institutions of pluralist interest intermediation lead to responsiveness among actors from both sectors and policy integration, especially in times when the context is favorable and demands such action. The results partially confirm this hypothesis. There are clear signs of professional activism in politics showing that the medical profession and also the public health profession are politically active. This means that the argument is partly right, namely that high professionalism leads to more political activism among professional organizations.

However, it does not always lead to more responsiveness, even though when we expected this to be the case. In a nutshell, the results show that conflicts between the professions of both sectors prevailed during the first half of the twentieth century, whereas this changed after the establishment of the NHS. From the turn of the century until the end of the Second World War, there were conflicts about the formation of health policy in general and the distribution of resources. This changed during the post-Second World War period, when the medical profession began to take new public health problems into consideration, such as tobacco control policy, and the medical and public health fields converged. There was some degree of responsiveness between the two sectors beforehand, but this was mainly responsiveness through policy integration.

Furthermore, the theoretical chapter hypothesized that the context was very favorable for sectorial responsiveness during t0 and t3, but less so throughout most of the twentieth century (t1, t2). Health care and public health should be noncoupled, especially during the post-Second World War period, because there are few incentives for sectorial responsiveness and the integration of the two sectors. The results also show a different picture in this case. Rather than following changes in the contextual demands, the health care and public health sectors coevolved in a different way than expected from the discussion of the context. The assumption regarding the context was only entirely correct concerning t3. These results show that the contextual elements played out differently than expected. They do impact the policy output that relates to both sectors, but not necessarily the relationship between the professions of both sectors.

5.5.2 Competing Explanations

How can the aforementioned differences between the theoretical expectations and the parts of the results concerning the coupling between the health care and public health sectors be explained? In the following, the chapter puts forward two competing theories that might help to illustrate the evolution of the coupling of the health care and public health sectors.

1. *Complementarity:* Chapter 2 discussed the literature on historical institutionalism and presented four empirical implications of the

theory for the coupling of the health care and public health sectors. Among these, one element is particularly interesting for understanding the coevolution of the health care and public health sectors, namely the theory of institutional complementarity. One assumption of this literature is that institutions emerge rather randomly and not in coordination with other institutions. However, institutions evolve toward complementarity over time because they improve their combined output for society through learning and increasing coordination (Yamamura and Streeck, 2003; Crouch et al., 2005). This insight is important with regard to the coevolution of health care and public health in the United Kingdom. Indeed, the creation and implementation of health care and public health legislation did not occur as part of major plan from the outset, but as a reaction to the most pressing health problems and technological possibilities at the time. Specifically, the first public health laws emerged in the late nineteenth century and health care legislation followed in the early and mid-twentieth century. Professions and other private actors subsequently fought for their place in these new institutions and for their share of the "cake," rather than only cooperating when the context demanded this. According to the results, the coevolution of the health care and public health sectors followed a logic of complementarity. Health care and public health in particular were differentiated from one another during the early time periods and became more specialized. After that, interest groups and professions in each sector sought their place within the institutional development and the emerging and differentiating modern state. The NHS eventually created an institutional equilibrium between health care and public health, which can be seen as the result of the preceding conflicts and developments, rather than as one contingent event. The responsiveness between health care and public health began to increase during the postwar period and the strong medical profession in the United Kingdom contributed to cooperation between both sectors. Since the emergence of "new public health" in the 1980s, learning and the coordination between health care and public health increased in the United Kingdom, mostly as a result of the activities of the professional community. In that sense, the coevolution of health care and public health followed a similar pattern as described by the literature on the complementarities of capitalist institutions. Institutions within both sectors emerged rather randomly; throughout their evolution they adapted to one another, and learning and coordination increased.

2. *Policy learning:* These findings point to another field of literature that is important for the understanding of public policy, namely contributions regarding policy learning (Bennett and Howlett, 1992; Gilardi and Radaelli, 2012; P. Hall, 1993; May, 1992; Dunlop, Radaelli, and Trein, 2018). In particular, these authors reflect on how innovations and new ideas enter the political process and become part of public policy. The results of this analysis show that the relationship between the health care and the public health sectors as well as the evolution toward sectorial complementarity entail a process of policy learning. The strong politicization of health professions that became apparent in the coevolution of the two sectors shows that high professionalism comes along with more policy learning and therefore better policy integration. This is particularly the case regarding the tobacco control policy in the postwar era and the new public health as of the 1980s. Public health policy in its broader sense played an important role during this period and the medical and public health professions both contributed to lifting these issues into the political agenda. This implies that there should be less policy learning in countries with low professionalism, especially regarding tobacco control policy and new public health.

5.6 Conclusion

This chapter analyzed the coevolution of the health care and public health sectors in the United Kingdom, based on an evaluation of the secondary literature. I selected this country because it has a relatively unified government and high professionalism and therefore tight coupling should be present in case the context is favorable to sectorial responsiveness. The results confirm the first hypothesis that unified government leads to the institutional integration of health care and public health, which remained constant over time. However, the link between politicized professions and responsiveness of the policy sectors only holds for the second part of the analysis, namely the postwar period. It was only during the Second World War that the responsiveness between health care and public health increased, i.e., the presence of a discourse coalition, notably between professional actors from both sectors. Similarly, the context also did not impact the findings exactly as hypothesized. In particular, the economic dimension was dominant and caused conflicts between the professions of both sectors, even when the context was favorable to responsiveness and integration. This became apparent in the first two time periods, when there were still struggles about a national paradigm of health policy. However, this changed after the NHS was introduced and increased the responsiveness between the health professions and public actors increased considerably. The results show that there are two further theoretical dimensions that are important for understanding health care and public health: institutional complementarity and learning. The former becomes apparent in the coevolution from noncoupling to tight coupling over time, which shows that there has been increased interaction and cooperation between both fields, in comparison to the first two time periods, when conflicts have dominated. Policy learning is the second element that comes along with high professionalism, namely that innovations enter the political process quickly and without being filtered as much by partisan conflicts.

6 | Australia: Politicized Professions and Tight Coupling of Health Care and Public Health

This case study analyzes the coevolution of the health care and the public health sectors in Australia. Australia is different from the United Kingdom mainly because it is a federal state, but there are similarities between the two countries. Australia's parliamentary system is similar to the United Kingdom's, although there has been proportional voting for the Senate since 1948, which represents the territorial dimension. At the same time, Australia has a pluralist system of interest intermediation and is a liberal market economy; therefore, it should have politically active health professions like the United Kingdom. Against this background, I expect the health care and public health sectors to be institutionally unified. In addition, there should be responsiveness between actors, such as discourse coalitions between the medical professions and public health organizations, especially once the context permits this. The historical analysis shows that there is distinctiveness and responsiveness (loose coupling) in the early time periods (especially t0). Nevertheless, both sectors coevolved toward tight coupling throughout the twentieth century. The results offer some support for my hypotheses that unified government leads to the unification of policy sectors and that politicized professions come along with responsiveness of health care and public health.

6.1 Loose Coupling in Times of Sectorial Emergence (1850–1918)

During the late nineteenth century, health policy in Australia was a matter for the colonial governments, which "came together" into the Australian Commonwealth in 1901. The colonies were originally founded as penal colonies of the British Empire and their governors had considerable discretion, which they used to intervene in all matters of public interest, including health, when they deemed it necessary. During this period, according to the discussed theoretical expectations, the context was positive for responsiveness and policy integration of health care and public health.

6.1.1 Differentiation in Colonial Times

To understand the emergence of health care and public health as two related but distinct policy sectors in Australia, it is necessary to begin the analysis in the middle of the nineteenth century. At this time, population- and individual-based health policies were similarly important as the predominant disease pattern made this necessary and the respective medical supplies were not available. In the nineteenth century, health policymaking in Australia was, above all, public health policymaking. As the overview in the appendix of this book shows, the colonies, and later on, the national government, passed a series of public health acts that focused on population health issues.

Thereby, Australian policymakers and interest groups oriented their actions according to the public health tradition in Great Britain. Public health legislation emerged in England during the late nineteenth century, specifically taking on two dimensions. On the one hand, it entailed actions to control disease by policing and isolating risk groups, which were essentially the poorer parts of society, and, on the other hand, entailed a more progressive approach aiming to generally make society a fairer place by investing in programs to adjust living conditions (Ross, 1991; Bryder, 1994).

Britain's influence on health policy in Australia also extended to the medical area, as many doctors pursued a post-graduate education in Great Britain. At the same time, British experts were present when the Australian government wanted to pursue reforms (Bryder, 1994). Since the colonial governments wanted to attract more new settlers, they avoided policies that would have been an obstacle to that, including health warnings and regulations (Bryder, 1994, 272–273). However, once introduced, public health legislation was similarly to the British Public Health Acts (Woodruf, 1984; Curson and McCracken, 1989), yet with the exception that the responsibility for administering public health lay with the central colonial boards of health rather than the local health administration. This was the basis for the strong involvement of state governments with public health after the creation of the Commonwealth of Australia in 1901 (Baum, 2008).

During the pre-First World War period, there was no national institutional framework in Australia to connect health care and public health across the colonies. Health care and public health were relatively separated institutionally as individual care occurred through private organizations and provisions.

The first public health legislation mainly covered quarantines and vaccinations. The Victorian Central Board of Health was created in 1854. Due to the many immigrants, the authorities had become very concerned with a possible increase in infectious diseases (M. Lewis, 2003a). Other states followed until the end of the nineteenth century. Health legislation mostly originated from acts against specific infectious diseases and was then followed by comprehensive public health acts (M. Lewis, 2003a, 71). Along with the public health acts, infrastructure was built to push back infectious diseases. For instance, epidemic measles and scarlet fever in the 1870s and typhoid in the 1880s led to the creation of a sewage system. At the beginning of the twentieth century, legal enactments concerning food safety were passed by state legislators. Again, the most populated states – New South Wales and Victoria – took the lead, with other states following (M. Lewis, 2003a, 2008).

In 1889, Victoria passed an amendment to the Victorian Public Health Act creating a public health department responsible to a minister and increasing penalties for offenses against the existing public health legislation. The creation of the board clearly followed the ideas of the municipal officials who were important in the English public health system. As in Great Britain, disease reporting was also part of the public health system, for instance, South Australia created a mandatory reporting system for various diseases in 1898 (M. Lewis, 2003a). At the turn of the twentieth century, all Australian colonies had passed public health legislation in the English style and each colony's central administration controlled and imposed preventive health policies (M. Lewis, 2003a).

Whereas these acts and legislation connected prevention and primary care for some problems, such as excessive drinking, health care was organized differently at the colonial level and was not under the same institutional umbrella. The individual-focused health care system, which plays the most important role in today's health policies, was different at the time and much less developed than today. Until the First World War, the Australian health care system had three pillars: (1) charitable hospital care for the indigent population; (2) contract practice through friendly societies for the provident working and lower-middle classes; and (3) private fees for services for wealthy patients (M. Lewis, 2003a).

To sum up, health care and public health were institutionally distinct during t0 in Australia. This holds from a national point of view because health policy was primarily public health policy. Individual health care was, for the largest part, privately organized at the time and separate from the institutions of the health care sector. What is more, we can also refer to institutional distinctiveness with respect to the differences among the colonies and the fact that there was no common institutional framework of national health policy at the time. This will be discussed in more depth, following analysis actor responsiveness during the first time period.

6.1.2 Actor Responsiveness between the Two Sectors

In 1872, the first association of health officials was founded in Victoria, which essentially was the forerunner of a public health professional organization. In 1889, Victoria began to appoint health professionals to the Department of Health. The University of Sydney had appointed its first lecturer in preventive medicine six years before, in 1883, which indicated the emergence of professional roles in the public health sector. Other states followed. Although based on a medical education, public health professionals had a different professional mission than doctors. Whereas doctors are a free profession, public health professionals are hired by the state as bureaucrats. During the first years of the nineteenth century, local governments and health authorities employed the first official health visitors, who began to individually consult patients in order to teach them about healthy behavior to prevent diseases. This was adapted from the British model. Australian officials later became public health nurses in the fields of infant health, school health, and tuberculosis. During the First World War, the demand for health care and public health professionals continued to increase among wounded soldiers and invalids as well as for treatment and prevention of communicable diseases among returning troops (Bryder, 1994; M. Lewis, 2003a).

The medical profession and nongovernmental organizations (NGOs) played an important role in health policy during the nineteenth century and gained more political influence during this period. Thereby, these professionals explicitly demanded more public health policies and publicly funded health care schemes. Nevertheless, colonial governments relied on friendly organizations and NGOs to finance health care for poorer people and to provide health care. Only a few medical graduates and immigrants entered the public services, which employed limited health officials to keep expenditures down. Campaigns against diseases were often inefficient as not enough doctors were involved. In this situation, doctoral organizations and public health boards argued in favor of more public provisions, which were seen as the path to the nationalization of medicine (M. Lewis, 2003a).

During the late nineteenth century, actors from both sectors were responsive to one another; for example, GPs and public health officers agreed on the health policy agenda and provided mutual support, such as when doctoral organizations advocated for public health measures. The presence of medical officers of health (MOsH) increased the public health sector's professionalization and formed a distinct actor coalition to demand more public health interventions. The medical profession was open regarding public health legislation, such as sanitary measures. Other actors joined the coalition for more state intervention in health policy during the recession and large strikes of the 1890s, which brought "middle-class Liberal reformers and the Labor party into a pragmatic alliance to achieve social justice through such [public health] intervention" (M. Lewis, 2003a, 140).

What do the results of the two preceding sections imply for the previous argument? This book hypothesized that Australia is a case of tight coupling between health care and public health because professionalism is high and the government is unified. Beginning with the latter case, the results are clear. During most of this time period (until 1901), Australia was not a nation-state and had no national government. Therefore, the institutional unification of health care and public health at the national level was impossible. Yet, looking at the colonies, we cannot find clear signs of institutional and organizational unification of health care and public health policy. The reason for this is that, at the time, what we would describe as health care policy was a private service that doctors provided and friendly organizations supported patients financially. Concerning responsiveness, between the two policy sectors, public health reformers, and the medical profession played an important role in politicizing public health problems and demanding more public health action. The medical profession did not oppose public health policies and joined a coalition with progressive reformers and politicians of the Australian Labor Party. Doctoral support for public health-related measures is an indication of mutual political support between the health care and the public health sectors. Indeed, this time in Australia was a period of state formation and the creation of political institutions of the modern state, including public health services. Since the national government only emerged at the beginning of the twentieth century, the state was not very strong and professions and interest groups – including public health officials that the state had hired – played an important role in demanding more public health policies. In this situation, the context indeed played out as expected before, namely that health care and public health actors show responsiveness in times of threatening infections, limited medical possibilities, and competition between nations.

6.2 Nation Building and the Unification of Health Care and Public Health (1918–1945)

The second sequence regarding the coevolution of health care and public health covers the interwar period. During this period, the context changed and the global economic crisis and improvements in the possibilities of medical care should have reduced incentives for actors from both sectors to cooperate with one another. At the same time, there was still competition among nations, which, as expected theoretically, gave high priority to public health policies.

6.2.1 *Toward Institutional and Organizational Unification*

During this period in Australia, the distinctiveness of health care and public health diminished as a result of reforms that moved both sectors toward a unified institutionalized framework at the national level. In 1921, the Commonwealth of Australia Department of Health was created, which increased the CW's control even further in national health policies. The department was in charge of administering the Quarantine Act, which granted the CW powers to intervene in case an epidemic broke out. Furthermore, it had the power for investigating diseases and setting up necessary facilities to that end, administering the CW's serum laboratories, collecting sanitary data, investigating health within companies, educating the public in public health matters, controlling the Australian Institute of Tropical Medicine, controlling infectious diseases among troops, and leading the Division of Sanitary Engineering (Bryder, 1994).

The idea for a federal health care system became prominent in the political debate in 1923, and some actors demanded the creation of a national health insurance based on the British model. The medical profession fiercely opposed the establishment of such a scheme. What is more the political parties could not agree on a national health care policy scheme. This decision was also a blow for the plans of public health reformers, for example, national hygienists who wanted to create an encompassing national public health service that would have integrated preventive and curative health policies. Furthermore, there were conflicts between the CW and states about how to share responsibilities for health policy. The conflicts in the partisan and federal arena made it easy for doctors to successfully oppose the introduction of a comprehensive national health service (Bryder, 1994; M. Lewis, 2003a).

After the demise of national health insurance, the NHMRC took over leadership in health policy. It had been founded in 1926 and held its first meeting in 1937. Its main responsibility was to encourage public health and medical research that was mostly linked to public health issues.[1] Most of the council's members were national hygienists, but there also were some members who represented the British Medical Association.

The idea of a national health insurance returned to the political agenda in the 1930s when private health care financing became more difficult as a result of rising unemployment. The ruling Conservative United Australia Party introduced legislation for a national health insurance, but Labor opposed it as it wanted to have a tax-funded health insurance system. Doctors also opposed the introduction of a comprehensive health insurance as they were afraid of losing their business. National hygienists opposed a health insurance scheme because it simply provided financing for curative medicine but did not have prevention and preventive means (M. Lewis, 2003a). Due to the lack of compromise among political parties and the strong opposition by interest groups, the establishment of health insurance legislation failed prior to the war (M. Lewis, 2003b). This secured the importance of private practice in Australia, parallel to state health policies concerning prevention and research, and it demonstrated the power of doctoral organizations to organize political opposition. Nonetheless, parliament passed the National Health and Pensions Insurance Bill in 1938, which covered basic health care costs for indigent groups (M. Lewis, 2003a, 251).

In 1944, the Commonwealth attempted to legislate for the provision of free pharmaceuticals through the Pharmaceutical Benefits Act of 1944. Benefits were to be restricted to medicines listed in the Commonwealth Pharmaceutical Formulary, a precursor to the Pharmaceutical Benefits Advisory Committee. However, the Australian Branch of the British Medical Association (BMA) challenged the act and the High Court subsequently declared it unconstitutional because the Commonwealth did not have the power to spend money on the provision of medicines. This finding led to an amendment to the constitution allowing for the Commonwealth to provide pharmaceutical benefits. Subsequently, the new Pharmaceutical Benefits Act was passed in 1947. The medical profession continued to oppose the act and few doctors participated; however, the 1944 and 1947 acts laid the groundwork for the development of the Pharmaceutical Benefits Scheme (PBS) by establishing it as a component of a state-controlled health system (M. Lewis, 2003a; Lewis and MacPherson, 2008).

To sum up, the relationship between health care and public health changed in Australia during the interwar period. Notably, the National Ministry of Health and the NHMRC were two important institutions that connected health care and public health. However, there was no encompassing national health service or national health insurance, but only a pension scheme covering health care costs for the indigent and the Pharmaceutical Benefits Scheme that originally had voluntary participation. Such policies did not pass because of the opposition by the medical profession who wanted to uphold free practice and the dominance of private health care, among other reasons. On the other hand, national hygienists demanded a national health service that integrated prevention and cure. Yet, a compromise could not be found and health care and public health remained institutionally separated because individual health care for the majority of the population remained in private hands and the national government focused on a public health policy. Nonetheless, the first steps toward institutional and Organizational unification had been made through the PBS and the health care payments for indigent groups.

6.2.2 Conflicts and Responsiveness during the Interwar Period

The battles of the First World War had a lasting impact on the agendas of health policymakers with consequences for the relationships between health care and public health, both in Europe and in Australia. The Holman Labor government appointed a minister for Public Health in New South Wales in 1914 while still at war. Following the First World War, the CW's responsibilities in health matters increased, especially in the area of quarantine. Consequently, many doctors were more eager to pursue preventive work. Many of them returned to Australia with great enthusiasm about public health, such as for bacteriological analyses, which had been well accepted in the army. However, there was a strong sense of disillusion when it came to the implementation of these ideas as a result of the obstacles of administrative processes (M. Lewis, 2003a, 181).

In the following years, the medical profession and national hygienists demanded more prevention and more activity in the area of health care, whereby population engineering played an important role. For national hygienists the central factors for successful settlement in Australia were: (1) the successful institution of adequate measures of preventive medicine, (2) the exclusion of lower races, and (3) an increase in locally born inhabitants (M. Lewis, 2003a). Yet, the racist discourse in Australia did not lead to the implementation of racist public health policies that were comparable to those other countries, such as in Germany (Garton, 1994, 2010).

During the Second World War, the NHMRC produced two important recommendations for a national health service that would integrate curative and preventive medicine. It even contained proposals for a replacement of free doctoral practice by salaried public health doctors. In the years 1941–1943, national hygienists' vision of an integrated health service that provided curative and preventive medicine, with a staff of salaried doctors, dominated the political debate. Specifically, an NHMRC subcommittee report proposed establishing a national system of hospitals and clinics staffed by salaried doctors that would officially supervise the preventive work of private practitioners.

However, these plans failed after a change in the institutional landscape in 1943, when the Centre of Health Planning moved from the NHMRC to the Treasury. The goal of the policy changed from "socialization" to the payment of cash benefits in order to buy services from private practitioners. This was the end of the plans that the previously quoted report had proposed. However, these ideas were not put into place because the national Labor government had made health a part of a larger social welfare-based scheme (M. Lewis, 2008, 230).

There was some responsiveness during the interwar period among the actors from the health care and the public health sectors. Notably, there was an increased professionalization and institutionalization of public health. The creation of a national ministry of health and the establishment of the NHMRC occurred with the support of both the medical profession and national hygienists. However, there was disagreement between doctors and public health professionals on state intervention in health care. Public health professionals demanded a national health service that connected public health with health care, whereas doctors opposed such plans because they wanted to retain free practice. In the end, the government and national parliament followed the argument of the medical profession, although the creation of the PBS showed that this position was not unanimous.

What do these findings reveal for the main hypotheses of this book? Depending on the dominant contextual element, there could be either tight coupling or noncoupling because Australia is a case with a unified government and high professionalism as well as more pluralist interest intermediation. During the interwar period the number of formal national institutions of health care and public health increased but no actual unification between both sectors within state institutions because health care remained largely private. In that sense the theoretical expectations do not hold up. As far as professionalism and interest group inclusion were concerned, the expectation was that Australia had politically active health professions in public health and health care. However, although there were favorable conditions for responsiveness, there were also conflicts between the professions in both policy sectors, especially regarding matters of health care. Actors from both sectors supported common public health legislation. Nonetheless, as predicted based on the possible contextual confounders, the actors did not fight over the distribution of public funds, but rather on whether there should be any publicly funded and regulated health care scheme or insurance. The medical profession opposed the latter and wanted to retain free practice. Given the absence of institutional unification, and the presence and absence of responsiveness, we can conclude that health care and public health were loosely coupled with regard to a national public health policy but decoupled concerning questions of health care.

6.3 Dominance of Medical Care in the Shadow of Tight Coupling (1945–1980)

The context for the coevolution of health care and public health changed after the Second World War, which was about a century after the first public health acts had been introduced in many countries, including Australia, e.g., due to decreasing mortality rates and better medication (Chapter 4). Due to these changes in context, I hypothesized that the contextual conditions for responsiveness among both sectors were not the same as in the preceding time period. Given the reduced demand for public health policies, I expected to find less responsiveness in health care and public health.

6.3.1 Postwar Coevolution of Institutional Relations

In the period following the Second World War, opposition against publicly regulated and funded health care and the further unification of public health and health care continued. In 1946, the High Court ruled that the PBS was unconstitutional because of the action by the medical profession. Subsequently, the court forbade the CW from taking pharmacists and doctors under civil conscription, which basically meant that a national health service, as had been proposed by national hygienists, was no longer possible (M. Lewis, 2003b). In 1948, the resistance of doctors, insurance companies, and pharmacists prevented the introduction of a national health service based on the British model. One particular reason for this was the opposition from the medical profession. The proposed bill by the Australian Labor Party suggested that the NHS would only allow GPs to bill their activities to the state, but not to individuals. Subsequently, the Commonwealth parliament passed an amendment (Art. 51) that allowed doctors to operate independently under the Australian constitution (Alford, 1975; Palmer and Short, 2010; Wilde, 2005) (Int-AUS-4).

In the postwar period, doctors and politicians were convinced that health policy should focus on health care, specifically individual care for the sick. The national minister for health of the Menzies government from 1949 to 1956, Earl Page, who was a surgeon and a member of the BMA, clearly spoke against public health care schemes and the NHS. He contended that "any such scheme should contain elements of self reliance and a sense of personal responsibility. Also it should stress the obligation of the individual to make a [*sic*] least a part of his contribution directly to the ... cost of the scheme." In another case he stated, "No disease runs an exactly similar course in every person. Its course is determined by the constitution and heredity, previous diseases and condition of other organs. It is obvious, therefore, that human disease cannot be overcome by mass treatment" (M. Lewis, 2003b, 14). After the failure to implement a general national health service framework, the CW Labor government worked on an alternative to the coalition government's national health service during the 1950s (M. Lewis, 2003b). As a consequence, Australia remained one of the few countries without comprehensive health insurance during the era of liberal governments from 1950 to 1972 (Wall, 1996). Yet, aside from the public health sector, private health insurance has always been – and is until today – an important pillar of the health system. Its political representation is through the Private Health Insurance Administration Council (PHIAC) and the Private Health Insurance Ombudsman (PHIO). The private health insurance market is highly regulated. Since 1953, the community ranking of private health insurance ensures that private insurance is affordable, regardless of risk. However, private insurance coverage declined after 1984 when Medicare was introduced (J. Hall, 1999).

The Labor government introduced the National Health Service in 1974, which was dismantled by the liberal Whitlam government in 1978 but was reintroduced in 1983 under the name of Medibank and has prevailed since then. The system is financed through income tax. Yet, there was strong opposition against the system; consequently, Australia is the only country that introduced a national health service and dismantled it again afterward (Palmer and Short, 2010; Duckett, 2007). The implementation of a national health service was the continuation of a process and debate that had begun during the Second World War. Nevertheless, Medicare and still contested politically to this day (Boxall and Gillespie, 2013; Carey and McLoughlin, 2016).

After the Second World War, the institutionalization of public health continued under the same institutional umbrella as before, namely through an increasing responsibility of the central government (CG). For instance, from 1945 to 1949 the Commonwealth Health Department carried out a national campaign against tuberculosis under the Commonwealth Tuberculosis Act; this action was coordinated with the member states to combat the prevailing epidemic (Dundas, 1952). Medical prevention mainly drove the campaign against tuberculosis. (Mass radiography was the key to detection.) This is an example of coordination between the Commonwealth and the states. It included a massive flow of funds from the CG to the states, which subgovernments used to construct annexes to state hospitals (M. Lewis, 2003b). For public health policymakers, the advancements in pharmaceutical policy provided an opportunity for large immunization campaigns (M. Lewis, 2008). Public health measures were again extended in the context of the Community Health Program (CHP) in 1973 as part of the Medibank scheme, which aimed at introducing complementary health insurance in Australia (Sax, 1984, 106–107). The CHP had put into place preventative health policy innovations under the auspices of the national government; however, there were differences at the state level regarding their interest in prevention programs. Nevertheless, the program remained reasonably coherent, as a review in 1986 showed that the program mainly provided tertiary and secondary prevention (Baum, 2008, 45).

To summarize, the institutional relationship between the health care and public health sectors changed incrementally following the Second World War. Due to a number of reforms, the state, notably the CW government, gradually increased its responsibilities regarding health care regulation and provisions. It augmented the scope of the public provision of health care with the establishment of the PBS through the establishment of a health care scheme for pensioners. Along with these changes, public health policy became increasingly nationalized. In a nutshell, the centralization of health care and public health increased, along with the institutional unification of both fields, and the states and the CW coordinated public health policies. A more formal institutional and organizational unification occurred with the establishment of national health insurance in 1974 (although it was dismantled for a short time in the late 1970s).

6.3.2   Responsiveness Despite Transgression

Despite the dominance of medical care in the postwar period, there was responsiveness between the health care and public health sectors, with mutual support among actors from both sectors on public health policies. The medical profession had become one of the most prominent players in Australian health policy during the 1940s. Medical organizations in Australia were organized as branches of the BMA until 1962, and the *British Medical Journal* was part of the organization's membership services (Bryder, 1994). The profession had successfully opposed the introduction of a national health service as well as urban and rural health centers (M. Lewis, 2003a). The empowerment of doctors also had consequences for priorities in health policies. The main topic in health policy after 1945 was the provision of access to individual care.

However, once individual care became the core of health policy, the activities of doctors were also extended to individual prevention and counseling about lifestyle, especially smoking. The NHMRC recommended in 1962 that the CW and states ceasing all tobacco advertisements. Moreover, it recommended that the CW work on risk-reducing strategies with other countries. In 1965, the Australian Cancer Society brought together representatives of the Australian Medical Association (AUSMA), the Royal Australian College of Physicians (RACP), the Royal Australian College of Surgeons (RACS), Australian College of Pathologists, National Heart Foundation, and National Tuberculosis and Chest Foundation to call for more health education and tobacco control policy from the federal government, especially bans on tobacco advertisements (M. Lewis, 2003b). Health foundations supported this undertaking of doctors, such as the Anti-Cancer Council (Dick, 2001). Other organizations, such as the National Heart Foundation, also participated in the political advocacy regarding prevention (Int-AUS-11) (M. Lewis, 2003b).

Public health changed significantly during the postwar period from a focus on infectious diseases to noncommunicable diseases. However, public health professionals did not gain the same importance as doctors did in the health care sector and they were less politicized. Although there was political action in the public health sector, activities were now much more focused on specific health issues, such as tobacco consumption, but political action was much lower for other issues, such as environmental problems and alcoholism. In the 1970s, the Action Council on Smoking and Health, Australia in Western Australia employed the first full-time lobbyist in the public health sector. Other organizations emulated this step, particularly the cancer councils and the Heart Foundation in Victoria, which employed lobbyists that pursued agendas for more health promotion. Together with the Australian Medical Association, committed academics, and interested politicians – mostly doctors from both political parties – these lobbyists successfully pursued a political agenda for more regulation in the areas of tobacco, alcohol, and, more recently, obesity (Montague, Borland, and Sinclair, 2001; Chapman and Wakefield, 2001; Wise and Signal, 2000)(Int-AUS-10).

Responsiveness between both sectors resulted in a series of public health measures and policy integration of both sectors, for example, when prevention was transferred to individual health services with the creation of community health centers (CHCs), which provided primary health care. What is more, during the 1970s, the Cancer Council in Victoria ran several campaigns against skin cancer (Montague, Borland, and Sinclair, 2001). Due to the research provided by health NGOs, the state governments began to introduce more public health measures. Governments created the first preventive measures for cancer in the 1960s, for example, mammography screening (Int-AUS-12). Further measures followed in the 1970s. For instance, Victoria introduced compulsory seat belts in 1971, the first smoking bans during the same decade, and bans on tobacco advertisements at the state level in the 1980s (M. Lewis, 2003b, 2008). In addition, in the late 1970s and early 1980s, the state governments created more anticancer activities, such as the Flip-Flop-Flap campaign (Int-AUS-4, Int-AUS-6).

To conclude, regarding responsiveness between both sectors, the analysis reveals that political activities of the medical profession and doctors increased considerably during the postwar period. This specifically concerns the impact of the profession on health care policymaking, such as the opposition against a UK-style national health service. Doctors successfully defended the predominance of the private health care system, which included their right to exercise free practice and to be economically independent. At the same time, they participated actively in the creation of more public health policies, which included the establishment of organizations that supported public health policies along with health foundations, but also the direct support of more public health policies, such as immunization and tobacco control policies. At the same time, public health underwent a significant change, both in terms of its professional role and the policy instruments that were applied.

The formulated theoretical expectations regarding Australia held that both sectors would have institutional unification and responsiveness as a result of the unified government and high professionalism. Again, the expectations were partly confirmed. Concerning the effect of unified government, there was an increasing centralization of health policy after the Second World War. This was true for fiscal policy in general, but the analysis also showed this in the field of health policy. In particular, there was more national legislation in the fields of health care and public health, including improved coordination among both policy fields. This came along with an institutional and organizational unification of both sectors in the political administration of the national government, which administered both sectors under the same institutional umbrella. Particularly following the unification of the health care and the public health sectors with the establishment of the national health service, Australia fulfilled the discussed conditions for sectorial unification. Concerning professionalism, there was political activity among the medical profession in general, as was expected from the theoretical discussion of professionalism. However, there was also a political investment by doctors in matters of public health and cooperation between actors from both sectors. Therefore, there was responsiveness between the health care and public health sectors during the postwar time period in Australia. As the analysis in the previous chapter on the United Kingdom and the preceding sections of this chapter show, the conditions does not necessarily play out as expected in all countries. Although the postwar period reduced the demands for public health policies regarding how they were made during the late twentieth century, there was no increase in conflicts between both sectors, but rather continuing responsiveness.

6.4   Tight Coupling of Health Care and Public Health (1980–2010)

Regarding t3, I hypothesized that tight coupling between health care and public health in Australia would be found. Apart from the professional and governmental dimensions, the hypotheses discussed expected that the change in the context would cause different dynamics in the responsiveness of both sectors. The reason for this was that during the 1970s, the pattern of prevalent diseases changed toward a higher prevalence of noncommunicable diseases – such as heart attack, stroke, and cancer – which needed the prevention of risk factors and screenings. On the other hand, criticisms concerning the existing concept of health policy became louder, demanding a refocusing of health policy, with a greater emphasis on matters of health policy.

6.4.1 Consolidating Unification and Re-separation

The institutional and organizational unification of health care and public health continued in Australia from the 1980s onward. The eventual implementation of a national health insurance scheme in 1983 moved the Australian health insurance system from one with a purely private character to a tax-funded public health insurance that granted universal coverage and fixed the unification of health care with public health. The universalist principles introduced into the Australian health care system entailed access to public hospitals and rebates for private health insurance. Nevertheless, private elements remained important in health care financing and provision (Carey and McLoughlin, 2016; Trein, 2017c), such as levels of patient contribution in the PBS. Overall, reprivatization of the Australian health care system increased in recent years (Boxall and Gillespie, 2013; Kay and Boxall, 2015).

Beginning in the 1980s, the CW, member states, and health foundations began to introduce public health strategies aimed at combating risk factors in order to avoid chronic diseases at later stages. These entailed policies against alcohol and tobacco as well as traffic accident prevention and policies against skin cancer. One example is the draft for a national alcohol policy that the National Standing Committee of Health Ministers put together in 1984, or the National Road Safety Strategy 2001–2010. These were very successful health education measures that changed public opinion and behaviors toward cancer (Chapman and Wakefield, 2001). At the same time, some of the states (e.g., Victoria, South Australia, Western Australia) established health promotion foundations that used tobacco tax money to promote better health as well as for cultural and sports activities (Baum, 2008).

Public health policies also extended to the national level. For instance, in 1992 the national parliament banned tobacco advertisement in print, only sponsoring of international sports events was allowed (and eventually banned in 2006) (M. Lewis, 2008). Regarding indoor smoking bans, the government of the Australian Capital Territory (ACT) led the way and introduced the first law in 1994. Other governments soon followed thereafter (Chapman and Wakefield, 2001). In Australia, there is high public acceptance for health promotion measures, such as smoking regulations, vehicle passenger safety restraints, gun control, fencing regulations for private swimming pools, and alcohol regulation policies (Hawe, Wakefield, and Nutbeam, 2001). Apart from these public health activities aimed at noncommunicable diseases, there were many public health developments in the areas of infectious diseases, such as strategies against SARS and funding for more vaccines. Interestingly, fears about SARS spread all over the news in 2003, but most of the national headlines in Australia focused on obesity; both issues concerned the Australian Health Ministers Council (AHMC) (Lin and Robinson, 2005).

The dynamics regarding the unification of health care and public health services seem to have fostered unification at the ministerial level since the 1980s. More and more departments were integrated in the national ministry of health since the 1980s, for example, the Department of Community Health Services in 1987. Further departments followed. Nevertheless, there were also instances of disintegration; overall, however, the responsibilities of the ministry of health grew during the last twenty- five years.[2] What is more, the Labor government created the Australian National Preventive Health Agency (ANPHA) in 2011 with the responsibility for large public health programs regarding the most important risk factors in health policy, such as tobacco, alcohol, and obesity (APHTF, 2009). Again, this reform separated public health from the national ministry of health; however, the liberal government abolished the agency again in 2014.[3]

To summarize, the institutional relationship between health care and public health remained unified during t3. The CW government regained a central role in both sectors since the 1980s. Although there were some reforms, such as the establishment of a national public health agency, this did not lead to a strict institutional separation between health care and public health. Therefore, institutional distinctiveness remained absent during this time period. Given that public policymaking in Australia underwent even further centralization during these times, this development is not surprising.

6.4.2 Broad Responsiveness and Policy Integration

Health care and public health remained responsive in the sense that there was policy integration and discourse coalitions among actors and interest groups from both fields. The previously discussed health foundations are important for this development. During the 1960s and 1970s research showed increasing deaths due to environmental factors, such as asbestos and cigarette smoke. In order to bring these findings into politics, Australian health foundations, such as the heart foundations and cancer councils, advocated for more public health policies or created organizations designed only for advocacy, such as ACOSH in Western Australia and ASH in Victoria as well as at the national level (Int-AUS-32). Such activities were often supported or initiated by doctors who were interested in preventive health policies. For instance, the Cancer Council Victoria is staffed with a medically trained faculty that pursues research in health promotion and clinical treatment, and it pays full-time lobbyists to support public health policies (Int-AUS-12). Liberal health ministers in South Australia supported smoking bans in public dining and coffee places (Int-AUS-2), and a liberal Commonwealth health minister created the first National Tobacco Strategy in 1997 (Int-AUS-19; Int-AUS-1) (Baum, 2008).

Although the medical profession played an important role in placing many public health issues on the political agenda, such as tobacco and road-traffic issues, there had been conflicts and less support from doctors with regard to the mixtures of certain policy instruments. There are still debates between the community health side, which mostly entail health foundations and the medical profession, regarding which population-based instruments are appropriate, such as whether it is better to employ educative responses or environmental and legislative approaches (Int-AUS-31). Community health doctors sometimes neglect medical prevention measures because they want to avoid sending patients to hospitals (Int-AUS-2). However, there is also resistance against the increase in preventive health policies. One of the major problems with many public health measures is that they are designed to have long-term effects and aim at risk factors. One interview partner put it the following way: "This is not the same as if you had a major outbreak of malaria or cholera, when the media would be storming the minister's office and asking about what is [being] done to prevent the disease" (Int-AUS-24). Contrariwise, health care issues are more likely to receive attention, such as prices for pharmaceuticals or waiting times in ambulances, as well as other life-threatening health issues in Australia's system that become front-page stories (Int-AUS-27). Despite these differences, Australia has developed strong public health advocacy for many health issues in the last thirty years, which includes actors from the health care and public health sectors in a discourse coalition regarding many areas of health policy (Daube, 2006).

In addition, the policy integration of health care and public health increased during the period after 1980. For instance, disease-related programs and strategies became important in health policy. These were policies that entailed an explicit combination of public health and health care measures. In other words, they included strategies to cure the disease through the individual, but also a series of preventive measures aimed at health hazards among individuals, as well as population or settings-based measures. These strategies focused on specific health problems or diseases in general. A prominent example was the National Better Health Program (Anderiesz, Elwood, and Hill, 2006), which was put into place in the 1990s and demanded a focus on prevention and primary health care (Baum, 2008, 46).

The aforementioned National Preventative Health Strategy, with the stated goal to make Australia the healthiest country by 2020, is another example (APHTF, 2009). Other strategies were more disease focused. For instance, the National Cancer Strategies that existed on a national level since the early 1990s, was especially aimed at screening and immunization, but also financing, research, and the coordination of cancer treatment. Responses to the disease were institutionalized in the Cancer Australia Act 2006 (Cancer Australia Strategic Plan 2011–2014). These successful strategies are based on the capacities of the federal government to intervene in health measures as it is responsible for the PBS, cancer screening, and other areas, such as the provision of radiotherapy. In addition, the long-standing support from the NGO sector, especially in the name of many NGOs such as the cancer councils, plays an important factor in this regard (Anderiesz,

Elwood, and Hill, 2006). Another example of actor responsiveness and its positive impact on public health policy is Australia's response to AIDS. The first national AIDS strategy (1991–1995) was the result of a successful alliance comprising government officials, community health groups, and health care services. The path to the law helped to create a network of AIDS organizations for gay groups, drug users, and sex workers (Baum, 2008, 494). The strategy was renewed in the following years and some of the state governments created their own strategies.

To sum up, there had been responsiveness between the health care and public health sectors since the 1980s. Notably, the medical profession had been involved in creating and advocating for public health policies, alongside other actors that belonged to the public health sector, such as the cancer councils (although these organizations also take care of health care matters, they are very active in public health policy). The cooperation specifically concerned policies involving risk factors, such as tobacco and alcohol. Yet, as far as infectious diseases such as AIDS were concerned, there was also cooperation between actors from both fields. Another dimension of sectorial responsiveness pertained to policy integration. Health care and public health were integrated with regard to many health problems. This not only concerned specific risk factors, but also sicknesses such as cancer or diabetes.

The analysis of Australia confirms the expectations concerning the discussed hypotheses. More unified government comes along with the institutional unification of health care and public health. Although there were some attempts to differentiate health care from public health, especially by Labor governments, the national ministry of health retained both sectors under tight control and as institutionally unified. With respect to the connection between professionalism/institutions of interest intermediation and responsiveness between policy sectors, the results confirm the theory put forward. Notably, the medical profession had been very active in advocating for more preventive health policies. This time, the contextual conditions reinforced these efforts, because the demand for public health policies had become even more apparent to the professions and interest groups in health policy, in addition to parliamentarians and decision makers. The presence of many examples for policy integration enhances this finding even further.

6.5 Discussion

What does this analysis imply for the hypotheses regarding the coevolution of the health care and public health sectors in Australia? The following section will summarize the results and discuss the implications of this case study for theory.

The results (Table 6.1) show that health care and public health in Australia coevolved from loose coupling during the colonial period toward tight coupling. Both sectors were institutionally distinct from one another. This changed incrementally over the course of the twentieth century, notably through a series of small reforms that gradually increased the role of the state in health policy. In addition, this dynamic entailed the unification of both sectors at the national level with the implementation of a national ministry of health and a medical research council (the NHMRC) that combined health care and public health research. One consequence of these reforms was the incremental unification of these sectors during the post-Second World War period, especially with the establishment of a national health service during the 1970s that integrated health care further into the national institutional health policy framework. Moreover, the creation of the community health centers at the municipal level established further unification between health care and public health. Since the 1980s, health care and public health moved toward further unification of both sectors, especially because there was policy coordination, such as with disease and risk factor prevention strategies.

Regarding responsiveness, the analysis revealed significant evidence for cooperation between health care and public health on the levels of professions and interest groups, but also policy integration. Other than in the United Kingdom, there was responsiveness among health care and public health actors during the early time periods, prior to the Second World War. This means that despite the different professional roles in health care (essentially medical organizations) and public health (e.g., public health doctors, NGOs, and members of the administration), these actors responded to one another in the sense that they commonly advocated for health policies, specifically public health policies, both in colonial and in more recent times. Yet, there were also conflicts, especially between public health reformers, such as national hygienists and doctoral organizations, with respect to the implementation of a national public health service in the 1930s and 1940s, similarly to the United Kingdom. After the Second World

Table 6.1. *Coevolution of health care and public health in Australia.*

1880–1918 (t0)	1918–1945 (t1)	1945–1980 (t2)	1980–2010 (t3)
Loose coupling: Separation in colonies; health care mostly privately organized; a broad public health coalition; separation of health care and public health; actor responsiveness through the employment of doctors in public health services as well as political activity	*Decoupling (Loose coupling):* Less distinctiveness at the national level; responsiveness entailing conflicts regarding a national health service; coordination of policy outputs at the national level	*Tight coupling (Loose coupling):* Incremental increase of unification of sectors at the national/state level; actor responsiveness: transgression of health care on public health; broad public health coalition	*Tight coupling:* Continuing institutional unification at the national level; actor responsiveness: broad public health coalition; policy coordination and integration

135

War, health care actors claimed and secured most of the resources in health policy, including some discretion with respect to prevention. At the same time, however, actors belonging to the health care sector, such as doctors, publicly supported and demanded more public health policies, such as for prevention in general, but also specific risk factors, for example tobacco control policies. This broad coalition of actors in favor of health and public health entailed health foundations and doctoral organizations that lobbied for public health issues. Beginning in the late 1970s, policy coordination and integration between health care and public health emerged as there were specific health strategies connecting cures with prevention for certain diseases, such as cancer, as well as risk factors, for example smoking and alcohol.

6.5.1   Unified Government, Professionalism, and Interest Intermediation in Australia

What are the implications of these findings for the discussed hypotheses? This book argues that health care and public health in Australia are either tightly coupled or noncoupled, depending on political institutions and contextual conditions. The chance for tight coupling between sectors is generally high because there is high professionalism, a unified government, and competitive interest intermediation. To what extent do these expectations hold in light of the results?

Regarding the impact of unified government, the results for Australia are different than expected, especially for the first two time periods, when both sectors were relatively separated institutionally. This is not so surprising, given that the establishment of a national state and accompanying institutions occurred fairly late in Australia compared to other countries. Although Australia and the United Kingdom have similar systems of government today, there were differences in the late nineteenth and early twentieth centuries, as Australia was a federation coming together in which much discretion rested in the hands of state governments. This changed during the course of the twentieth century. Health policy reforms unified health care and public health institutionally, especially during the post-Second World War period. In particular, the establishment of a national health service was a consequence of the unified government that empowered the left party, which did not need to make a compromise in parliament to put this institution into place.

Health professions and interest groups took an important role in politicizing health policy matters. Notably, the medical profession was particularly active politically. This became visible with regard to the setup of public health. Doctors across parties supported state activity in the field of public health – with infections but also with respect to risk factors such as smoking. Regarding preventive health policies, the medical profession had the same ideas as public health actors and thus the same political goals. Consequently, doctors were active politically to promote legislation for matters of public health and formed a discourse coalitions with health care related actors. Responsiveness changed with respect to individual health care. The medical profession opposed too much interference of the state into matters of health care and thus a national health service that would have combined cure and prevention, which resulted in conflicts between national hygienists and the medical profession. Furthermore, the competitive manner in which interest intermediation works in Australia incentivized doctors to promote public health policies.

Along with the institutional unification and responsiveness between actors, health care and public health coevolved toward unification, which became visible in the integration of policies from both sectors, as the examples of the post-1980 period showed. These policies entailed preventive and curative measures regarding infections such as HIV, cancer, and diabetes, but also risk factors such as tobacco and alcohol.

The contextual conditions discussed did not play out exactly as expected, but the predictions were better than those for the United Kingdom. In comparison with the United Kingdom, the difference in Australia is the later development of the state and the hierarchical governance in health policy. A tentative conclusion regarding responsiveness could be that the state took an important role in public health policy more quickly in the United Kingdom, in the sense that it governs the relationship of health care and public health by means of hierarchical governance. In contrast, hierarchical governance in health policy emerged later in Australia. In this situation, high professionalism in the field of health policy and pluralist interest intermediation played an important role in the agenda setting of health policies, including public health policies. In this case, the combination of unified government and professionalism led to health care and public health becoming unified. Consequently, it seems that the mix of private and public intervention in public health is a significant element of the coevolution of health care and public health. This book will discuss this element, the timing of institutional emergence, and its interaction with professionalism in the comparative chapter.

6.5.2 Competing Explanations

Nevertheless, apart from unified government and professionalism, other theoretical elements emerged as important for the coevolution of health care and public health: sectorial complementarity, policy learning, and differences between political parties.

1. *Complementarity:* My analysis of the coevolution of health care and public health in the United Kingdom showed that both sectors coevolved toward complementarity of institutions, but also policies. The findings are similar with regard to Australia. Health care and public health institutions emerged as consequences of particular health problems, but not as a coordinated institutional arrangement. Yet over time, they coevolved toward complementarity, which means increasing policy integration and learning in both sectors. However, other than in the United Kingdom, this came along with fewer conflicts between the professions of the health care and public health sectors.

2. *Policy learning:* Policy learning is important concerning the relationship between health care and public health in Australia. The analysis of the coevolution of both sectors in the United Kingdom has shown that high professionalism comes along with policy learning. Notably, politically active professions adapt innovations regarding health care and public health policies and put them on the political agenda, including toward tobacco control policy, cancer prevention, and infectious diseases such as AIDS. Therefore, politicized professions not only come along with responsiveness between policy sectors but also policy learning, because professional organizations play an important role in transferring innovations into the political process.

3. *Party differences:* This impacts the role of political parties concerning the relationship between health care and public health. In Australia, there were conflicts between parties regarding health care institutionalization, notably in the creation of a national

health insurance in the interwar period. Both parties opposed this reform. Labor supported the creation of a state-governed health care service, whereas the Liberal Party just opposed this reform fiercely. Nevertheless, in later decades, regarding public health policies, there were no basic conflicts between both parties about the necessity of an encompassing public health agenda, especially in the 1980s. Naturally, we would expect that the Liberal Party would be more opposed to public health policies, because these instruments often target individual and corporate behavior and freedom. Nevertheless, in Australia, some of the ministers in the Liberal Party were doctors who supported an encompassing public health agenda. What is more, the AUSMA was part of the liberal conservative base of the party and advocated more public health policies.

6.6 Summary

This book focused on Australia as a case study because it expected to find tight coupling between health care and public health even though it is a federal state. The results of the analysis confirmed the hypothesis, notably for the more recent time periods. Health care and public health were separated institutionally during the late nineteenth century. Only during the 1970s did health care become the matter of a national health service and therefore a case of institutional and organizational unification. Alternatively, regarding responsiveness, the results showed that the medical profession, public health doctors, and private organizations concerned with public health matters were responsive and collaborated in health policy matters, such as the tobacco control policy. Similar to the United Kingdom, both sectors coevolved toward complementarity. However, there are differences between the two countries. In Australia, health care and public health institutions emerged later than in the United Kingdom, as did conflicts between actors and professions from both sectors. On the other hand, doctors and the medical profession were more politically active in public health policies.

7 | Germany: Dominance of Individual Health Care and Decoupling from Public Health

This chapter analyzes the coevolution of health care and public health in Germany. The case study examines the coupling of the two sectors against a backdrop of a combination of unified government and low professionalism as well as corporatist interest intermediation. My theoretical priors lead me to expect to find noncoupling of health care and public health, even if the contextual conditions are favorable to sectoral responsiveness. The results show that the political activity of the medical profession did not focus on broader health issues, i.e, it did not give nonmedical public health policies a high political priority. Nevertheless, there was policy integration of health care and public health since the policymakers followed the example of other countries. In contrast to my hypothesis, the analysis demonstrates that the federal structure of Germany has resulted in institutional fragmentation of the two sectors – despite the comparatively centralized structure of the German state. Nevertheless, there was policy integration of health care and public health since German policymakers started following the example of other countries.

7.1 Local Public Health in the Shadow of the National Health Insurance (1880–1918)

This book argues that during t0, the context should have been favorable for responsiveness between health care and public health because the increasing prevalence of noncommunicable diseases and the return of infections created a demand for preventive health policy. In Germany, due to weak professionalism, neither health care nor public health professions should play an important role in politicizing matters of health care and public health. Therefore, I expect that the change in the contextual conditions should have led to no increase in responsiveness between these two fields but that conflicts were likely to arise between health professions and other interest groups. At the same time, due to the relatively unified and centralized government, the fields of health care and public health should be unified institutionally and organizationally.

7.1.1 Institutional Distinctiveness on Three Levels of Government

During the second half of the nineteenth century, the institutionalization of public health in Germany entailed two aspects. On the one hand, there were institutions associated with the control of epidemics and health policing, which were situated at the state level. The tasks of the subgovernments were medical policing, sanitary policy, the admission of drugs, and psychiatric expertise (Labisch, 1982; Rosen, 1993 [1959]; Weindling, 1994). On the other hand, there were municipal health services at the community level. Health remained the responsibility of the states after the unification in 1871. Public health remained fragmented even during periods of time when national administration centralized. All the doctors that were trained by the state became district doctors, *Kreisärzte*, and were subordinate to the control of the civil service (Weindling, 1994). Different public health institutions emerged at the municipal level. In the late 1860s, the public health scholar Virchow encouraged the city of Berlin to build sewage and water supply systems. Other cities followed (Fee, 1994; Schmiedebach, 2002, 191–192).

Contrary to the public health sector, health care was institutionalized at the national level in 1883 when a national health insurance law was put into place. As in other countries, Germany had a voluntaristic tradition of health policy, which included the provision of health by local and voluntary organizations. Nevertheless, in the late nineteenth century national, social policies, such as sickness, disability, old age, and unemployment insurance, were put into place (Porter, 1999, 198). These reforms challenged the voluntaristic model of social policy by passing a number of interventionist policies that made Germany the forerunner of national social policy legislation in Europe. The motivations for introducing social legislation were to prevent socialist challenges to state authority from politically disenfranchised workers and to arbitrate disputes between employers and employees. Similarly, the purpose behind the introduction of

public health insurance was to protect the population from impoverishment to reduce political support for radical and politically organized groups of workers. It was against this background and to
respond to some of the political demands of the working class that
Kaiser William I passed a law introducing general health insurance in 1883 (Diederichs, Klotmann, and Schwartz, 2008), which
established compulsory health insurance. The local *Krankenkassen*
[health insurance funds] participated in the implementation. The *freie
Hilfskassen* [free relief funds] had been legalized since 1876 and
had served as an alternative form of compulsory health insurance
(Hennock and Peter, 1987; Mommsen and Mock, 1981; Porter,
1999).

Although the officially announced goal of the health insurance
was to prevent the impoverishment of workers in times of sickness,
they focused on the provision of medical services. The insurance
employed doctors under contract in exchange for their right to work
for individual fees. This regulation of the medical profession was a
subject of constant political quarrels between doctors and the state;
for instance, in 1913, the medical profession went on strike against the
poor working conditions and doctors were able to secure an agreement
(the Berlin Agreement) that allowed them to close a universal contract
that applied to all health insurance organizations (Porter, 1999, 199).
However, the inclusion of doctors reduced their political power as
a pressure group, because their position in the self-administration
of the insurance programs secured important benefits (Alber, 1982;
M. Schmidt, 2005b; Rosenbrock and Gerlinger, 2014).

To sum up, health care and public health were institutionally distinct
in Germany in the late nineteenth and early twentieth centuries.
To some extent this is not surprising because the German Empire
was newly reunited after the Franco-German War of 1870–1871.
Although Germany was a federal state, the national government had
a great deal of leverage in policymaking as a result of framework
legislation and centralized bureaucracy. However, this did not
lead to the institutional, unification of health care and public
health. Whereas the establishment of a national health insurance
was a nationalization of health policy, the same did not occur
with regard to the municipal and state public health services,
which remained the legislative responsibility of lower levels of
government.

7.1.2 Professional Differentiation and Political Inclusion of Doctors

Professionalization in the health sector generally increased in the late nineteenth century. The National Society for Public Health was founded in 1873 as an offshoot of the German Association of Scientists and Doctors. The members of this society had a strong admiration for British public health reformers. At the same time, public health research advanced considerably and became a thriving scientific discipline in Germany. The interpretation of the evidence for infectious diseases changed constantly (McKeown, 1979; Weindling, 1994). In the late nineteenth century, researchers found out that specific health conditions and the environment were mutually reinforcing causes of health problems. From this perspective, new preventive strategies such as social hygiene emerged. This form of prevention focused on certain disadvantaged groups and later became part of eugenics (Weindling, 1994).

Politically, public health sciences came along with demands for state-employed doctors. After the 1890s, especially doctors favoring eugenics, demanded schemes that made all doctors state officials, yet, in reality, full-time public health positions remained rare. Until the early nineteenth century, public health policies had been made by states and cities without the participation of doctors and sometimes even against their ideas. It was primarily the elites in city-states that determined the necessity for public health policy and eventually public medicine to sustain cities as social units (Labisch and Woelk, 2012, 61).

The literature argues that public health also had a political dimension, as will be discussed in the following. Many of the doctors who were employed in the communal public health services were part of liberal – and, after the First World War, socialist – political circles; they were often of Jewish origin (Labisch, 1982). For workers and voluntary organizations, public health was an important field to pursue political activities and to demonstrate political autonomy and resistance in the authoritarian *Kaiserreich* [empire]. For instance, in 1892 there was a boycott of the Royal Charité in Berlin after a cholera epidemic to protest against the poor public health conditions in the city-state. Oftentimes, public health doctors were simultaneously the leaders of strikes and boycotts and justified their political activities with public health concerns, such as sanitation (Labisch, 1985). Nevertheless, Germany did not have the same degree of professionalization and staff density as the British MOsH. Yet, proponents of social hygiene and social medicine – including left parties – demanded a more encompassing national health service (Porter, 1999, 109; Alber and Bernardi Schenkluhn, 1992; Huerkamp, 1985).

The introduction of a national health insurance also had an effect on the formation of the medical profession as well as on its political activity. With the introduction of the national health insurance in Germany, the state took a more important role in shaping the medical profession than in the United States. Licensing was rigidly regulated early on in Germany and doctors were integrated in the social health insurance system, which strongly controlled medical practice. Doctors wanted the help of the German state in order to protect their professional autonomy and degrees. This had consequences for the politicization of doctors in organizations of interest. In contrast, professional medical organizations in the United States emerged bottom-up from the cities and states, whereas in Germany they were created with a lot of organizational help from the state. In Germany the business of medical organizations focused on scientific exchange as well as friendly networking, while the self-regulation of the American organizations politicized doctors to a larger degree than in Germany (Gottweis et al., 2004).

The German health system was the prototype of a corporatist system of negotiations (Lehmbruch, 1988). It entailed the participation of a centralized interest organization in policy formulation and decision making from the very introduction of the health insurance system (Bandelow, 1998, 22). With the inclusion of the medical profession in the statutory health insurance, the state made a deal with the medical organizations. They were included in the administration of the health insurance and consequently reduced their political activities as pressure groups (Labisch, 1982).

To conclude, during the late nineteenth and early twentieth centuries, there was not much responsiveness between health care and public health. Notably, the medical profession negotiated a deal with the state and received a privileged role in the corporatist system of health care governance. In return, it did not act as a strong pressure group. Overall, doctors were politically less active regarding public health matters than, for instance, doctors in Australia were during the same period of time. German doctors focused mostly on matters that directly concerned their interests, such as health insurance legislation. Therefore, public health did not have a strong professional lobby because public health doctors and interest groups were rather weakly organized.

What do these results imply regarding the discussed hypotheses? I had assumed that Germany was a case of noncoupling of health care and public health because it had a relatively unified government and low professionalism. This book hypothesized that there would be institutional unification because of the framework legislation in place at the national level. Alternatively, the theoretical section argued that low professionalism would come along with the absence of responsiveness between the two sectors. The hypothesis regarding low professionalism proved to be correct. As argued in the theoretical section, the state controlled the education of doctors in Germany. The inclusion of the medical profession in the governance of the national health insurance system was an act of depoliticization in that it granted some employment to doctors. Thus, doctors were less politically active and did not defend public health policies and other matters in health policy as long as they did not concern their own material interests. Accordingly, there was less support for the agenda of public health from the medical profession, and partisan interests came into play in politicizing matters of health policy – notably, public health. Population health policies became a political demand of leftist parties only, without the substantive backing of the medical profession.

With unified government, the results were different from what was expected. Although Germany had a unified government, there was no institutional unification of health care and public health. Public health policies remained at the discretion of the subnational and municipal governments, whereas health care policy became a national matter. As expected, contextual elements were not important for the German case.

7.2   Conflicts and Unification of Health Care and Public Health (1918–1945)

The interwar period in Germany can be split into two phases: the post-First World War period, which lasted until the NSDAP came into power, and the period under the Nazi government, 1933–1945. The circumstances were both favorable and unfavorable to responsiveness between the health care and the public health sectors during this time. Infections were still the most pressing health problem, but earlier public health policies had some successes. At the same time, medical technology had improved and many diseases could be cured. The increasing possibilities for curative medicine should have reduced support for public health policies in the medical profession. What is more, after the economic crisis of 1929, government austerity measures could cause distributional conflicts between these two policy fields.

7.2.1 Between Institutional Separation and Unification

In the time after the First World War, fears of the biological and social degeneration of the population began to rise as a result of the large number of mentally and physically wounded soldiers after the war. Consequently, policymakers increased public health efforts after the war. The tasks of the public health services were prevention and primary care, especially regarding tuberculosis, alcoholism, genital diseases, and mental illness. However, the interest in preventive health policies was significant because the cure of many diseases was still difficult if not impossible (Schleiermacher, 2002). Public health measures had already become important during the war. For instance, the national government centralized the *Fürsorgestellen* [welfare or social care offices] into integrated health services (Porter, 1999, 192–193; Steindor, 2009). Nevertheless, the project to create a national ministry of health combining health care and public health failed. Health care financing remained part of the social insurance legislation and public health remained institutionally subordinated to it as it was organized at the state and municipal jurisdiction level (Schleiermacher, 2002).

Reforms in the German health care policy from 1910 to 1945 focused on the expansion of statutory health insurance financing and coverage. The health insurance legislation of 1911 (*Reichsversicherungsverordnung*) created a unified social insurance that comprised health, accident, and retirement insurance. At the same time the regulation of health insurance payments was unified. Originally, the goal of the health insurance was to compensate for loss of income in case of sickness. With the passage of this legislation, its profile changed and payments for health care services became more important

(Gottweis et al., 2004). The health insurances increased the scope of included groups; incorporating women and children in the health insurance resulted in a significant improvement of the coverage of the population as well as the state of the population's health in general (Steindor, 2009).

Rather than setting up a national ministry of health to pursue public health policies, reformers attempted to include prevention and public health in the statutory health insurance. In the mid-1920s, health insurance began to include preventive measures in their portfolios. The federal parliament decided in 1925 that doctors could bill for preventive measures, but only in case of concrete health problems such as tuberculosis or genital diseases (Labisch and Tennstedt, 1991). Yet, the inclusion of prevention and public health in the statutory health insurance came along with legal problems since – in principle – the health insurance had no permission to pay for services that were not connected to a diagnosed disease; however, preventive health policy aimed exactly at that (Moser, 2002; Steindor, 2009). Therefore, during the Weimar Republic health care and public health remained structurally separated; health care continued to be included in the social insurance institutions, whereas public health remained located at the subnational and the municipal levels of government.

Institutionally, the relationship between health care and public health changed after the Nazis came to power in 1933, which brought profound changes in health policymaking. In the health care sector, the new government curtailed the corporatist autonomy of the health insurance system and the power of medical associations increased. Specifically, self-governance of health insurance came under the supervision of the state, especially the department of labor, and corporatist structures dissolved (Alber and Bernardi Schenkluhn, 1992, 55). The coverage of health care services was extended for the population in general, but some groups were excluded, among them Jews, the disabled, but also members of the political opposition (Schwoch, 2002).

In the public health policy sector under the Nazi government, reforms entailed the inclusion of eugenic ideas in public health policies and the nationalization of the public health services. The institutional consequences of this development were a merger of the municipal public health services with those of the subgovernments of the federation.

(Germany officially became a unitary state in 1934.) One of the tasks of these new public health offices was the implementation of the new sterilization law of 1933, which was aimed at non-Aryan population groups. Furthermore, there were primary prevention policies such as tobacco control measures (although the military distributed cigarettes to soldiers at the front) (Proctor, 1996; Ellerbrock, 2002). These policies revived the tradition of medical policing that had been present in Germany during the nineteenth century; however, this time the policy was based on social Darwinism. As a consequence, centralized health institutions supported by the medical professions became crucial in the execution of the Holocaust (Weindling, 1994; Eberle, 2002; Rosenbrock and Gerlinger, 2009). These reforms reduced the dualism of health protection between the member states of the federation, which were responsible for prevention of and reaction to infectious diseases, and the municipal public health services, which had been in charge of secondary prevention and primary care at the individual level and had been an important element of the German public health sector (Labisch, 1982).

To sum up, the institutional and organizational relationship of health care and public health had two faces in Germany during the interwar period and the Second World War. During the Weimar Republic, health care and public health remained institutionally separated. Health care was governed at the national level because the national health insurance remained the dominant paradigm of health care policy and because such insurance was mandatory. Public health was managed at the state (health protection) and municipal levels (secondary prevention, health education). There were some attempts to integrate both sectors by trying to include public health and preventive policies in the health insurance, but this did not work very well because the principle of prevention was legally incompatible with health insurance. During the Third Reich, health care and public health were institutionally and organizationally unified. Health insurance carriers lost their dominant role and a national public health service was created.

7.2.2   Conflict, Cooperation, and the Decay of Public Health

Whereas health care and public health had been institutionally and organizationally distinct from one another during the 1920s, they were merged during the Nazi government period after 1933. As far as the responsiveness between these policy sectors was concerned, before 1933 conflicts and ignorance of interest groups and professional actors from both policy sectors belonging mainly to either the health care or the public health sectors prevailed, with more responsiveness during the rule of the Nazi government. Yet, the conflicts between the two policy sectors were solved by eliminating or expelling public health doctors and other workers in the public health sector who held different political opinions. At the same time, the laws on racial discrimination and the Holocaust can be read as policy integration of health care and public health, because they entailed a distinctively population-based approach to eliminating "sick" elements in the population and preventing the creation of new ones by banning interracial marriages.

After the First World War, public health played an important role in German politics and public health professionals demanded innovative public health policies. Drawing on physical and biological research related to hygiene, they argued that social components were essential to improving public health and demanded laws to reduce causes of ill health in the environment; however, they also argued that for some people, health improvement and prevention through health-based social intervention was impossible because of heritable information. Social hygienists were very clear in emphasizing that disabled and badly educated individuals are a cost factor for society (Schmiedebach, 2002). Social hygiene, which was the driving force of the public health sector in Germany, was increasingly connected to eugenics, which was concerned with the genetic improvement of humans. This stream of thought within the public health profession was an open door for the politicization of preventive health sciences by the Nazis (Weindling, 1989, 1994; Porter, 1999).

Nevertheless, demands for more public health policies came along with conflicts between medical doctors and public health doctors. For instance, in 1927 at the national meeting of German doctors (Deutscher Ärztetag) in Würzburg, Bavaria, the majority of the congress voted against more prevention and public health and was opposed to the recruitment of doctors responsible for public health measures. As a consequence, many public health doctors took this as an offense and increasingly favored the merging of the existing organizations of public health doctors into a strong national organization (Moser, 2002). However, the conflicts among public health practitioners and "free doctors" who were mostly panel doctors for the national health insurance could not be resolved – mainly because there was no ministry of health that could have regulated such conflicts (Weindling, 1994). During the financial and economic crisis of the 1930s, municipal health services became attractive employers for doctors because private practices were difficult to sustain (Eberle, 2002). At the end of the 1920s there was no change in the expenditures of the health insurance; they spent more on medical treatment and wage replacements for members than on preventive and public health measures (Moser, 2002).

After 1933 when the Nazi Party monopolized power and turned Germany into a unitary state with a dictatorship, responsiveness between the health care and public health sectors increased strongly. This did not occur because the new government adopted programs to increase understanding and unification between the two policy sectors, but rather because of the policies by the Nazi government against individuals with different ideological positions, ethnic origins, or religion, such as Social Democrats and especially Jews. As discussed before, the public health profession had many Jewish and leftist members, who were particularly affected by the racial and ideological purification policies; even voluntary workers were dismissed. Members of the profession either emigrated, ceased to work, or collaborated with the Nazi government in order to implement a racist population health policy. What is more, public health services were also experiencing financial problems (Weindling, 1994; Stöckel, 2002; Rosenbrock and Gerlinger, 2009).

The Nazi government reduced the political influence of the health insurances, but doctors retained their powers and extended them even further (Lindner, 2004b). In addition, researchers have argued that doctors and scientists were fascinated by the exclusive character of the national socialist racial hygiene and its ideas and phantasies of societal engineering by means of social and health policies (Ernst, 2001). Resistance to these practices was minimal as the Nazi government systematically controlled the medical power and resistance was met with the expulsion and incarceration of those who deviated from these ideas (Alber and Bernardi Schenkluhn, 1992; Ernst, 2001).

To sum up, in the interwar period there were conflicts between the medical profession and public health doctors on the inclusion of prevention in the national health insurance and the municipal public health services. Doctors opposed the merging of the two fields. After

1933, responsiveness between the health care and the public health sectors increased, although these dynamics entailed the expulsion of the public health profession. The part of the public health profession that was in conflict with the medical profession about the implementation of a more state-centered public health approach was subject to political persecution. The result was consolidation of the position of general practitioners, weakening of the health insurance, and elimination of all other interests that suggested alternative concepts of health policy. These were actors that could have questioned the dominance of private practice in health care – for instance, social hygienists and social medicine (Alber and Bernardi Schenkluhn, 1992, 55). What followed was a high degree of responsiveness, mainly with regard to racist health policies, which excluded minorities from health services and also helped to construct and implement the Holocaust.

What are the implications of these results for the hypotheses regarding Germany? This book has argued that health care and public health should be noncoupled, because of unified government and high professionalism. These results were partially confirmed. For the first half of the interwar period, namely from the First World War until Hitler came to power, health care and public health were decoupled. Despite some attempts and an increasing centralization of other fields of social policy, most facets of public health remained the responsibility of subnational governments and municipal governments. Policymakers tried to include secondary prevention in the health insurance at the national level, but without great success. After 1934 the Nazis set up a national public health service and unified it with the national health insurance. This was soon after the abolition of the *Länder* [states] governments. Consequently, there was also unification of the health care and public health sectors – however, mostly in the context of racist public health policies.

Concerning professionalism and interest group inclusion, this book expected that low professionalism and corporatism in Germany would above all lead to the absence of responsiveness and conflicts. During the interwar period the medical profession and other health professions were indeed politically active, but there were considerable conflicts between these professions not only regarding scientific questions, but also because they were often linked to political parties. Public health doctors were often socialists or belonged to the political left and the debate between health care and public health was politicized.

Ironically, in 1934 the Nazi government reformed the relationship of health care and public health, not as a reaction to the lobbying of public health doctors and the medical profession, but in an effort to centralize all of the state institutions, similar to what happened in the Soviet Union. At the same time, there was responsiveness between the medical profession and those public health doctors who stayed in the country. Tragically, the common ground of both sectors in Germany was the justification and execution of racist health policies, including the Holocaust. However, the political activity of health professions at the time focused on increasing their influence in the framework of the national health insurance. Politicization was different in Australia and the United Kingdom where the medical profession in particular gained enormous political influence and had a lasting impact on political decisions.

7.3 Decoupling and Subordination of Public Health (1945–1980)

During the postwar period, the context for health care and public health changed because of prior successes in health policy and the possibilities for curing infections. At the same time, notably in Western democracies, the focus of social policy shifted to benefits and services for the individual rather than the entire population. As far as the German case is concerned, the expectation expressed in this book is that as a result of weak professionalism and corporatist interest intermediation, these conditions would reinforce the absence of responsiveness even more.

7.3.1 Restoring Institutional Unification

Following the Second World War, health care and public health were institutionally (re)separated in the Federal Democratic Republic of Germany. National health policy was above all health care policy. Specifically, the health care sector was reconstructed in the postwar area along the lines of the German welfare state, i.e., the broad social insurance system. This meant that the federal government retained the most power concerning the financing of health care, whereas prevention and public health went into the portfolio of the subnational governments (Int-GER-17, Int-GER-18). At the same time, the (re)construction of the (West) German welfare state occurred in contrast to centralization, collectivism, and a unified health service because this was widely associated with National Socialism and left-oriented Socialism and Communism. Therefore, the government of West Germany followed the suggestions of the Allied occupying forces and the unions. The founders of the FDR eventually intended decided not to model their health policy on the British and Scandinavian welfare states (Hockerts, 1991, 363–364; M. Schmidt, 2005b).

Health policymaking in the new republic referred to competing policymaking between the *Länder* and the federal government. This meant that the federal government could interfere in areas of international agreements and health protection. The rest was in the power of the subnational governments (Lindner, 2004b, 39). With the foundation of the FDR in 1949, health policy became part of the concurrent legislation, but with a strong emphasis on the member states' role (Labisch and Woelk, 2012, 79). As a consequence, the municipal public health services, which were also the backbone of the public health sector during the Third Reich, were marginalized (Schmacke, 1993, 1996). Public health in the 1950s was mostly focused on pregnancy and education issues and was the domain of the panel doctors of the statutory health insurance (Int-GER-7).

Consequently, the federal government legislated very little on preventive health policy. For example, the federal government passed a law in 1953 on the protection from genital diseases, but the legislation was very broad and gave little power to the state to coerce patients (Lindner, 2004b, 327–329). In 1956, the German municipalities debated public health measures and proposed increasing help for mothers and children as well as patients with tuberculosis, genital diseases, cancer, and rheumatic and heart diseases. However, these efforts did not result in specific programs (Schmacke, 2002). At the federal level, there was little effort by the national government to invest in public health in terms of preventive health care (Lindner, 2004b), except in the field of infectious diseases.

The health care sector was governed by the ministry that was responsible for social insurance. There was no ministry for health at the national level until the mid-1960s. However, many actors in the health sector demanded that such a ministry be established in order to govern the health sector properly. In 1957, the German Centre for Population Health Care (Zentrale für Volksgesundheitspflege) demanded the establishment of a national ministry of health to invest more in public health matters, but the subnational governments (SG) did not agree (Soenning, 1957; Lindner, 2004b). Yet, demands for a national ministry of health increased. In 1961 the German Centre for Population Health Care again referred to the issue and argued there should be a national ministry of health. Consequently, they argued, the federal government in Germany needed to consider why it did not act in a similar way and created a national ministry of health (Lindner, 2004b, 42). In the same year a national ministry of health was created and public health competences were assigned to it. However, health care, i.e., health insurance, remained in the discretion of the ministry for social insurance and separated from public health (Lindner, 2004b). Therefore, health care and public health remained largely separated and the health insurance principle dominated.

To sum up, health care and public health in Western Germany were institutionally and organizationally separated after the Second World War. Health policy was essentially health care policy at the national level until the 1960s. No national ministry of health existed before that and public health was a responsibility of subgovernments. Even after a national ministry was set up, health care remained the responsibility of the Ministry of Social Insurances. Interestingly, this was in contrast to the GDR, where health care and public health were considerably more unified, for example, in the polyclinics.

7.3.2 Transgression and Ignorance on the Actor Level

After the war, the project to establish national schools of public health failed in Germany (Ellerbrock, 2002; Schmacke, 2002, 179; Brößkamp-Stone, 2003). There was strong opposition in the medical profession to primary prevention (Ernst, 2001). Panel doctors in the health insurance profited from the public health measures that were established – namely, measures to improve pregnancy consultation and prevent illness in mothers and children. When immunizations were introduced in the early 1970s it was also to the benefit of the panel doctors (Int-GER-7). And when these policies entered the political agenda in Germany in the 1970s, courses to stop smoking were offered in popular universities, but there was little legislation regarding population- or setting-based approaches (Int-GER-9). Another public health issue that received political attention during the 1970s was workplace protection, which had been a weak spot in the German health system. Before the Second World War and in the early years of the Federal Republic of Germany, there had barely been any focus on health and safety in the workplace. The first university professorship for workplace medicine was established in 1968. In 1976, a medical specialization in workplace medicine was created as a consequence of the workplace security law of 1974. The situation was much different in the GDR as workplace medicine had been established much earlier (Milles and Müller, 2002).

The institutional and professional differentiation between health care and public health was important and led to a loss of competences for the public health services, as in the field of health research and expertise. Courts and social insurance demanded public health expertise from specialized institutions in daily practice, such as experts in forensic medicine. Such tasks before then had been in the hands of the public health services. After the war this development led to conflicts between general practitioners and public health doctors in which the former accused the latter of being "public doctors," which was seen as derogatory because it made a connection to the role of public health professions during the Third Reich and to the health system in the socialist GDR (Lindner, 2004b, 39). Consequently, the majority of the medical profession opposed the concept of municipal public health services and disregarded the doctors working in them (Labisch, 1982). Population-based and group-based preventive measures subsequently lost their agency (Eberle, 2002).

To sum up, actor responsiveness between the health care and public health sectors was absent. The medical profession strongly opposed public health matters for economic reasons because doctors regarded public health professionals as competitors, but also for historical reasons as public health had an explicit connection to the Holocaust in the Third Reich. This argument became the justification against public health policies in the postwar era. However, the roots of minimal responsiveness between health care and public health had been laid before. In the late nineteenth century, the medical profession made a deal with the state and participated in the self-governance of health policy and, consequently, it had not become a powerful pressure group. What is more, there was only a weak connection between health care and public health at the universities and in the process of professional formation, especially after the war. Due to the negative experiences of public health during the war, the restoration of the pre-war situation strengthened the separation of the sectors even further.

What do these findings imply for the hypotheses regarding Germany? This book has expressed the argument that health care and public health should be decoupled in the interwar period – mainly, because of unified government and the absence of professionalism and the strong corporatist interest intermediation, which guaranteed the medical profession the possibility of participating in the governance of health policy. The case study partly confirms these expectations. During the postwar period, health care and public health remained institutionally separated. On the one hand, this was the case because public health was a task for the subgovernments, which in turn had very different methods of public health policymaking. On the other hand, despite the extension of the welfare state, public health policies remained separate from health care and relatively underdeveloped. In other words, it was exactly because the focus of social policy was on cash transfers in case of illness or poverty that the actual provision did not occur through the state as such, but was delegated to private actors. This paradigm overshadowed unified government in Germany and the central public health legislation that we expected to occur due to the "relatively" strong state. On the other hand, professionalism remained weak in Germany, in the sense that the medical and public health professions did not join forces against the state to advocate public health. The medical profession did not take the role of a politically powerful pressure group, but remained included in the health care governance system along with other interest groups of the health care sector. Doctors opposed public health professionals and their ideas for political reasons rather than trying to incorporate them in a national health policy agenda.

7.4 "New Public Health" in the Shadow of Sectoral Decoupling (1980–2010)

Beginning in the 1980s, public health returned to the political agenda in most countries across the globe as a result of changes in the health policy, such as the pressure of more noncommunicable diseases, increasing budgetary pressures due to rising expenditures, decreasing economic growth, and critiques of classical medicine. This led, in many countries, to changes in health policymaking with a focus on more public health policy. The following section will discuss how this change played out in Germany after the 1980s.

7.4.1   Public Health Policymaking in the Shadow of Institutional Distinctiveness

German policymakers reacted to the new demands for a preventive health policy by trying to include prevention in the social health insurance system, which lacked a legal basis for encompassing preventive health legislation, especially concerning primary prevention issues. Policymakers did not pursue major reforms to change health policy in a way that would have improved the legal basis for unifying health care and public health in a common legal framework. To the contrary, reformers sought to include public health and prevention into the existing national health insurance framework. For instance, the reform of the social insurance legislation, in 1989, extended the degree of preventive measures that were included in the public health insurance (SVRG, 1989). Nevertheless, some of the health insurances that are statutory bodies took their own initiatives to set up prevention projects, for example, the Aktion Gesundheit by the AOK (Allgemeine Ortskrankenkasse) in Mettmann, North Rhine-Westphalia. Nevertheless, these activities resulted in the same professional conflicts as during the 1920s and 1950s. Medical organizations claimed that preventive measures were their own business (Eberle, 2002).

Regarding health care reforms, a number of innovations passed that focused on cost containment and strengthened market elements in the provision of health care, such as the Kostendämpfungsgesetz in 1991. Further reforms followed in the 1990s and 2000s. Notably, reform projects increased the degree of liberalism and privatization in the health care system. The reforms entailed, for example, more options to choose a health insurance provider, DRG payments, co-payments, user fees, rationalization of benefits, and the merger of the occupational and public health insurances (Paquet, 2009; Carrera, Siemens, and Bridges, 2008; Rosenbrock and Gerlinger, 2014). Nevertheless, the main governing principle – corporatist self-administration – of the health care system was retained (Bandelow, 2004; Gerlinger and Stegmüller, 2009).

During the 1990s, public health was extended especially to workplace protection. The 1996 law on workplace protection extended public health to the prevention of health dangers in the workplace. Prior to that, this area of public health was in the hands of public insurance and the employers' liability insurance coverages. However, similar to the principle of health insurance, only accidents that had already occurred were covered by these arrangements. Based on the reform of 1989, in 1996 insurance providers received a mandate to pursue a preventive health policy following the European framework legislation regarding workplace protection (Int-7-Ger).

Following German reunification, the health policy was reorganized. Specifically, the national health insurance laws were transferred to the *Neue Länder* [new states]. In order to implement this reorganization, the Kohl government set up the Ministry of Health and made it responsible for health insurance – which had previously been under the purview of the Ministry for Social Insurances – as well as prevention and health protection. Preventive exams had already been integrated in the health insurance law in 1989. In 1991, the main competences for health policy at the national level were merged into a common ministry.[1] Since then, there has been more institutional and organizational unification of health care and public health; however, most tasks related to prevention and health education – such as infectious diseases, risk factors, and health education more generally are a competence of the federal agency for health education BZfGA (Bundeszentrale für gesundheitliche Aufklärung), which is a subordinate but separate agency to the Ministry of Health.[2] The decision to include preventive exams in the national health insurance was, however, repealed in 1996 and readopted in 2000.

Speaking from a legal basis, public health in Germany lacks a common ground for encompassing legislation as the responsibilities are separated among different ministries and areas (Int-GER-1). There is already separation between subgovernments and the central government concerning public health issues, but at the national level they also variation between various ministries. The public health sector, as discussed in previous sections, is distributed across many areas of the political system in Germany, but, importantly, it is separated from medical care (Int-GER-2, Int-GER-5, Int-GER-7, Int-GER-9, Int-GER-17, Int-GER-18). Thus, public health continues to reflect the corporatist model, which is highly inclusive and comprises different levels of government, nonprofit organizations such as the Federal Organization for Health and the Federal Organization of Health Promotion, and other self-help organizations as well as their legal entities on the regional and national levels, as well as consumer protection and sports clubs. Based on this, there is a large network of institutions and actors responsible for public health (Int-GER-5). Yet, at the same time it is a network with little power to rule hierarchically – unlike the United Kingdom, for instance (Int-GER-5, Int-GER-7, Int-GER-12), which renders the aforementioned collective action problems of public health even more important. In 2015, the federal parliament passed a law on prevention that aimed at unifying the fragmented public health sector but did not bring together health care and public health.[3]

Nevertheless, Germany adopted a number of public health policies. These were either tobacco control policies, namely tax increases, partial smoking bans, and partial regulation of tobacco advertising. These laws and regulations passed, however, as a consequence of the pressure by the EU Commission and European Directives (Duina and Kurzer, 2004; Reus, 2016; Trein, 2017b). An example for successful preventive health policies that were put into place without international pressure are responses to HIV/AIDS and health promotion within companies. Actors from both fields – health care and public health – supported these policies (Rosenbrock, 2001).

To sum up, health care and public health have remained institutionally separate since the 1980s in Germany; although there were some attempts to create a national public health framework legislation, which would have created the legal basis for nonmedical health policies at the national level and included them in the national Ministry of Health, such a law was not passed. Instead, policymakers tried to use the existing health insurance legislation to include preventive measures, with moderate success. The problems were the same as after the First World War – namely, that public health policies are difficult to integrate in a legal framework that was designed for individual health care and that the health insurance and doctors have few incentives to demonstrate and develop political interest in primary prevention measures. Nonetheless, some public health policies were put into place, notably regarding HIV and workplace protection; yet the landscape of public health policies in Germany has remained fragmented and different from those in Australia and the United

Kingdom. Only the more recent (since 2000) evolution of public health legislation has moved in that direction.

7.4.2 Conflict and Coordination in the Shadow of Subordination

Medical and public health doctors did not develop into a politically strong and active discourse coalition for public health, although during the early 1990s the federal government supported the establishment of new schools of public health at several universities, for example, in Hannover, Bremen, Hamburg, Bielefeld, Düsseldorf, Köln, Dresden, München, Ulm, and Augsburg as advanced technical colleges (*Fachhochschulen*) (D. Braun, 1994; Maschewsky-Schneider, 2005). Due to the structure of the corporatist health care system and the subordinated role of public health research, there was little responsiveness between policy sectors. The main stakeholders in public health had neither strong financial nor professional support from the main players in health policy, such as health insurance and doctoral organizations, nor were they supported by a medical profession putting forward public health issues. Doctoral organizations are obviously interested in public health issues, yet it is not a foremost priority for them, especially primary prevention (Int-GER-1). At the same time, there are strong conflicts between nonmedical health sciences and the medical profession. Although conflicts between different professions happen in all areas, the example of health care and public health in Germany is striking in this sense, as there is remarkably little coordination and responsiveness in the sense of cooperation and mutual support between doctors and public health actors when it comes to health issues (Int-GER-7). Priorities in health research reflect this strategy. The health research that is put forward and funded by the Ministry for Science and Education in Berlin is more strongly focused on natural sciences and individual health problems than on nonmedical aspects of health problems (Int-GER-2, Int-GER-17, Int-GER-18) (DGfPH, 2012).

There are of course doctors who support public health policies, especially in the context of their daily practice as GPs. However, there is generally not strong pressure from doctoral organizations for a general public health concept (Int-GER-8). The health insurance's interests, which are to a large extent responsible for preventive health policies, entail mostly individualized programs such as health counseling and individual health promotion. In addition, some subdisciplines of the medical profession in Germany, such as pediatricians and lung and throat specialists, are active in demanding more public health measures. However, from a general point of view the support from these organizations for the medical profession is not strong as they do not publicly put strong pressure on elected officials (Int-GER-17).

The weak responsiveness between health care and public health is also apparent with regard to one of the most politicized public health issue of the last fifty years: tobacco control. The evidence that smoking is bad both for smokers and for those in the vicinity of smokers has been overwhelming since at least the early 1990s.[4] Whereas many countries began to pass laws that restricted smoking in public, Germany remained a laggard in international tobacco control (Raw and Joossens, 2006, 2010; Joossens and Raw, 2014), especially in comparison to other European countries (Studlar, 2006; Studlar, Christensen, and Sistari, 2011). Along with other factors (Grüning, Gilmore, and Mckee, 2006; Grüning and Gilmore, 2007) is due to the lack of political activity by the medical profession for tobacco control policies (Hirschhorn, 2000; Bornhäuser McCarthy, and Glantz, 2006).

As in other countries, health strategies and goals, which aim at coordinating and integrating preventive and curative elements with regard to a specific health problem, have been passed at the national as well as the subnational level in Germany. As a reaction to the increasing international debate concerning the connection of cure and prevention in health strategies, some of the German *Länder* began to pass health strategies. The first member state to pass a health strategy was Hamburg in 1992, followed by North Rhine-Westphalia (NRW) in 1995. Most other states passed health goals in the years after 2000. At the time of this writing, NRW has the largest number of health goals (10 in 2012). What is more, health goals are heterogeneous with regard to their content. Most common are the following topics: health of children and adolescents (9 MS), health of elderly (7 MS), cancer (7 MS), and tobacco prevention. Nevertheless, a common strategy to implement these health goals – from a national perspective as well as a coordinated approach by the *Länder* – is lacking (Thietz and Hartmann, 2012). The national government has also passed health strategies and there have been attempts to coordinate health strategies by the subgovernments (Maschewsky-Schneider et al., 2009).

To sum up, these results show that responsiveness between the health care and public health sectors happens through policy integration, which has been established at the subnational and the national level, although later than in Australia, but in similar areas. However, regarding health professions and interest groups, there is little responsiveness (cooperation, discourse coalitions) among the policy sectors. There is a lack of mutual support for policy proposals and a strong voice from the medical profession to implement more encompassing public health laws. In Germany, contrary to Australia, health strategies and progress in primary prevention (especially tobacco control policy) has occurred as a reaction to international political pressure and a change of the discourse therein. The establishment and implementation of health strategies is discussed as a consequence of the changing international discourse and the EU has played an important role in establishing tobacco control policies on the international agenda.

What do these results imply for the hypotheses regarding the relationship of health care and public health? This book's argument has been that unified government and depoliticized health professions should lead to the noncoupling of health care and public health in Germany. Similar to the preceding section, the analysis of this time period reveals that there was no full unification of health care and public health, as a national law for preventive health did not pass parliament before 2015. The political activity of the medical profession remained limited to its interests in the health care sector; public health professionals did develop into a politically powerful group and did not receive support from the medical profession. Despite the decoupling of health care and public health, there was to some extent policy integration during this time period – as a result of pressure from the EU in tobacco control policy, for example, but more so because of policy learning and the adoption of innovative ideas in health policy to deal with pressing health problems, such as noncommunicable diseases in general.

7.5 Discussion

What can we retain for the theoretical discussion from this case study? The results of my analysis show that, overall, health care and public health in Germany coevolved in a decoupled way in which both sectors were institutionally distinct but at the same time did not respond to one another (Table 7.1). With the exception of the Third Reich, health care and public health had separate institutions, horizontally as well as vertically. For instance, it was mostly the national government that was in charge of financing and implementing health care policy, whereas subnational governments and municipalities were responsible for governing public health. The origins of this separation are to be found in the nineteenth century, when the foundation of the social health insurance shifted health policymaking at the national level toward individual care and separated it from public health policy, which had been located at the member states and municipalities level. This separation remained in the post-First World War period until the Nazi government came into power. Under Hitler the public health system was integrated into a national public health service; actors from both sectors played important roles in the Holocaust in designating targets of euthanasia and implementing these policies. After the Second World War, in the FDR, health care and public health returned to the pre-NS institutional separation. The health care financing system at the national level was separate from public health (especially everything that went beyond disaster management) and was the responsibility of the subgovernments as well as the municipalities. At the federal level, competences for public health emerged only gradually and remained separate from the health insurance administration, which was part of the ministry for social insurances. In 1991, the government created a ministry for health, which formally unified health care and public health. However, most competences and expertise in public health remained in the BZfGA, the federal agency for health promotion. BZfGA is a separate agency but subordinate to the federal ministry of health.

As far as the responsiveness of health care and public health was concerned, my analysis shows little communication and support between the two policy sectors' actors. During t0 there was few interaction between them because doctoral organizations had been included in the administration of the health insurance and were also employed by them. However, they had not many connections to the public health profession at the municipal level and public health doctors who supported and demanded more public health policies. After the First World War, professional support for public health policies increased, especially from public health professionals who

Table 7.1. Coevolution of health care and public health in Germany.

1880–1918 (t0)	1918–1945 (t1)	1945–1980 (t2)	1980–2010 (t3)
Decoupling: Separation in three levels of government: national health insurance, public health, and prevention on the state or municipal level; mutual ignorance or competition of health care and public health actors; political differences (left/right)	*Decoupling (Tight coupling):* Separation in three levels of government: national health insurance, public health, and prevention on the state or municipal level; unification of public health during National Socialism; Conflicts between health professions during Weimar Republic; public health profession virtually "extinguished" during NS	*Decoupling:* Separation in three levels of government: national health insurance, public health, and prevention on the state or municipal level; transgression of health care on public health; weak public health coalition	*Decoupling (Noncoupling):* Separation in three levels of government: national health insurance, public health, and prevention on the state or municipal level; little communication, interaction between health care and public health; policy integration

164

were among the world's leading researchers in this field (especially social hygienists). However, many researchers in Germany refused interventionist public health actions such as large immunization campaigns as they were advised by international representatives of the profession. Conflicts arpse between the medical profession and public health researchers concerning more public health services and preventive examinations, especially concerning the question of whether preventive exams should be financed by the national health insurance. During the Third Reich, responsiveness between the health care and the public health sectors increased, but this came at the price of a large part of the public health profession emigrating or being subject to political persecution. At the same time, during the beginning of the Nazi period, the medical profession reinforced its deal with the state and took a leading role in the governance of health care.

After the war, the health care policy was connected to the expansion of the welfare state in Germany, which disconnected it from public health. Public health, as defined in this book, took a minor role, especially in Western Germany. This development also entailed decreased responsiveness between health care and public health and resulted in a weak coalition connecting the two sectors – a problem that remains prevalent to this day.

7.5.1 Unified Government and Professionalism in Germany

To what extent do these results confirm or refute the hypotheses regarding the German case? It has been assumed in this book that unified government and low professionalism led to the institutional and organizational unification of health care and public health and a lack of responsiveness between both sectors. Consequently, there should be noncoupling of health care and public health. At the same time, contextual elements should not play an important role.

In a nutshell, my results show that there is indeed weak responsiveness between these sectors due to professionalism, but no institutional unification as a consequence of (relatively) unified government. The federal structure of Germany's political system significantly impacts the lack of distinctiveness between them, because public health is to a large extent a task of the subnational governments; this did not change throughout the observed periods, except for marginal changes during the Third Reich.

Germany's political system has been a relatively centralized federation, except for the twelve years of Nazi rule, in the sense that the national government handles legislation and the member states have a more administrative role. Therefore, this book expressed the expectation of finding more unification of health care and public health at the national level. However, as my analysis shows, this is not the case; the two sectors have remained institutionally separate from one another. It was the second chamber of the national parliament, the *Bundesrat*, that had blocked national public health legislation, especially after the Second World War and again since the 1980s. Members of the subgovernments sit in this chamber. Oftentimes, its political majorities are different from those of the first chamber where the governing parties have a majority and control the political agenda. However, unlike Australia, which also has two parliamentary chambers but a different electoral system, it is much more difficult in Germany to forge parliamentary alliances – especially regarding policy integration of health care and public health.

One reason for this is the weak professionalism of and the absence of responsiveness between the two sectors. This is especially visible with regard to the medical profession's interest in and support for public health. This research shows that the political activities of German medical professionals regarding public health are different from those of their colleagues in Australia, for example. It seems that physicians' organizations are much less active in lobbying and suggesting preventive measures going beyond secondary and tertiary prevention. The German medical profession focuses mainly on the individual and is much less concerned with new public health perspectives, which put a strong emphasis on environmental factors. The big medical organizations are less politicized than in Anglo-Saxon countries and less interested in public health policies. Most active in this area are pediatricians, but pulmonologists and cardiologists are also politically active, especially concerning smoking. For instance, there is a physicians' working group against smoking that has been active for quite some time in Germany. It is often the case that doctors are against community-based interventions because they are afraid to lose their dominant role in health policy (Int-20-Ger). Another important factor in Germany is that there are no strong health foundations like the cancer councils and heart foundations existing in English-speaking countries that include doctors engaged in public health research, deliver public health education, and serve as important organs in the area of lobbying for public health policies. In Germany, there are organizations concerned with these diseases, but they are less independent from state money and less powerful as political pressure groups (Int-2-Ger).

Overall, however, the medical profession is not very active politically in cooperation with public health professionals. This is rooted in the low professionalism that entails a strong role of the state in protecting employment by establishing the national health insurance that guarantees doctors' employment. Consequently, the medical professional association is not politically active and does not support public health policies. Therefore, matters of public health are often partisan issues.

7.5.2 Competing Explanations

However, regarding the preceding case studies, there are competing explanations and important theoretical elements that need to be mentioned and discussed in terms of the coevolution of the two sectors in Germany. Notably, these are the following elements:

1. *Complementarity:* The German case study provides interesting insights with respect to the impact of the general relations of health care and public health. Although the health care and public health sectors are decoupled and public health remains to a large extent subordinate to health care, there is to a certain extent complementarity, especially if we take policy integration into consideration. The fact that the German national government initiated national health strategies and disease management programs that combine health care and public health shows that, despite the institutional separation of the two sectors and the weak responsiveness between professions and interest groups of the two policy sectors, there are common policy outputs that also exist in other countries with different degrees of sectoral coupling. However, the adoption of these policies is the consequence of diffusion mechanisms rather than of the domestic responsiveness between the health care and public health sectors. With regard to certain public health policies,

such as the tobacco control policy, the lack of responsiveness between the two sectors is a big problem and leads to reduced policy outputs.

2. *Policy learning:* Germany shows an interesting dimension of policy learning regarding the relationship between health care and public health. As far as Australia and the United Kingdom are concerned, this book has demonstrated that as a result of high professionalism there is policy learning, because the political activity of the medical profession leads to the infusion of new ideas in the policy process. According to this logic, there should be no policy learning in Germany, at least not by the medical profession. Nevertheless, there has been coevolution toward the complementarity of health care and public health. Yet, in this case, the adoption of new ideas such as public health policies has occurred through international pressure – for example, from the EU – but also by means of policy learning from international institutions and other countries, following the logic of the policy diffusion (Gilardi and Radaelli, 2012). For example, the adoption of national health strategies has not occured as a reaction to the pressure of the medical profession, but by means of learning from international organizations and other countries.

3. *Partisan differences:* Germany is also an interesting example of partisan differences regarding the relationship of health care and public health. As argued in the preceding sections, there was a partisan difference regarding public health. Left parties supported public health policies, whereas conservatives and liberals opposed them. The reason for this is that public health reformers could not manage to forge a coalition across political parties due to the lack of professional support. Unlike in Australia, where many doctors played an important political role in the liberal party and supported more public health policymaking, such a dynamic did not occur in Germany.

4. *Autocracy–Democracy:* The German case has another particularity that might be important for understanding the coevolution of health care and public health: the impact of autocratic and totalitarian government. There are two ways in particular in which these factors affected the coevolution of the two sectors and changed the impact of my main explanatory variables. First, it came along with a centralization of government, notably the abolition of federalism.

Soon thereafter, this led to the institutional unification of health care and public health. Moreover, after the Nazi government came into power, there was a shift toward authoritarianism and an erosion of human and political rights. This had consequences for health professions, which adapted and conformed to the ruling Nazi government. Many doctors joined the NSDAP, whereas public health professionals had to leave the country or were jailed, either because of their political ideals or because they were of Jewish origin. During that time, the government institutionally and politically unified health care and public health in a national health policy. Specifically, there were policies that combined both fields, including racist public health policies such as the national health service and sterilization laws and, eventually, the Holocaust. However, the responsiveness of interest groups and professions of the two policy sectors, as conceptualized in the theoretical chapter, did not play an important role because it demanded the presence of a democratic polity. During the Third Reich, professionals were politically more active than before – not because they chose freely to defend their interests, but because they feared oppression – as membership in the NSDAP and participation in its political rallies were advantageous for their physical and economic security.

7.6 Summary

This chapter analyzed the coevolution of the health care and public health sectors in Germany. This book includes a case study on Germany because of the country's combination of a relatively unified government and weak professionalism; the expectation was that this combination would lead to noncoupling of the two sectors. However, the results are different than expected regarding sectoral coupling. The proposed hypothesis concerning professionalism is correct in that the medical profession did not act as a very strong pressure group and did not vocally support public health actors. Consequently, doctors did not act as interest groups that competed for the attention of policymakers in the service of public health issues, but rather guarded their privilege and defended the autonomy of the corporatist game. Policymakers thus did not see a necessity to become more active concerning the institutionalization of public health under a general institutional framework at the national level, and political support for public health across partisan divides remained limited. The fact that Germany still had strong veto rights with legislation at the national level, as well as the demise of German public health sciences during the Third Reich, increased decoupling of the two sectors in the post-Second World War period. Nevertheless, despite the decoupling of health care and public health in Germany, both sectors coevolved toward complementarity and there has been policy learning and policy integration between health care and public health.

8 | Switzerland: Institutional Fragmentation, Depoliticized Health Professions, and Noncoupling

Switzerland is an important case study for this book's argument because it combines the absence of professionalism and the presence of corporatist interest intermediation with a relatively fragmented and decentralized government and competences in policymaking. Therefore, based on the theoretical predictions, I expect to find decoupling of health care and public health. The analysis of the Swiss case will proceed similarly to the studies of the other countries. I will start by examining the distinctiveness and responsiveness of both policy sectors in the late nineteenth and early twentieth centuries. Then I will focus on the interwar and Second World War period. After that, this chapter will examine the relationship of both sectors in the post-Second World War era. The last section will analyze the coupling of both sectors in what has been labeled the "new public health" era. 5

8.1 Decoupling at the National and Cantonal Level (1850–1918)

The story of the Swiss case begins in the second half of the nineteenth century. As for the other countries in this sample, this was a period in which the demand for public health policies was high. Notably, the most pressing health problem was infectious diseases and it was difficult to cure them based on the medical technology of the time. At the same time, the emerging nationalism provided an intellectual and policy context that was favorable for the integration and coordination of both sectors.

However, according to the theoretical argument outlined previously, these contextual elements should not have an effect. Since there is low professionalism – and health professions are not very active politically – sectorial responsiveness between actors should be absent, even if the context is favorable to integration as in t1.

171

8.1.1   Sectorial Emergence: National and
Cantonal Health Policies

As in other countries of Western Europe, in Switzerland, health policy differentiated (specialized) into health care and public health policy sectors during the late nineteenth century (Achtermann and Berset, 2006). Given that Switzerland has been a decentralized federation, health policy infrastructure was established at the cantonal and the municipal level. In the early nineteenth century, medical care in hospitals was already becoming more important. Subsequently, big (municipal) hospitals were put under the responsibility of the cantons (for instance, in Lausanne in 1806). Nevertheless, since not all cantons could fund health care to the same degree, there were differences in the quality of care between the cantons (Achtermann and Berset, 2006, 20–21).

The first forms of health insurance in Switzerland emerged in the early nineteenth century. During the second half of the nineteenth century, in the context of industrialization and social changes, a plethora of health insurance providers were founded, mostly at the cantonal and municipal level (Kaufmann, 2010). Nevertheless, in contrast with Germany, no national compulsory health insurance was established; a legal proposal failed in a popular referendum (Alber and Bernardi Schenkluhn, 1992; Degen, 2008; Kaufmann, 2010). In 1911, the national government adopted a reduced version of the law that entailed a subvention to health insurance providers (if they complied with federal supervision), as well as obligatory accident insurance, and granted the right to the cantons to introduce compulsory health insurance for part or all of the population (Vatter and Rüefli, 2003; Degen, 2006, 2008; Vatter and Rüefli, 2014; Santésuisse, 2014). This reform shaped Swiss health policy and no major modification of the Swiss health insurance system occurred until 1994 – when a national legislation created an obligatory health insurance (Uhlmann and Braun, 2011).

Public health fell (at least partially) under a different jurisdiction than the health care sector. The federal constitution of 1848 trans-ferred the responsibility of combating dangerous epidemics to the federal government. Thus the national government began to legislate on public health issues. The federal government used this right to pass laws in workplace protection (1877) and matters concerning epidemics (1887) (Achtermann and Berset, 2006, 21). The Federal Office for Public Health (BAG – Bundesamt für Gesundheit) was established in 1893. Its task was to implement federal laws on public health. Parallel to the public health legislation at national level, the cantons passed their own laws concerning population health, for example, on health polices, health of cattle, and hygiene of water and meat as well as the regulation of health jobs. At the cantonal level, however, health care and public health were in the hands of the cantonal health departments and therefore both sectors were under the same institutional and organizational umbrella. A doctor was hired in the bigger cantons to oversee and implement public health measures (*Kantonsarzt*) (Achtermann and Berset, 2006, 21).

Aside from the separation of control between the cantons and the national government, however, public health also had a private component. Following the principle of subsidiarity, Swiss officials left the implementation and adoption of specific programs for prevention to private actors, such as doctors, nurses, and public health doctors. For instance, the national cancer league, tasked in 1913 with informing the population on cancer through publications, talks, and exhibitions, published its first flier. Interestingly, however, in one of the their meetings the cancer league board declined the suggestion of one of their members to prepare a leaflet for doctors on possible preventive measures, deciding to serve only as a point of information for interested doctors (Kauz, 2010, 11–13).

To sum up, this overview of the institutional emergence of health care and public health shows that health care and public health were institutionally separated in late nineteenth-century Switzerland. The federal office for public health was in charge of public health but did not administer the national law on social insurance, which had been a responsibility of the federal office for social insurance after being formed in 1912.[1]

8.1.2 Responsiveness between Jurisdictions rather Than between Sectors

It is difficult to evaluate the responsiveness of the health care and public health sectors in the late nineteenth century in Switzerland because it is hard to identify the different groups that were responsible for health care or public health and whether they communicated with one another in the political realm. The development of interest groups and professional roles in the health sector – such as doctors, dentists, and nurses – occurred in a similar manner as in English-speaking countries and Germany. However, it was different with regard to public health (Brändli, 2008). Voluntary organizations in Switzerland, such as the cancer leagues, emerged as functional equivalents to the public health profession. These organizations were nationalized, but they were not politically active pressure groups. Although doctors were involved in the provision of public health, for instance, as cantonal public health officers, there is little evidence of large political public health coalitions before the First World War.

Similarly to the Swiss federal state, political organizations of doctors emerged from cantonal organizations that had been formed in the first half of the nineteenth century. Medical doctors founded the first federal medical organization in 1788, the Helvetic society of corresponding doctors and surgeons (Helvetische Gesellschaft korrespondierender Ärzte und Wundärzte). The unification of all physicians' organizations occurred in 1901 with the forming of the Association of Swiss Doctors (Verbindung Schweizerischer Ärzte) that became a powerful political pressure group. Doctors in Switzerland already had an important influence on political life, but with the forming of a national medical organization, the political activities of the medical profession could be united under a common umbrella (R. Braun, 1985, 350). Medical organizations were politically active, for example, when they resisted state intervention in their business, such as attempts to regulate public health insurance. This is different from the case of Germany where doctors and medical organizations are more under state control (R. Braun, 1985, 356–357).

However, there was no large public health coalition in Switzerland, which meant that public health doctors and administrators and medical organizations demanded more public health policies, as was the case in Australia. This was because of the absence of the professionalization of public health, as was the case in Australia where the first postgraduate diploma of public health was established in Melbourne in 1906. In Switzerland, the professionalization of public health began in the second half of the twentieth century. The first courses in public health were taught in the early 1960s when an academic title was created (Bern, Geneva, Lausanne, and Zurich then established institutes for preventive medicine).[2] As mentioned before, the tasks of public health that were in the hands of the state mostly referred to policies against epidemics, but apart from that, subsidiarity (the delegation of public tasks to private actors) played an important role. We therefore need to look at nongovernmental organizations to understand the public health sector in Switzerland. As mentioned before, the *Gesundheitsligen* (leagues to combat certain diseases) were important in this field, such as the cancer league and the lung league. One example of this is the activities of the league against tuberculosis in the canton de Vaud, which started activities against cancer in the early twentieth century and helped to advocate for a national law on tuberculosis (Achtermann and Berset, 2006, 41; Kauz, 2010, 11–13).

To conclude, based on the review of the secondary literature, there was limited responsiveness between the health care and public health sectors. The medical profession was not very active politically beyond its proper interests. Public health was also not very well developed as a profession and the organizations that served as functional equivalents were not politically active either.

What do these results imply for the hypotheses on Switzerland? I had expected to find decoupling of the two sectors because of institutional fragmentation and low professionalism. The results confirm this hypothesis. First, because of the distribution of legislative power between the cantons and the federal government, there was no institutional integration of health care and public health at the national level and the cantons remained in charge of the majority of health policy. National health policymaking remained fragmented. The national office for public health was in charge of some of the policies related to public health. Second, there was no national health insurance to connect public health to health care policies. Although there was a proposal to implement national health insurance, the proposed law failed in a popular vote. The only health care legislation that passed was a law that permitted additional payments by the federal government to the cantonal health insurance providers, yet the administration of this legislation was the responsibility of the ministry of social insurance.

As expected, theoretically, the absence of responsiveness between sectors was a result of low professionalism of the medical profession. Doctors, public health professionals, and health foundations did not form an alliance that advocated more public health policy, but medical organizations served as a platform for scientific exchange with little impact on the political integration of prevention and health care. Despite a favorable contextual situation for responsiveness and integration of health care and public health, contextual elements did not have a strong impact on the relationship between the two sectors.

8.2 Decoupling of Sectors, but Coordination between Cantons (1918–1945)

The next section turns to the interwar and Second World War periods. It was argued before that during this time the context for the coevolution of health care and the public health sectors changed. Demands for public health policies altered because more sophisticated medication was available and conflicts over the distribution of resources between actors of the two sectors were likely, especially because of the economic crisis in the late 1920s. In Switzerland, these factors should increase conflicts between the two sectors even further.

8.2.1 Institutional Separation at the National Level

During the interwar period, health care and public health remained two separate policy sectors at the national level because their institutions were relatively independent. The federal office for public health administered public health laws and the national office of social insurance took responsibility for the national part of the health care legislation. It remained difficult to draw a distinction at the cantonal level between the two sectors. In larger cantons, there was a cantonal officer for public health (although named *Kantonsarzt*), who was specifically given responsibility for public health and prevention, whereas this role did not exist in the smaller cantons. Many cantons built cantonal and university hospitals in the interwar period, resulting in the cantonal governments getting increasingly involved in financing or co-financing hospitals as their demand for cash increased in the modernization process (Achtermann and Berset, 2006, 22). Nevertheless, the competences in health policy remained separated between the federal government and the cantons. The remainder of the legislative powers over health policymaking stayed with the cantons, which legislated in the following areas: sanitary, hospital planning, planning of care, and prevention of noncommunicable diseases (Achtermann and Berset, 2006, 31). The law of 1911 remained the only legislative milestone for health care at the national level during the interwar period. There were quite a few attempts to reform the law that failed in several instances during the 1920s and the 1930s (Degen, 2008; Santésuisse, 2014). Health insurers' economic situation worsened after the First World War. As a legislative reform was not possible, the federal government paid additional subsidies to health insurers and the insurance providers increased out-of-pocket payments (Alber and Bernardi Schenkluhn, 1992, 186–187).

The cantons played an important role in national health care legislation. After the establishment of the Conference of Cantonal Directors of Public Health (CDP), the cantonal directors for public health had a platform to put health policy issues on the national political agenda, for example, legislation of pharmaceuticals governed by a concordat, i.e., an inter-cantonal agreement (Minder, 1994). However, the CDP was more active with public health policies, such as food transport, birth rates, improvement of drinking water provisions, improvement of waste disposal and water provision regulations, and health in schools (Minder, 1994). At the same time, the cantons took care of public health topics such as health protection and prevention, especially with regard to environmental factors. They were concerned with issues such as infectious diseases, childhood mortality, alcoholism, improvement of drinking water supply, improvement of living hygiene, trash, and health in schools. In addition, they implemented the public health legislation of the federation (workplace protection, legislation regarding epidemics). They oftentimes played an important role in putting public health problems on the agenda of the federal government, for instance, with regard to the federal law against tuberculosis (1928) and the federal law on alcohol (1932) (Achtermann and Berset, 2006, 22–23).

To sum up, health care and public health remained institutionally separated during the interwar period. National health policy was mostly public health policy. There was an extension of the state's role with regard to its interference in matters of health policy, especially with regard to infectious diseases. The CDP performed an important role in advocating more public health policies. The cantonal ministers of health connected the high rate of TB infections with housing problems. They also recognized the necessity of improving primary care and individual prevention and they saw that economic growth is good for public health. However, the conference did not have the means to implement these policies. Prevention was the most important paradigm in the discussion of the Swiss health system before and during the war. Yet, it was understood as a paternalistic method of intervention. It was not really implemented because in the mainstream liberal and conservative parties population-based health policy was discredited as a result of the racist population health policies in the fascist states, especially in Germany (Minder, 1994). Alternatively, there were no reforms of the existing health care legislation that would have increased the regulatory power of the national state. The only adaptations were the national government's reforms that increased health care co-payments.

8.2.2 Coordination of Cantonal Governments rather than Responsiveness of Health Professions and Interest Groups

What happened with the responsiveness of the health care and public health sectors during t1? Public health issues were put on the political agenda by the CDP during the First World War. The founding of the organization in 1918 was a consequence of the war (Minder, 1994) as it was the war that caused the health issues. Although Swiss troops did not participate in battle, military mobilization involved sanitary challenges, such as the potential spread of infectious diseases as a result of the movement of troops and the gathering of many people that came along with it. The cantonal directors of public health noticed that infectious diseases that were already known became even more virulent in wartime. Consequently, sanitary conditions became even worse and epidemics broke out, for example, smallpox, cholera, dysentery, spotted fever, typhus, influenza, genital disease, and malaria. To get a grip on these problems, the national and the cantonal governments communicated on how to improve the coordination of public health policies (Minder, 1994).

In the CDP, coordination of public health policies occurred between the cantonal governments and the federal government. However, my analysis of secondary literature did not reveal evidence of responsiveness from the health care and public health sectors in the sense of communication and coordination between interest groups or professions of the two sectors, such as the medical profession on the one hand and public health doctors on the other hand. Although the national medical organization in Switzerland developed a more professional organization during the 1920s,[3] it was not very politically active.

In fact, it was the CDP that set the agenda for health policy, including public health issues. In 1933, the CDP proposed to the federal department of domestic affairs to draft a national law to combat epidemic diseases. The trigger for these activities was the smallpox epidemic from 1921 to 1926 and the increasing incidence of polio in the second half of the 1930s (Minder, 1994). The CDP itself also became an important arena for discussing issues of population health, which included references to ideas of social hygiene. Nevertheless, these concepts did not play a very important role and, if anything, their focus was on supporting weak and sick individuals rather than selecting the healthiest groups in the population. However, during the 1930s and 1940s, members of the CDP more explicitly articulated eugenic ideas for population health policies, for example, with family protection (Minder, 1994). It is not surprising that we find such arguments in Switzerland given that eugenic ideas were widespread at the time and that some Swiss cantons had implemented sterilization policies (Mottier, 2008). However, after the war – and the events in Germany during the Holocaust – support for these policies quickly dwindled in Switzerland (Minder, 1994).

In Switzerland, there was also policy integration of prevention and care regarding the prevention of accidents in the workplace and the provision of treatment facilities and payment in case of accidents. In 1918, the Swiss Accident Insurance Company (SUVA) was set up. It is an independent company under public law that insured all employees in Switzerland against workplace accidents and is responsible for workplace accident prevention and reimbursement of insured workers. One reason for the establishment of SUVA was that companies were not really interested in regulations for the prevention of accidents as these were considered as normal incidents. In addition to developing regulations for workplace protection, SUVA also developed technologies to prevent accidents (SUVA, 1993). SUVA is charged with the implementation and supervision of workplace security in companies (Achtermann and Berset, 2006, 22). Nevertheless, SUVA was not part of the federal administration, but was a public company that operated independently under supervision of the federal government (SUVA, 1993).

To sum up, this analysis did not find significant responsiveness of the health care and public health sectors as two different policy sectors in Switzerland. The previous chapters have discussed support for public health policies from physicians' organizations as a main indicator for responsiveness between health care and public health. In the Swiss case, however, it seems that the interaction between cantons played an important role in understanding the relationship between health care and the public health sectors. Since public health was in the hands of the cantons, coordination between cantons is the key to understanding public health policymaking as opposed to responsiveness of policy sectors.

What do these results imply for the argument of this book? We hypothesized for the Swiss case that health care and public health are decoupled because government is fragmented and professionalism is low. The analysis confirms this assumption. As far as sectorial distinctiveness is concerned, health care and public health were separated, notably at the national level. On the one hand, the federal and cantonal governments shared public health legislation, yet the residual powers remained at the cantonal level. On the other hand, health care, notably health insurance legislation, was a cantonal responsibility. At the national level, there was a health insurance law that only subsidized health insurance. Any obligations were a cantonal responsibility. The national health insurance legislation was a responsibility of the social insurance department, but not the federal public health office. Decentralization of the legislative competences and many veto points made up the institutional context, which caused the separation of both sectors.

At the same time, there was little responsiveness between sectors in the political arena. There was little political activity from the medical profession and patient organizations in general. At the same time, public health had not emerged as a profession similar to that of doctors in the health care sector. Therefore, private and professional interest groups did not play important roles in putting health policy issues on the political agenda and, consequently, they did not forge an alliance across sectors. The cantons, however, played an important role in politicizing public health problems and coordinated these activities in the CDP. Responsiveness for both sectors occurred at the cantonal level, if at all, but this dimension is beyond the scope of this book.

8.3 Decoupling and Subordination of Public Health to Health Care (1945–1980)

Following the Second World War, the context for health policymaking changed globally. The focus shifted to health policies aimed at individuals, rather than on the population in general. The reasons for this were the success of public health policies, pharmaceutical innovations, and prominence of public (population-focused) health policies in authoritarian states. These elements would also have an impact on health policies in Switzerland by aggravating the absence of responsiveness in the two sectors.

8.3.1 *Institutional Separation and Subordination*

After the Second World War, national health policymaking in Switzerland focused on individual health care, which was separate from public health. Shortly after the war, the discussion regarding a "complete revision" of the federal law on health insurance returned to the political agenda. However, the national government's main idea of creating mandatory health insurance for needy groups was soon abandoned as the economic situation and problems of financing the existing health insurance were already a pressing problem. Furthermore, the proposal did not pass in the national referendum (Kocher, 1967; Alber and Bernardi Schenkluhn, 1992; Vatter and Rüefli, 2014). During the 1950s, the federal government abandoned the idea of completely revising the national health insurance and only aimed at a partial revision of the health insurance legislation that increased the obligatory services that insurance companies had to provide and adapted federal subventions. However, the reform did not include a national health insurance obligation or more strict regulations of medical practice (Vatter and Rüefli, 2014).

The national government partially revised the national health insurance law in 1964. The reform created new services, especially for mothers, changed the regulation for subventions, and included insurance against tuberculosis. According to researchers, in this revision of the health insurance law, doctors and health insurance acted as "countervailing powers" and neutralized each other in the public debate. Therefore, the parliament and the administration in particular had a large influence in the process (Kocher, 1967; Santésuisse, 2014). Another revision failed in a popular referendum in 1974. The same happened with a proposal by the national government concerning a proposal for the health and mothers' insurance in 1987 (Alber and Bernardi Schenkluhn, 1992; Vatter and Rüefli, 2014). These reform proposals aimed to increase a national obligation to institute health insurance, but they all failed. In this context, medical organizations were indeed politically active, but in coordination with right-wing and liberal parties. Therefore, the regulation of health insurance providers remained at the cantonal or even the municipal level, which resulted in a different landscape of health insurance regulations (Uhlmann and Braun, 2011, 85). There was no further transfer of rights in health insurance legislation to the national level and consequently no further integration of health care and public health at the national level.

Public health remained institutionally and organizationally separate from health care at the national level and the federal office for public health retained some specific competences in public health policymaking. One attempt to increase the national public health legislation was made directly after the Second World War. In the context of its annual conference, the CDP proposed an amendment to the 1928 national law on tuberculosis. The proposition entailed mandatory testing for tuberculosis for the entire population. In a popular vote on May 22, 1945, the voting population refused the proposal with a large majority. The result of this vote is yet another example that policies which are perceived to constrain individual freedom (in this case to decide whether to be immunized or not) are difficult to implement in Switzerland. Another reason for the rejection of the law is that mortality from tuberculosis was already declining at the time and therefore the population did not perceive this as a really pressing problem that needed to be regulated immediately (Minder, 1994).

While there were no political majorities for more public health policies at the national level, the cantonal governments took action in that respect. For instance, in 1962, the CDP discussed prevention of dental caries because some dentists had demanded that health education include dental hygiene in schools. The canton of Zurich considered introducing mandatory toothbrushing for school kids, and the CDP recommended using fluoridated salt (Minder, 1994). As in the United Kingdom, smoking and its possible health effects became part of the debate among those in the medical profession. The national cancer league also discussed smoking as a health problem in its national report of 1962. However, despite much evidence to the contrary, many observers regarded smoking especially dangerous for youth, whereas it was seen as a deserved enjoyment for the elderly and pensioners (Kauz, 2010). Despite the scientific debates on cancer, I found little evidence that the medical profession or other pressure groups made these policies a political priority.

Most public health policymaking activity occurred at the cantonal level, yet it did not turn into comprehensive public health legislation at the cantonal and national levels and there were no outspoken or strong public health campaigns by the actor groups of the two fields. There was some timely national public health legislation, such as an increase of tobacco taxation (1969) (Achtermann and Berset, 2006, 23), the ban of tobacco advertisements on TV (BAG, 2014), and a new law regarding epidemics (1970) (Federal Council of Switzerland, 2010). As in Germany, there were some attempts to legislate public health by including preventive exams in the catalog of services paid for by health insurances (mostly at the cantonal level), which the CDP had demanded in the context of the revision of the health insurance legislation of 1972. As a consequence, a foundation for health education was created, which distributed materials concerning health education and preventative exams in schools, doctors' offices, and public places and ran an office for the documentation of health education. Furthermore, cantonal governments passed preventive health policies, for example Ticino and St. Gallen (Achtermann and Berset, 2006, 26). Yet overall, preventive approaches to health policy received less political attention compared to other issues in health policy, such as the financing of hospital reforms and deficits (Achtermann and Berset, 2006, 23).

To sum up, following the Second World War, health policy making in Switzerland changed in a way that put the focus on individual health care policy, as was the case in other countries. The public health agenda, which had been weak before therefore lost even more credit. The institutional separation of health care and public health was retained because there was no main institutional reform of health policymaking and at the national level there was no legal basis (such as a legislative framework) for public health policymaking (except for disaster management).

8.3.2 Continuity of (Non)Responsiveness between Sectors

As I will explain in the following section, there was little responsiveness between the health care and public health sectors in the sense of common policy advocacy and coordination of interest groups and professions. One reason for this was that public health, understood as preventive medicine, was established at Swiss universities in the mid-twentieth century, which was relatively late in international comparison. The first public health school emerged in the late 1950s when the vice-director of the federal office for public health returned with a Master of Public Health degree from the United States and accepted a teaching position at the University of Zurich. About ten years later, in 1968, social and preventive medicine became part of the general exams for medical doctors. The content of the subject "Sozial- und Präventivmedizin" [social and preventive medicine] involved mostly medical aspects of occupational health, but not many other concepts and instruments of preventive health policy. In the following decades, the universities of Zurich, Lausanne, Geneva, and Bern established institutes of public health and preventive medicine (Int-CH-13).[4]

However, the new field did not achieve the same status as public health in the United States. Doctors of clinical medicine did not appreciate the new field or easily integrate it with classical medicine. For instance, at the University of Bern, many professors of the faculty of medicine regarded the first professor for social and preventive medicine as an intruder. What is more, the fact that the new subject had been introduced as a decree by the federal government caused fears in the medical profession that this would come along with the establishment of a state medicine system (such as a national health service). Therefore, public health turned into a negative label (Int-CH-13, Int-CH-25) and did not receive strong political support from the medical profession.

Nonetheless, public health issues entered the political agenda and the public debate, as explained in the previous section. Thereby health-related NGOs, such as the Swiss Heart Association (nationalized in 1967) and the Swiss Rheuma League (nationalized in 1958), were somewhat active in public health agenda-setting because they promoted such policies to policymakers. In the postwar period, the policies advocated by these actors focused on individuals, for example, cancer screening. The health leagues, such as the Swiss Cancer League, collected money for cancer research, prevention, and cure and informed the population on the matter (Kauz, 2010). However, the politicization of public health and lobbying activities concerning these issues were not deemed professional. For, example, the federal office for public health and the national cancer league organized a commission for public health relations, which had the goal of informing the public on cancer problems and run projects to collect money for cancer research. However, in the literature, these political activities of the public health sector have been regarded as unprofessional. The commission for public health relations noted that, compared to Anglo-Saxon countries, Switzerland is lagging behind with public health information campaigns, including political activity on this matter (Kauz, 2010).

Although the medical profession did not act as a powerful pressure group on public health issues, doctors were interested in public health issues. For instance, in 1966, the president of the national cancer league, Martin Allgöwer, and Meinrad Schär from the University of Zurich published an article in the Swiss newspaper for doctors defending the usefulness of cancer registers as a means to learn more about cancer as well as to better prevent and cure the disease and they demanded a better coordination of the cantons. However, until the mid-1970s, only the cantons of Geneva, Vaud, Neuchatel, and Zurich (the last only temporally) had cancer registers (Kauz, 2010). The CDP played an important role in the nationalization of public health policy. In 1967, it demanded to be informed about the funding for Swiss health research that had been created at the time and demanded for it also to be used for social and preventive medicine, as well as to research economic, sociological, legal, and statistical problems of population health. The CDP demanded to create a section for this purpose in the Swiss National Science Foundation, which had been set up in 1970 (Minder, 1994).

To sum up, postwar health policy created serious challenges for health policymaking in Switzerland. There was strong opposition toward national public health policies in the population. Consequently, most national health policy projects focused on health care, whereas public health and prevention played a subordinate role. However, the increasing complexity of health policy problems in general made coordination of health policy and care as well as prevention more necessary, especially because many financially weak cantonal governments could not afford such policies anymore. With regard to the responsiveness of health care and public health, the lack of public health professionalization and the orientation of the medical profession toward individual care, also with regard to political activity, supported the subordination of public health under the health care sector.

What do these results imply for the hypotheses on the Swiss case? I hypothesized before that, in Switzerland, health care and public health are decoupled because government was fragmented and general political activity of health professions was low. These results mostly confirm this hypothesis. Regarding institutional distinctiveness, legislative decentralization and the many veto points and players at the national level were crucial for less institutional and organizational integration of health care and public health. The cantons kept many of their prerogatives in health policy, whereas the medical profession and popular opposition prohibited further state regulation in the field of health care. Consequently, there was less institutional integration of both sectors under the public umbrella. The low professionalism in Switzerland was caused by little political activity from the medical profession and health foundations resulting in no political responsiveness from the actor constellations of both sectors. Nonetheless, public health issues were on the political agenda, but only for some specific problems.

8.4   Noncoupling and Policy Integration (1980–2010)

Public health returned to the political agenda in Switzerland during the 1980s as it did in other countries. This was due to the changing contextual conditions, discussed in Chapter 3. As a reminder, during this time period the focus shifted back to public health because the pattern of dominant diseases evolved to more noncommunicable illnesses. What is more, the ever-rising cost of individual health care led to demands for more prevention for reasons of cost containment. This section will discuss how health care and public health coevolved in a changing context, in Switzerland.

8.4.1   Nationalization of Health Policy

In the early 1980s, health care infrastructure, specifically hospitals, began to change in Switzerland. This entailed the construction of big university hospitals, which were either newly constructed or modernized (the situation was similar for regional hospitals). Applied medical technology changed at the same time and became increasingly expensive. Consequently, the demand for more efficiency in medicine increased and critical voices became louder, demanding fundamental changes in the health system. Critical questions included how the rising health expenditures could be stopped. Specifically, the effectiveness of traditional medicine was called into question as was the role of companies in medicine, such as the pharmaceutical industry (Achtermann and Berset, 2006, 23; Kocher, 2010; Vatter and Rüefli, 2014).

In the early 1990s, the old model of a voluntary social health insurance, which was based on predominantly local health insurance, did not function anymore because of the increased mobility of citizens with "good risks" and cost pressure. Politicians throughout the 1980s tried to regulate these issues with decrees, but for experts it became clear that the best solution was to create obligatory health insurance (the majority of the population already had some kind of health insurance) and to regulate the insurance market (Int-CH-22) (Achtermann and Berset, 2006, 22). A national health insurance law passed in parliament in 1994 as well as a referendum. The new law created an obligation for each resident of Switzerland to have health insurance and required health insurance providers to accept everyone irrespective of health status and age. Nevertheless, insurance premiums are not calculated according to income (regressively) and employers do not have to pay a health insurance contribution (Bertozzi and Gilardi, 2008; Cheng, 2010; Indra, Januth, and Cueni, 2010; Böhm et al., 2012; Uhlmann and Braun, 2011). Since its establishment, the national health insurance law, the main instrument for governing health policy nationally, has been revised regularly with regard to some problems that have occurred, such as risk equalization between cantons and health insurance carriers (Uhlmann and Braun, 2011; Bonoli, Braun, and Trein, 2013).

New public health policies emerged at the cantonal level in the 1980s and 1990s. Cantons created their own sanitary units, programs for preventive health or health protection, and some cantons renewed their legislation on health. There was a change toward encompassing programs of health prevention instead of only having sectoral approaches in many cantons. However, there are large differences among the cantons with regard to expenditure for prevention (Achtermann and Berset, 2006, 26) (Int-CH-16, Int-CH-21, Int-CH-25). The national government also increased public health activities in this period. A national program to prevent AIDS was implemented in 1985 (Kübler, Neuenschwander, and Papadopoulos, 2001; Achtermann and Berset, 2006) as well as an ordinance for clean air (Achtermann and Berset, 2006). The federal office for public health created a "prevention" section in 1987 (tobacco, alcohol, drugs, and immunization). In the same year, the national government established more than ten national research programs to improve research on preventive health and to complement the medical research done by private and academic actors (e.g., the prevention of cardiovascular diseases). Nonetheless, clinical research remained dominant, although it received less public funding and more private financing (Achtermann and Berset, 2006, 24). Federal activities in the areas of HIV and drugs led to an increase of public health activities in the cantons that either implemented federal programs or made their own (Kübler, Neuenschwander, and Papadopoulos, 2001; Kübler and Wälti, 2001; Kübler, 2001).

In the 1990s, the federal government pursued more programs and activities in the field of public health policy. A national program to prevent drug use was established in 1991 (Achtermann and Berset, 2006), but some parliamentarians demanded more, such as a national law to prevent drug addiction.[5] The aforementioned Swiss Public Health Foundation published a national action program to replace the missing national health strategy. The federal government, the cantonal conferences for public health, and the national conference of health leagues supported this program (but not explicitly the medical associations). The program advocated better use of resources in the health sector for the optimal development of the health potential in the society by improving quality of life through the prevention of diseases (Domenighetti et al., 1993; Minder, 1994).

The government's public health activity was a reaction to increasing figures in the consumption of drugs, tobacco, and alcohol as well as the renewed attention to public health issues. However, the national legislation covered only illegal drugs, such as the federal law on narcotics that was approved in parliament in 1995. There were no majorities in parliament or popular referendums for national laws regarding tobacco and alcohol. For instance, a proposal to ban tobacco and alcohol advertising in 1993 was emphatically turned down in a popular vote (Cornuz et al., 1996; Achtermann and Berset, 2006; Vatter and Rüefli, 2014). The defeat of the proposition for a national ban of tobacco and alcohol advertisement was a strong blow to the ambitions of national public health policymakers because it underlined how little support public health issues had in the population and that the "anti-public health regulation coalition" was able to mobilize much stronger support among voters (Cornuz et al., 1996) (Int-CH-2, Int-CH-30). However, many of the cantonal governments became active and passed regulative policies in the fields of tobacco and alcohol after 2000 (Mavrot and Sager, 2017; Sager, 2003, 2004; Trein, 2017b).

In 2004, the federal department for domestic affairs demanded that the federal office for public health should evaluate the possibilities for a new national law on preventive health and should find out if it would be possible to integrate the existing public health programs and decrees into a national legal framework. There was, however, strong opposition to such a law. For instance, Swiss business corporations and organizations set up a platform that advocated modest prevention and opposed most forms of national public health legislation.[6] Another attempt to pass a national law for prevention (tabled in 2009) failed again (Int-CH-9, Int-CH-16).[7] Nevertheless, public health reforms on infectious diseases were possible in Switzerland (Achtermann and Berset, 2006, 24; Paccaud and Chiolero, 2010). For example, the national law on epidemic diseases underwent a general reform in 2011 (Int-CH-17).[8]

Important for this analysis, the administration of health policy became more centralized. The administration of the national health insurance legislation was integrated into the federal office for public health in 2003. According to the criteria that I discussed before, this can be regarded as an instance of institutional and organizational integration of both sectors because both sectors are in the same ministry. The effects of this reform have been evaluated differently. Some policymakers praised this as a good idea because it brought together health care and public health (Int-CH-19). However, others did not think that this reform was useful because it took all the attention in the federal public health office away from public health in favor of health care (Int-CH-9). This reform caused conflicts and irritation within the administration, especially in the area of public health. Nevertheless, the responsible minister argued that this reform was necessary to improve the coordination of both sectors (Int-CH-19). Alternatively, some of the personnel who were responsible for public health and prevention at the time complained that this reform shifted the internal preferences in the office to health care policymaking and that there was little room for public health policymaking (Int-CH-9, Int-CH-16).

To sum up, the institutional relationship of health care and public health evolved during the fourth time period. Due to the continuing decentralization of legislative competencies, health care and public health remained to a large part institutionally separated because the national government as well as the cantons had responsibilities for health care and public health. The most important institutional dynamic at the time was the increasing centralization of health policies in health care as well as public health. For example, the nationalization of health insurance matters and more national public health strategies showed that the national integration of both sectors increased considerably. Horizontal integration, health care, and public health had been institutionally separated until the administration of the national health insurance law was integrated in the federal office of public health. As a result, health care and public health were institutionally integrated in Switzerland, although the fragmentation of competencies between levels of government remained a problem.

8.4.2 Many Voices, but Little Harmony: Struggle for More Public Health Activism

The situation has changed since the 1980s with respect to the responsiveness between the health care sector and the public health sector, notably as far as the coordination between the cantons was concerned. Along with the discussed nationalization of health care and public health policy, the interaction between the national government and the cantons increased through coordination in the CDP as well as the national dialogue on health policy. As far as the interaction of professional actors was concerned, that is, medical doctors and public health doctors, there is less evidence for activities than in Australia.

With the return of public health to the political agenda during the early 1980s, public health gained more importance. Accordingly, prevention was also included in the national health insurance law, which passed parliament in 1994. An article of the new health insurance law (Art. 19 Abs. 1 KVG) includes prevention in the national health insurance. However, for preventive health policies to be reimbursed by health insurance, their effectiveness needs to be scientifically proven, which is the case for all services that health insurance can pay. In addition, the law demands that the national government and the cantons create an institution that coordinates prevention and health education nationally. The aforementioned Swiss foundation for preventive health has been charged with this task (Rosenbrock and Gerlinger, 2009). In Switzerland, about 50 percent of the public health measures are funded by public money (from the federal government, cantons, and large municipalities). The other half of the money comes from nonstate organizations such as the Swiss Public Health Foundation or the health leagues as well as directly from health insurance providers and households (Paccaud and Chiolero, 2010).

The integration of prevention and public health in the national health insurance law created national legislation in the field of public health and more funds for public health (Int-CH-16). Yet, as discussed in the chapter on Germany, this form of public health law subordinates public health to health care because it only regulates the financing of public health and does not give additional regulative power to the state, which is an important part of public health policy. It is done this way because the corporatist health insurance providers, as in Germany and Switzerland, have few competences and little interest to make public health policy.

With respect to the interaction of health care and public health as professions and interest groups, Switzerland is quite similar to Germany. Public health groups and the medical professions did not advocate public health issues, as was the case in Australia. Although the professionalization of public health has increased in Switzerland since the 1970s, for instance, by creating more study courses on public health, Switzerland is still seen as lagging behind with regard to the inclusion of public health in medical education (Brauchbar, Chastonay, and Mattig, 2014). At the same time, public health research has not resulted in more public health legislation, especially with regard to risk factors. Despite the slowly increasing professionalization of the public health sector and louder demands for more public health policy, increasing education and science have not led to a more coherent and politically active public health coalition including the medical professions (Int-CH-32). The newly created preventive health activities have often not been very professional with regard to the implementation of public health policies, but also with respect to lobbying activities. Of course, there are groups of doctors, such as the (Vereinigung Schweizer Ärzte gegen Drogen (VSAGD)), and interested citizens who lobby for more systematic public health legislation, such as in Geneva (Int-CH-25). However, this group did not have the financial means to pursue lobbying and lacked the full support of the national medical organization. Consequently, it was the federal office of public health that set the public health agenda, such as with the fight against the HIV epidemic (Kübler, Neuenschwander, and Papadopoulos, 2001).

Another potential important actor for more substantial public health lobbying is the health leagues, such as the cancer league and the lung league. During the 1990s, these organizations began to professionally organize their activities. For instance, the national cancer league pursued more professional donation campaigns, produced merchandising articles to increase donations for cancer activities, and increased the political lobbying in the national parliament (Kauz, 2010). However, traditionally, the cancer leagues had been organizations that focused on patients' social and psychological support rather than cancer prevention. Today, this development has changed, and the leagues are trying to gain attention by being outspoken against smoking (Int-CH-15).

Like other countries, Switzerland began to pass a series of health strategies regarding important diseases such as AIDS, cancer, and eventually tobacco and alcohol abuse. The national cancer league was involved in the establishment of the national programs for cancer (Kauz, 2010). The federal government recently passed a national health strategy, Gesundheit 2020, which entailed various general topics, such as prevention of risk factors, long term care, and workplace safety (Bonoli, Braun, and Trein, 2013).[9]

To sum up, there has been more public health policymaking since the 1980s, but no similar increase in responsiveness of health care and public health. Notably, there was little political activity by the medical profession or by the health foundations and other actors that could advocate more public health policies as private actors. Doctors, on the other hand, did not really support public health policies because many members of the medical profession questioned the effectiveness of these instruments. Scientific debates prevailed over political activism in professional organizations.

What do these results mean for the hypotheses that have been discussed earlier? It was argued before that health care and public health should be decoupled in Switzerland because of the fragmented government and low professionalism. The results of this analysis partially confirm this contention. Until 2003, health care and public health were institutionally and organizational separated, but then the national government decided to institutionally integrate the two sectors. Nonetheless, the institutional separation of health care and public health remained between cantons and the national government. Any project to integrate both sectors further failed because of political opposition. The integration of health care and public health could be undertaken through a governmental decree. However, further political integration was not possible. Concerning responsiveness, professional organizations were not politically active but focused on scientific controversies, for example, concerning the effectiveness of public health policies. Yet they did not forge a political alliance that advocated changes in health policy. Health policy issues, especially problems of public health, were therefore politicized along partisan lines.

8.5 Discussion

Health care and public health in Switzerland coevolved differently than in Australia and the United Kingdom and similarly to Germany. On the one hand, from the 19th century onwards, there was decoupling of health care and public health because both sectors remained institutionally and organizationally separated until the early twenty-first century. At the same time, there was little interaction between health care and public health by interest groups and professions. On the other hand, since the competences in health policy – individual care as well as prevention – were distributed between the national government and the cantons, there had been increasing interaction between both levels of government with regard to health care and public health issues, as well as the integration of both sectors (Table 8.1).

The results show that health care and public health coevolved in a decoupled manner in Switzerland. Throughout most of the time period, the two sectors were institutionally distinct from one another. In general, responsibilities for health policymaking were distributed

Table 8.1. Coevolution of health care and public health in Switzerland.

1880–1918 (t0)	1918–1945 (t1)	1945–1980 (t2)	1980–2010 (t3)
Decoupling: Separation of competences between the national and the cantonal government; informal interaction; no interaction between sectors	*Decoupling:* Sectors remain institutionally separated; very little interaction horizontally between health care and public health, but increasing coordination between cantons	*Decoupling:* Sectors remain institutionally separated; very little interaction horizontally between health care and public health	*Decoupling (noncoupling):* Centralization of health policies – regarding health care and public health policy; little responsiveness between actors

between two different levels of government, the subnational and the federal government. Yet at the same time, they had different institutions from a horizontal as well as a vertical perspective. The federal office for public health was responsible for public health and the federal office for social insurance had the task of administering the national health insurance legislation. This changed in 2003 with the inclusion of the national health insurance law in the federal office for public health. However, health policy still remained institutionally separated between national and cantonal health policy. Although there was considerable centralization of health policy, especially since the 1980s, the demand for coordination between the national and the cantonal government was still high.

Switzerland is similar to Germany with respect to the absence of responsiveness in both sectors. Since the emergence of health care and public health as two different policy sectors, there has been a lack of responsiveness of health care and public health regarding political activity and the interaction of professions and interest groups of both sectors. GPs have never taken an important role in advocating public health policies, a task that had been fulfilled by members of the administration. This does not mean that doctors were not interested in public health issues or prevention, but they did not act as the most powerful pressure group in this area, along with public health foundations or other actors. To the contrary, support for public health initiatives often came from members of cantonal governments or the public administration, such as the national public health administration or cantonal directors of public health, especially those who were active in the CDP. These actors, however, did not create the same political pressure as doctors and health foundations in other countries. Doctors were mostly concerned with the administration and inclusion of the health insurance providers, but as well as opposed to a mandatory national health insurance (until 1994). Health foundations were not very active with their support for public health, an issue that only changed in the 1990s.

8.5.1 Fragmented Government and Absence of Professionalism

What are the implications of these findings for this book's argument? We hypothesized previously that health care and public health in Switzerland should be decoupled. The reasons for this are the absence of a unified and centralized government and low professionalism. These results should hold independent of whether the contextual condition is favorable or unfavorable for responsiveness between the two sectors.

The decentralized structure of the Swiss federation and the multitude of veto points at the national level have impacted institutionalization in the field of health policy. The residual powers to legislate in health care as well as public health were originally on the side of the cantons. Competences were only gradually transferred to the national government, first concerning public health and then regarding health care. Thereby, the cantons jealously guarded their competences. This dynamic contributed to the institutional fragmentation of health care and public health and created coordination problems in the Swiss health system that still exist today. Nowadays, since health policymaking has become ever more complex, the cantons in some cases even want the federal government to take on new tasks in health policy because they do not want to pay for it. The decentralization of legislative power was a key argument for the opposition to a comprehensive national health insurance, which would have signified institutional integration of the two sectors. Such a reform only passed in 1994, but had failed many times before in parliament with popular votations.

Another feature of the coevolution of health care and public health is the absence of political responsiveness from the two policy sectors' actors in Switzerland. Notably, this is due to two reasons: the professionalism is low overall compared to other countries. Public health, in particular, did not evolve as a profession in a similar way to the United Kingdom, Germany, or especially Australia. For example, a university education in the field of public health was only established in the middle of the twentieth century. At the same time, the medical profession was very active politically, except for matters regarding its own interests. In other words, doctors did not stand out for being politically active with regard to health policy. This concerns health care specifically, but also public health more generally. The medical organization did not participate in forging alliances that spanned across the health care and public health sector. However, the absence of political activity also holds for other actors of health policy, notably health foundations and more public health-focused organizations.

Contextual elements were not important for responsiveness from actors and interest groups of the two sectors because the necessary predisposition, namely high professionalism, was lacking. With respect to the international context, Switzerland was in a peculiar situation. On the one hand, its proximity to Germany and the decay of public health in the Third Reich, in which population health policies became a key justification for the Holocaust, were a negative example for encompassing public health policies (Minder, 1994). On the other hand, the diffusion effect after the development of an international public health paradigm beginning in the 1980s had an effect on Switzerland and as a result public health policies were adopted, although the national public health coalition was rather weak. Nevertheless, contextual elements played a role, and especially since the 1980s, there had been a renewed impact of international elements, such as WHO strategies, on the relationship of both sectors.

8.5.2   Competing Explanations

As in the three preceding country studies, there are other theoretical elements that are important to the coevolution of health care and public health that I have discussed in the previous sections. Notably, these are sectorial complementarity, policy learning, and the difference between political parties.

1. *Complementarity:* Health care and public health in Switzerland coevolved toward two complementary sectors, although this did not entail extensive responsiveness between professional actors of the health care and the public health sectors and interest groups or much policy integration. A comparison of health care and public health between the late nineteenth century and today shows that there is more coordination between both sectors, for instance, regarding various health strategies. However, the development toward complementarity occurred by adapting new ideas regarding public health policies from other countries and international organizations, such as the WHO. At the same time, the main challenge of health policymaking in Switzerland is the coordination between the cantons and the national government. Therefore, all efforts in national health policy need to be coordinated between the levels of government. The coevolution of health care and public health in Switzerland is also part of the history of the changing interaction between the national and cantonal governments

and an increasing centralization of the competencies in health policymaking.

2. *Policy learning:* Policy learning in Switzerland occurred differently than in other countries with regard to the coevolution of health care and public health. Policy learning did not happen as a transmission of innovations on the coordination of health care and public health by the national medical profession and the public health profession, but rather through international channels. Swiss policymakers adopted WHO norms and ideas in order to pass innovative health policies that connected ideas of care and prevention. According to the literature, there are good reasons to assume that the adoption of new innovations in health care also occurred in the context of policy diffusion rather than based on domestic experiences only (Gilardi, Füglister, and Luyet, 2009).

3. *Party differences:* In the Swiss case, partisan differences in health policy also became apparent. This book has argued before that low professionalism came along with politicization of important issues in the party arena. If health professions were politically inactive, political parties played a more important role in putting problems on the political agenda. Many of the discussed health policy reforms were subject to large differences between the political parties, especially concerning public health policies. The medical and public health professions did not play a politically integrating function as in other countries. Thereby, the ways in which parties differed are not very surprising. On the one hand, left-wing parties supported more public health policies and more public health care services, such as a nationalized health insurance. On the other hand, the liberals and the Christian democrats supported less public intervention.

8.6 Summary

As theoretically expected, health care and public health in Switzerland coevolved in a decoupled manner. Due to the fragmentation of government, health care and public health were institutionally and organizationally separated between levels of government. Low professionalism and little political activity of the medical profession led to the absence of responsiveness between the two fields. As in the two other countries, the salience of public health issues changed with the aforementioned business cycle of public health. In the late nineteenth and early twentieth centuries, infectious diseases were rampant and public health became important. As in other countries, individual health care became the main paradigm of health policy after the Second World War, but after the 1980s the issues returned more prominently to the agenda of health policy in Switzerland. Nonetheless, both sectors were decoupled at the national level and only integrated in the federal office of public health after 2000. In contrast to Australia and the UK, and similarly to Germany, the medical profession in Switzerland did not think in terms of public health but rather focused on individual care and prevention. Consequently, it had a prominent role in the governance of health care, which occurred in a corporatist manner, traditionally at the local and cantonal level (until the 1990s). Public health activists themselves were not as professionally organized or backed up by a strong professional coalition of medical and public health doctors.

9 | United States: Politicized Professions and Loose Coupling of Health Care and Public Health

This chapter discusses the coevolution of the health care and the public health sectors in the United States (US). I selected the US for a case study because it combines a fragmented government with high professionalism as well as a competitive system of interest aggregation. Therefore, I expect that health care and public health should coevolve in a loosely coupled manner; in case the contextual conditions are favorable for responsiveness. In other words, if policy demands require an integration of health care and public health, or more public health policies, there should be responsiveness between the health care and public health policy sectors, in the United States. The results of the case study partially confirm my initial hypothesis. During t0, the two sectors were loosely coupled, coevolved toward decoupling, and shifted back toward loose coupling during the later time periods.

9.1 Emergence of Public Health in the Municipalities and States (1880–1918)

As in other countries, the most pressing problem for US health policy-makers involved infectious diseases during the first time period. At the same time, the possibilities of pharmaceutical technology were very limited. Therefore, I expect that there is an incentive for policymakers and interest groups to connect health care and public health policies. Given the competitive system of interest intermediation and politicized professions, interest groups and professions of the health care and the public health policy sectors had strong appeals to work together in order to deal with the most pressing health problems of the time.

9.1.1 Institutional Separation

Contrary to the English model, in the United States public health legislation emerged bottom up, often initiated by voluntary efforts.

200

Instead of being created by professionals, public health law originated from Puritan ethics on social cleanliness and godliness; the idea of a centralized health service never overcame the tradition of criticism of the central state and the belief in the superiority of local rights (Porter, 1999, 147). Thereby, the establishment of public health services began in cities in the southern and eastern parts of the country. This public health legislation, however, needed some form of coordination between different geographical areas. Consequently, statewide and regional boards of public health were set up, for example, in the state of Louisiana or New York City (Porter, 1999, 153–154).

Although the first state board was established in Louisiana in 1855, it was Massachusetts that set up the first effective board of public health in 1869. The Massachusetts board was different because Lemuel Shattuck, a statistician, had been recruited to set up the board. He understood that in order to achieve a solution for the pressing health problems, a more rational and systematic approach was needed. Massachusetts created a board of public health that was allowed to pursue investigations but not make reforms. The work by Shattuck was inspired by the British public health reformer Edwin Chadwick and Shattuck conducted similar works in the United States. Health departments or boards of public health were established after the 1860s in forty states (Institute of Medicine, 1988). Due to its efficient water supply, Massachusetts became the model for health boards in many other cities. However, most of the public health facilities that were established before 1890 were ineffective and only after the mentioned introduction of statistical exams did decision makers understand that a more scientific and rational government was needed in health policy (Porter, 1999, 155), to achieve improvements in public health.

At the national level, the institutionalization of public health occurred punctually and with regard to specific problems. Congress created the National Board of Health in 1879, which existed until 1883 (Gottweis et al., 2004, 74). However, the board was not transferred into a national public health agency because the responsibility for public health had been distributed among many agencies that did not want to give up their powers (Mullan, 1989). At the time, the Department of Internal Affairs dealt with sanitary conditions and hygiene in schools. Health in factories and housing was the responsibility of the Census Bureau and the Department of Commerce and Trade. The Surgeon General in the War Office conducted epidemiological research and was responsible for the health of the US Army. When the legislation for a new public health service came on the congressional agenda, the National League for Medical Freedom opposed health legislation that was supported by the American Medical Association and others. They argued that such legislation would create a medical trust controlled by a federal elite with federal authority and they campaigned successfully against national health legislation. Congress passed a law in 1912 that transferred the Marine Hospital Service to the United States Public Health Service. By 1915, the US Public Health Service and the Rockefeller Foundation were the major players involved in public health services. They were supplemented by a web of local state and city departments for health (Fee, 1994, 198; Institute of Medicine, 1988; Fee, 1994; Jonas, Goldsteen, and Goldsteen, 2007). Although sanitary reforms were largely accomplished by local initiatives and organizations, the Surgeon General received the power to demand annual meetings of the public health services in all states and to ensure universal standards. US public health officers, on the other hand, did not have anything to do with the engineering revolution in the states but instead provided biomedical assistance and managed the disease collectively (Porter, 1999, 285).

During the late nineteenth century in the United States, health policy was mostly public health policy. The regulation and financing of individual health care were in the hands of the market and the actors operating it. Thereby, the nongovernmental and not-for-profit sector played an important role in the expansion of the health care infrastructure. The running costs of hospitals were financed by nongovernmental organizations, religious groups, churches, and the state, whereas private hospitals were founded much later. Most hospitals were funded as a result of the public initiatives at the municipal level. The federal government only financed hospitals for the military, especially the Marines. Out-of-pocket contributions played an important role in the financing of medical care and hospitals. These institutions of health care provision were simultaneously a place of social control in the sense that being able to afford medical care in hospitals meant that the individual or the family had achieved an elevated social status and that hospitals could sanction sick people in order to protect the community. In contrast, burglars, prostitutes, and simple workers had to go to "almshouses" in order to get medical care (Schlesinger, 1997). Public assistance for health care payments existed only for indigent groups, such as soldiers and widows, yet a national health insurance – as, for instance, in other countries – did not find a political majority (Skocpol, 1995).

To sum up, health care and public health were institutionally separated in the United States during the second half of the nineteenth century. Institutions of public health were established at the levels of states and municipalities, such as public health boards and public health services, whereas individual health care was a responsibility of private actors and was barely regulated by the state.

9.1.2 Responsiveness of Health Professions and Interest Groups

During the last decade of the nineteenth century, social reformers tried to respond to the social conflicts in the country, including in the field of health policy. The Progressive Movement in the United States had a large influence on all areas of public policy at the turn of the century (Porter, 1999, 156–157). These reformers ideally imagined an institutional unification of health care and public health because investments in a healthy population entail not only prevention, but also primary care measures. In principle, the newly founded national public health organization also supported this cause. A group of engineers, physicians, and citizens created the American Public Health Organization in 1872. It was not a professional organization but rather a nongovernmental organization (NGO) based on goodwill (Porter, 1999, 156; Fee, 1994, 188–189). By 1884, the American Public Health Association had increased its influence and attracted members from Canada, Central America and later also Mexico. Its goal was to coordinate and standardize public health practices among authorities while, the same time, it was difficult to agree on the standardization of public health services (Porter, 1999, 153). Many of the members were organized in the American Public Health Organization (Porter, 1999, 158–159). Doctors were the most prominent group in the national public health organization. In addition, there were engineers and public-spirited citizens with an interest in improving sanitary reforms (Fee, 1994, 190–198).

The predisposition for public health policy changed significantly at the end of the nineteenth century. Between 1880 and 1890, bacteriological research produced new insights on the origins of diseases and provided new possibilities to prevent their outbreak. In the eyes of many researchers it offered an even more efficient approach to counteracting infectious disease compared to environmental reforms. In addition, the new science cast doubt on the arguments of those advocating for social reforms (Fee, 1994, 194), while many public health reformers, who supported ideas by the Progressive Movement for social intervention, embraced the new techniques and preventive health officials used this method to justify their challenge of clinical (curative) medicine. Many doctors and the medical elite embraced it but were skeptical about the immediate effect of preventive bacteriological interventions (Fee, 1987), especially by those who had been trained as engineers (Porter, 1999, 160; Fee, 1994, 192). Bacteriological methods, however, helped with responsiveness to infectious diseases, which were a crucial public health problem, for example, during military campaigns such as the Spanish-American War (Fee, 1994, 194–197; Porter, 1999, 157).

Consequently, by the early twentieth century there was a high demand for well-trained public health specialists (Fee, 1994, 198) to use army methods as widely as possible for domestic purposes. For instance, the Marine Hospital Services and the state health board in Louisiana successfully used public health techniques developed by the army during an epidemic of yellow fever (Porter, 1999, 157). The coordination of health services had been in the hands of the Marine Health Services since the late eighteenth century. A corps of officers had been providing public health services to communities during periods of crisis since the 1870s. The corps gradually became a force on which officials could call in times of crises. By 1902, the Marine Hospital Service was the largest single agency in the federal government (Porter, 1999).

Although health care and public health in the United States, from a general perspective, were institutionally separated in the sense that the state (i.e., a hierarchical bureaucratic logic) governed public health whereas the market (i.e., a competition of regulators and providers) governed health care, there was interaction between the fields, for example, regarding the professionalization of health in general. With the increasing interest of states and the federal government in public health, the demand for education and specialized training rose. Public health was concerned with medicine, engineers, lawyers, economics, and nursing, yet medicine had the strongest position. By 1912, twelve states demanded that all members of their boards of health be physicians, and twenty-three states required at least one physician to be on the board. The other states had no requirements. From the mid-nineteenth century to the early twentieth century, physicians were eager to participate in public health activities because this offered them intellectual distinction – for instance, with participation in social reform movements – or as the job came along with an income above and beyond what they received through their activities as doctors; in other words, working in the public health sector was economically attractive (Fee, 1994, 199).

Another indication of responsiveness between health care and public health is the establishment of public health schools, for example, at Johns Hopkins University, Harvard University, Yale University, Columbia University, or the University of Toronto – to name a few. Those schools had a preference for physicians, but members of other health professions were also admitted. The plans of studies mostly emphasized biological and laboratory sciences, which further institutionalized the biomedical paradigm in public health (Porter, 1999, 198) and fostered responsiveness of health care and public health professionals. There was often some interaction between actors at the highest level of health care and public health policy sectors; for instance, Rupert Blue became head of the US Public Health Service (Surgeon General) as well as the AMA (Mullan, 1989). He supported the demands for the creation of a national health service, although this endeavor eventually was not successful (Porter, 1999, 287).

In the decades after its foundation (1847), the American Medical Association (AMA) became politically very active in national health policy as it had to defend itself against state interventions (Gottweis et al., 2004, 177). Whereas the medical profession in Germany was already established as a professional and scientific organization at the beginning of the twentieth century, in the United States, there were debates on whether it is necessary to have the medical profession as an organization controlled by the states or if it is sufficient to have professional self-control. The key conflict between doctors and the state in the United States was whether the government should intervene in the regulation of doctors, whereas this issue had already been regulated in Germany long before the end of the nineteenth century. In Germany, due to the inclusion of doctors in the national health insurance program, the connection between doctors and the state was much closer than it was in the United States, and German doctors were much less politicized. Whereas doctoral organizations in Germany focused on scientific exchange as well as friendly networking, self-regulation of the American organizations was more politicized earlier on (Gottweis et al., 2004, 111–114). As a consequence, medical organizations opposed universal health care but supported more public health policies, which did not touch upon their special interests.

To sum up, beginning in the late nineteenth and early twentieth centuries, the medical profession developed into a politically active and strong professional organization that successfully opposed public health care or a national health insurance program. However, doctors supported prevention-related public health policies notably because they wanted to avoid public action in the health insurance sector. Along with health reformers of the Progressive Movement, a group of public health specialists even developed activities and lobbied for a national public health program that combined primary care services with structural measures in order to improve environmental conditions for health. The plan failed as a result of the opposition of the federal government.

What do these results imply for the presented hypotheses regarding the coupling of health care and public health? This book has argued that the sectors should be distinct from each other because legislative competences are separated between different levels, and many veto points exist at the national level, but there should be responsiveness as a result of the high professionalism, which implies that professional organizations are politically active. The results partially confirm my hypothesis. Regarding the fragmentation of government, the analysis clearly shows that the decentralization of competences had an effect in the sense that local and state governments took action with regard to public health policy instead of the national government. Because many veto possibilities exist at the national level, a national health service could de facto not be implemented against the resistance of the states. Concerning professionalism, the medical profession and public health organizations were politically active in order to represent the interests of their members. A side effect of this was that doctors and public health reformers cooperated and advocated more public health legislation. There were some conflicts between medical practitioners and public health reformers about treatment in public health services, but, overall, actors from both sectors cooperated with one another.

9.2 Cooperation and Conflict in the Interwar and Second World War Period (1918–1945)

The contextual condition changed slightly in the interwar period. The prevalence of infections notably declined and the technical possibilities for the cure of diseases increased. What is more, particularly due to the difficult economic context, there was a potential for conflicts between the two policy sectors.

9.2.1 Continuing Institutional Separation

As of the 1920s, health care, especially clinical practice, gained strength and became more important than public health with regard to policymaking in the United States. Salaries from private practice increased considerably, whereas those in the public health sector stagnated. Medical technology and practice improved significantly and became more scientifically grounded, technologically advanced, and dependent on hospitals. This development attracted physicians aiming for professional status and income, whereas positions in the public health sector became less attractive because of low income and little professional autonomy. Health departments subsequently no longer required degrees in public health because they wanted to attain physicians at any price. This reduced the incentive to take a degree in public health even further (Fee, 1994, 200). The increase in the salaries of physicians augmented their prestige as a profession and contributed to the following success of medical science, which had its onset in the 1920s. It was in the same decade that the organization declared its general opposition to any compulsory health insurance system based on contributions with the purpose of organizing payment for treatment. The rising membership of doctors in the organization confirmed this policy. (In 1901, about 7 percent of physicians were members of the AMA and about 65 percent were members in 1930) (Hacker, 1998).

A number of health care policies passed during the interwar period. For instance, the Sheppard-Towner Act of 1921 provided federal funding for maternal and child health, which was an extension of the previous US social policy schemes that provided services mainly to veterans and widows (Fee, 1994; Skocpol, 1995). At the same time, however, private health insurance remained an important element in the American health system. At the time of the Great Depression (1929), noncommercial health insurance organizations dominated the markets, such as Blue Cross for stationary care and Blue Shield for ambulatory care (Gottweis et al., 2004, 179). The AMA opposed any regulation of insurance organizations and also did not agree to voluntary health insurance policies. Consequently, the medical societies set up their own insurance policies during the 1930s; however, this policy was dropped soon thereafter (Starr, 1982; Hacker, 1998).

Most important for the relation of health care and public health during the interwar period in the United States was the New Deal legislation of 1935. Amid the pressing economic crisis of the 1930s, the national government passed a series of social policies, such as retirement insurance, unemployment insurance, and support for families (M. Schmidt, 2005b). The New Deal legislation of 1935 introduced new public health legislation as it provided a means for the financing of public health programs at the state level, but it did not introduce mandatory comprehensive health insurance. The proponents of the law decided to omit comprehensive health insurance from the reform because otherwise it would have been hard to find enough support for the New Deal legislation, even among the Democratic majority in Congress and especially the AMA, who managed to organize enough support against the introduction of comprehensive health legislation to cut it out of the legislative package. It was a coalition between Republicans and southern Democrats, in particular, that was susceptible to lobbying by the AMA (Hacker, 1998; Schild, 2003). The conservative coalition defeated it in Congress even though the law was very popular among the public (Marmor and McKissick, 2012).

With the New Deal and Social Security Act of 1935, the "state" played a stronger role in public health. The law provided new grants for the states to develop public health services (as a consequence, municipal public health services more than tripled between 1934 and 1942, from 541 to 1828, and declined again to 1322 after the war), federal funds for health education programs by the states, and federal regulations for minimum public health qualifications for personnel employed with federal grants. As a consequence, state universities offered more public health programs, as there was a high demand for public health education because private practice had become less profitable during the economic crisis of the 1930s. The programs, which were based on federal funds, enormously increased the capacity to deliver public health measures (Fee, 1994, 204). Although compulsory health insurance was not included in the New Deal Act of 1935, the program established grants for aid, which the United States Public Health Service (USPHS) used to establish local health departments (Porter, 1999; Institute of Medicine, 1988, 287).

The situation for health insurance legislation improved during the Second World War. In 1942, the War Labor Board permitted companies to include benefits in working contracts in an effort to attract employees to the labor market. Consequently, enrollment in hospital insurance plans that were sponsored by employers increased dramatically, even more so after the war when the unions secured the possibility of including health benefits in collective bargaining, with these health benefits being exempt from federal taxes. Consequently, the number of Americans who had some type of private health insurance plan increased sharply in the postwar area (from 12 million in 1940 to 76.6 million in 1950) (Hacker, 1998; Gottweis et al., 2004). Yet, from the 1920s until the 1960s, the medical profession in the United States successfully blocked any encompassing (towards universal coverage) health insurance legislation (Gottweis et al., 2004). This shows, first, that health care and public health remained institutionally separated as health care remained attached to the market; and second, that doctors were a much stronger veto group than they were in Germany, for example, in terms of political activism.

Before and during the Second World War, prevention of infectious diseases continued to play an important role in public health policy. Federal grants for the control of venereal diseases were set up in 1938. During the Second World War, national health policy received another expansionary move. Policymakers understood that in order to win the war it was necessary to have a healthy population (Fee, 1994, 204). In 1940, the USPHS greatly expanded its grant program to states and counties and sent personnel to very needy areas. What followed was the largest public health survey ever conducted in the United States. The Selective Service Board examined 16 million young men and found 40 percent to be physically or mentally ill. Although mortality rates from infectious diseases had declined since the beginning of the century, morbidity levels remained high. Mobilization efforts required the creation of large training campuses and industry plants, which, in turn, needed infrastructure and workers. These facilities were often placed in southern areas where sewage and canalization were inadequate for such large industrial complexes. To counteract malaria, a Center for Controlling Malaria was established in the war areas. After the war, these facilities were transformed into Centers for Disease Control, which later on became important institutions for public health (Fee, 1994, 205–206).

To sum up, during the interwar and Second World War periods, health care and public health remained institutionally separated. There were more and new public health policies, such as programs by the state public health departments, with regard to infections and health education. On the health care side, policymakers also created new policies, such as federal funding for child and maternal care. However, comprehensive health insurance, which was on the table during the New Deal debate, did not find a majority in Congress. Consequently, both fields remained institutionally separated because the market governed most parts of the health care sector, whereas public health remained in the hands of the state.

9.2.2 Conflicts between Health Care and Public Health

The discussion of the distinctiveness between policy sectors also showed some insights on the responsiveness between policy sectors. First, during the period of the economic crisis, there was no evidence of major conflicts between the interest groups and professional actors of both policy sectors that occurred as a consequence of the crisis, but, rather, in times of economic hardship, the public health sector provided interesting career opportunities for doctors who did not dare to enter private practice. Second, conflicts occurred, however, with regard to other problems; for example, doctors opposed any state intervention in the area of medical care. Above all, this entailed a fierce opposition against the proposed health insurance that was supposed to be included in the New Deal. The medical profession also opposed any policies, even if they just seemed to transgress in their discretion, such as measures of individual prevention. Yet, they did not oppose state activity regarding health education and promotion that targeted groups or settings.

Responsiveness occurred with regard to the exchange of professional members between public health schools and medical schools. Candidates from both fields occupied jobs in the public health sector and implemented the discussed public health measures. Contrary to its opposition to national health insurance, the medical profession did not oppose public health measures concerning infectious diseases and it participated in and supported the training of new public health personnel as well as the establishment of new public health departments during the New Deal legislation.

As mentioned before, the medical profession fiercely opposed the establishment of national compulsory health insurance. The reason for this opposition was the slow but steady increase in the competences of the state health departments. Doctors had resisted the provision of health care services by state public health departments since the late nineteenth century. Plans by local health departments to provide treatment for general diseases have especially received strong opposition. The medical profession was generally successful in obstructing these efforts throughout the entire twentieth century. Personal health care services by the public health departments extended mainly to areas in which private physicians were either not competent (TB, sexually transmitted diseases), not interested (certain routine exams), or not available (remote areas) (Jonas, Goldsteen, and Goldsteen, 2007).

After the second decade of the twentieth century, however, professional conflicts arose among nonmedical public health professionals and doctors. Yet, at that stage, only sanitary engineers were strong enough to challenge the dominance of physicians. They contributed significantly to the reduction of infectious disease. At the time, they complained successfully about the medical monopoly in public health. Physicians were willing to concede responsibility for public sanitation and water supplies, but not much else (Fee, 1994, 199). However, during the expansion of public health activities in the early twentieth century, health departments began to pursue activities beyond urban and sanitary reform – for instance, activities involving the control of infectious disease. The medical profession recognized the competition and shifted from strong support to criticism of and open hostility toward public health policies. Public health officers understood that cooperation was necessary and took into account occasional conflicts among the clinicians and public health officers, but they often avoided conflicts (Fee, 1994, 200).

However, during the 1930s, the relationship between the medical profession and public health officers became increasingly conflictive. The economic crisis during this period limited possibilities for private practice because an increasing number of physicians could no longer afford living on out-of-pocket fees from patients. Consequently, support for a national health insurance scheme and a national health service increased. But, we have seen before, the former failed and was excluded from the New Deal legislation in 1935. However, in the decade between 1935 and 1945, the USPHS supported the creation of a national health service. In 1938, a conference took place in Washington, DC, which united representatives of labor as well as farmers and public health professionals. The results of the conference became the basis for a bill that failed in 1939 but reemerged in the 1943 Wagner-Murray-Dingel Bill proposing a national program for the provision and financing of health care. Although the bill of 1943 failed again, the results of the conference became the substance of the battles between the AMA and the PHS over the introduction of state control in medical care (Mullan, 1989, 109–110; Porter, 1999, 287).

To sum up, the two decades of the interwar period were highly contentious with regard to health policy, as the medical profession vigorously opposed any public interventions by the state in the field of health care policy, whereas public health reformers demanded more public health interventions (Fee, 1994; Skocpol, 1995). Therefore, responsiveness between the two sectors was mostly absent. On the other hand, public health professionalization continued to establish a separate profession that was concerned with population health matters, which was different from the medical profession (Starr, 2009). Although both groups competed for research money and the attention of policymakers, medical organizations also supported population-based health policies as long as they did not touch their core competencies, such as free individual practice.

What do these results imply for the discussed hypotheses? This book has contended that health care and public health should be loosely coupled or decoupled. On the one hand, there should be institutional separation because government is rather fragmented. On the other hand, there is high professionalism, which is a good context for sectorial responsiveness, as professions are politically active on a broad array of topics. Yet the contextual condition at the time changed and the economic crisis should have led to conflicts between the two fields. The results confirm these hypotheses. Although there were legal proposals to integrate health care and public health, the respective laws failed in Congress, not the least because of the opposition of the medical profession, which particularly opposed a national health insurance law but also any other law it suspected of diminishing free practice. However, the medical profession was politically very active. It supported public health policies that did not interfere with the material interests of its members, such as actions against infections, but it opposed the intervention in its core business. The post-crisis period did not spark opposition against public health generally, but, at the time, the number of proposed laws that demanded more unification of health care and public health increased, and so did conflicts between the two sectors, for example, between the AMA and the USPHS.

9.3 Dominance of Health Care in the Shadow of loose Coupling (1945–1980)

This section will turn to the coevolution of the health care and public health sectors during the postwar period. Based on the discussion on the contextual conditions, there should be a decoupling of health care and public health even though professionalism is low. The reasons for this are that the demands changed and public health problems were much less virulent than they were in the two preceding time periods.

9.3.1 Toward more Institutional Unification

There were many different health care policy reforms in the United States after the Second World War. Congress passed the Hill-Burton Act (Hospital Survey and Construction Act) in 1946. The law had the objective of constructing hospitals in rural areas and bringing medical care to everyone. Under the act, the federal government paid one-third of the expenditure for hospitals (USD75 million yearly for the first five years) and it became the most popular health program in the United States. The law met the demand for nationwide health care without touching the prerogatives of the medical profession. Some authors, such as Fee, argued that the creation of local public health departments could have been achieved with a fraction of the cost, yet public health advocates lacked a strong lobby and health care gained most of the available public resources (Fee, 1994, 208). Nevertheless, the AMA successfully opposed any reforms that would have increased universality of health insurance (Hacker, 1998).

The main reform in American health insurance policy occurred in the 1960s. The establishment of Medicare and Medicaid in 1965 was part of a new wave of social policy led by the then President Lyndon B. Johnson and was called the "War against Poverty" (Schild, 2003). However, the reform did not introduce the type of encompassing health insurance that reformers had demanded in previous decades, but, rather, it proposed limited insurance for hospitalization for pensioners and the disabled (Medicare) and for some parts of the impoverished population (Medicaid). The passage of this law is significant for health policy in the United States in several ways. First, it is the result of reaction by advocates for social security to the failure to introduce comprehensive health insurance in the second part of Truman's term in office. Looking back on the failed proposals to establish comprehensive health insurance in the 1930s and 1940s, supporters of the reform introduced a proposal that extended health insurance coverage to more indigent groups – in this case, the elderly, poor, and disabled. Second, they ended a long ideological battle concerning the need for government to establish health insurance, by creating this exact legislation for a segment of the population. However, this reform was, again, an incremental increase of health insurance coverage, which fitted into the pattern of previous social policy legislation that had especially been extended to indigent groups, such as veterans (Hacker, 1998; Marmor and McKissick, 2012).

With regard to the coupling of health care and public health, the reform of 1965 reduced the institutional distinctiveness of the health care and public health sectors. The legislation concerning Medicare and Medicaid underlined once more that the United States had taken a different course concerning health insurance policy, as the majority of its welfare state policies, including health insurance, were privately organized. At the same time, several public programs provided health care for the indigent. However, in contrast to the United Kingdom, in the United States, there was no national public health care scheme to cover the lower, working, and middle classes, which entailed the majority of the population and were very important for the economy (Hacker, 1998). Health insurance was largely provided as employer-based schemes of health insurance, which are part of the private health care system (Seeleib-Kaiser, 1993).

Public health policy in the United States underwent significant changes in the postwar period because of contextual changes, such as different patterns of diseases (Fee, 1994, 209). As a consequence, public health policy ideas had particular problems to find political support during the immediate postwar era. One reason for this was the magnitude of activities that needed its attention, such as chronic disease rehabilitation, mental health, industrial health, accident prevention, and environmental issues, or to put it differently, the lack of clear policy priorities. Many public health departments had few ideas about what to do and continued to run the same programs as before the war – except New York, Virginia, and Minnesota, where the states ran research laboratories for the prevention and treatment of chronic disease. Public health programs focused more on screening and the early detection of disease than on actual preventive measures. According to Fee, the field lost its social orientation and "seemed to be merging with clinical preventive medicine" (Fee, 1994, 209–210). Yet health departments implemented some measures, such as the fluoridation of water supplies to protect children's teeth. Although scientific authorities and professional organizations almost unanimously supported these measures, the political climate at the time was extremely unfavorable to these kinds of policies. The political right especially denounced public health policies as socialist and communist interventions and the measures were halted. One great success of the 1950s was the development and mass-scale implementation of the polio vaccination. Yet this occurred as a result of massive private funding and a huge PR campaign by the Foundation of Infantile Paralysis (Fee, 1994, 210), rather than a coordinated public health initiative by the state. At the time, completely new health problems arose. Public health officers were overwhelmed with many tasks, such as visiting child health stations, tuberculosis clinics, and venereal disease clinics; operating immunization sessions; and completing communicable disease diagnoses. They therefore had no time for community health education, the study of health problems, diabetes and cancer control, rheumatic fever prophylaxis, nutrition education, and radiation control. As a consequence, positions often remained vacant and could not be filled and medical practitioners had to provide these services on the side (Fee, 1994, 206–211).

However, not all accounts are as critical of US public health policy as the one by Fee who claimes despite all criticism that the role of public health policy nonetheless remained important in the postwar era and that investments in public health policy also increased with the establishment of new sections in the National Institute for Health (Pratico, 2001). In a book on the history of the USPHS, Mullan insisted that USPHS played an important role in national health policy in the postwar era and particularly under President Dwight Eisenhower, when the Federal Security Agency (FSA) was replaced by a ministry of health and education, which had an impact on the USPHS because the Surgeon General now reported to the new minister. Moreover, this author underlined the allegedly important role of the US public health service in the polio vaccination campaign and the considerable public criticism of the service because of accidents with the vaccine that caused some children to die. Consequently, it was hard to defend the need for more public health policies, and the support of private actors for the immunization campaign was extremely important for funding public health campaigns (Mullan, 1989).

During the 1970s, further public health reforms were put into place in the United States. The Occupational Safety and Health Act of 1970 aimed to improve health and working conditions for workers in general (Morey, 1975). At the community level, the public remained the most important provider of classic public health services, such as the supply of pure water, sanitary sewage disposal, inspection of food and drugs, and control of communicable diseases (i.e., immunization and the control of sexually transmitted diseases) as well as health statistics and the protection and regulation of the environment. Some of these functions were provided in conjunction with private actors, such as the American Cancer Society and the American Heart Association, that were active in public health education, whereas others had an important role concerning health science education and research. The Sierra Club and the Natural Resources Defense Council participated in environmental protection (Jonas, Goldsteen, and Goldsteen, 2007).

Nongovernmental organizations played an important role in the provision of smoking control policies. These were smokers' rights groups that advocated tobacco control policies, especially those policies that would protect nonsmoking citizens from smoke. From the outset, public opinion was rather favorable for smoking bans to protect nonsmokers. The argument that smokers would place other individuals at risk allowed the movement to bypass accusations of being paternalistic and to demand a "Nanny State." Consequently, the first successful public health policies were already passed during the 1970s. In 1973, seats of smokers and nonsmokers were separated on domestic flights. In 1974, the Interstate Commerce Commission decided that 20 percent of the seats on interstate busses had to be smoke free. In 1977, Berkeley was the first community in California to limit smoking in restaurants and at other public places (Bayer and Colgrove, 2004).

To sum up, health care and public health remained institutionally and organizationally separated during the postwar period. The state was responsible for public health policies, notably the subgovernments, whereas the national government was in charge of health care for the indigent, whereas individual health care was privately governed for the majority of the population. However, there has been an evolution of both sectors toward more unification, specifically with the state assuming a stronger role in institutionalizing individual health care than had been the case during the previous time period, most notably with the Medicare and Medicaid legislation. Nonetheless, the majority of the population had private or employer-based health care plans, which left both sectors largely institutionally independent.

9.3.2   Responsiveness and Subordination

After the war, many public health reformers hoped to unite medical care and public health as this was appropriate for combating chronic diseases under the conduct of health departments. Thereby, the reformers forgot the strong resistance of the medical profession against any intervention of the state in curative medicine. Social medicine was also regarded as another possibility for combating chronic disease and integrating curative medicine and public health. Some in the profession, however, were cautious and warned of the widespread anti-state attitude in the United States when it came to medical care. At the same time, a new specialty in public health arose, which was placed between public health and clinical specialties. Its representatives were private practitioners who conducted clinical prevention, such as providing screening tests and advice on the individual level. In order to increase their influence, they wanted public health departments to refrain from preventive action against chronic diseases, such as cancer, diabetes, and cardiovascular disease. Public health officers had no unanimous position as some favored tax-financed medical care, whereas others were more loyal to the medical profession and held that the combination of health care and public health services would disturb the existing structures of medical care. At the same time, the American Hospital Association and the American Medical Association strongly pushed for legislation to support the building of hospitals (Fee, 1994, 206–208). The subordination of public health with respect to the health care sector increased during the 1950s. Theoretically, social medicine proposed efficient and viable alternatives to the sole focus on clinical cures; yet, these ideas were not translated into actual health policies as public health departments lacked budgets and political support. During the postwar period, there was massive investment in biomedical research, hospital construction, and the payment of health care by private insurance providers, whereas public health services were neglected. The reasons for this were that basic sciences and clinical medicine established the research priorities and public and social services caused immediate suspicion of creeping socialism or even communism. In this context, the integration of public health and health care, as envisioned by social medicine, was perceived as a threat (Fee, 1994, 208).

The creation of Medicare and Medicaid legislation shifted public health in the direction of individual care. It covered medical costs and social security for the poor but failed to provide adequate preventive services. The programs were built on the coordination with private providers of medical care and increased the costs for medical treatment. Programs, such as the anti-poverty programs that were intended to encourage community participation, were seen as competition with private interests and did not function as well (Fee, 1994, 214). At the same time, there was an institutional evolution of the public health service. The USPHS was not included in the debates on Medicare. The USPHS and the local health departments did not receive additional resources, but the grants in aid were offered by the Office of Economic Opportunity to fund new neighborhood health centers. When Medicaid and Medicare were put into legislation in 1965, the Department of Health Education and Welfare assumed the responsibility of administering the acts (Porter, 1999; Institute of Medicine, 1988, 288).

The reforms in the United States upheld the central principle of the health care financing system, which was the market. Like governments in other countries, the United States needed to save health care costs in the 1970s and 1980s. Yet, other than in the more statist systems in the United Kingdom and Canada, the US government faced much more difficulties with establishing second-level agency relationships, such as with the professional standards review organizations. The 1960s were characterized by the War on Poverty and the growing urban power of the civil rights movement and riots: anti-poverty efforts as well as other social policy reforms passed by the Johnson administration focused on medical care, i.e., access and hospitalization, especially for the elderly. Many of the social and health programs of the 1960s bypassed public health departments and set up new agencies mediating between the federal government and the local communities, as state governments were seen as too conservative to deal with the problems in an egalitarian and progressive manner. In addition, neighborhood health centers and community-based mental health services were established without reference to public health agencies. Environmental issues that attracted political concerns in the 1970s were organized in the Environmental Protection Agency at the federal level. Mental health was, again, included in a different program. As a consequence, "Public health further lost visibility and clarity of definition" (Fee, 1994, 214–215).

Nevertheless, health care and public health in the United States were still very responsive compared to other countries. There was a successful public health coalition with regard to tobacco control policy, the connection of fluoride to dental caries, and the prevention of coronary heart disease through physical exercise. However, the context of health policy had shifted its focus toward individual health care. Particularly, public health professionals and interest groups were not prepared for the relative disappearance of infectious diseases and the advent of noncommunicable disease. At the same time, federal expenditures on medical research increased from USD28 million in 1947 to USD186 million ten years later. Most of this money was spent on clinical and laboratory research and little on epidemiology. The schools of public health had not dealt adequately with the arriving chronic diseases and followed the research guidelines of the National Institutes of Health, who had little interest in the practical problems of public health departments (Fee, 1994, 212–213).

In other fields, the USPHS and particularly the Surgeon General continued to make important contributions to public health policy. This occurred especially based on the reports by the Surgeon General that focused on certain health problems in the United States. For instance, in 1964, the Surgeon General published the report "Smoking and Health: Report of the Advisory Committee of the Surgeon General of the Public Health Service," which sparked a huge debate on tobacco control policy and was the onset for more public health policies.[1]

The publication of the Surgeon General's report on smoking and health had immediate policy implications. The federal commission of trade, which had been prepared for it, immediately released regulations concerning warning labels on cigarette packs and restrictions on tobacco advertising. However, the opposition in Congress and opposing interest groups blocked the adoption of a comprehensive tobacco control policy (Bayer and Colgrove, 2004). Yet, the Surgeon General's reports continued to emphasize the need for more tobacco control policies. Historically, the agricultural committee in Congress controlled tobacco control policy in the United States. The US Department of Agriculture (USDA) and some interest groups closed the subsystem. This was the dominant iron triangle in the first half of the twentieth century, but it changed thereafter through reports by the Surgeon General in 1964 and following reports in 1986 and 1988 in the sense that the medical profession became one of the strongest advocates of tobacco control policy (Bayer and Colgrove, 2004). One policy consequence was the strengthening of warning languages in 1970, 1985, and 1996; the Federal Cigarette Labeling and Advertising Act; and the fact that health warnings on billboard ads became mandatory (Worsham, 2006).

To sum up, there was responsiveness between health care and public health during the interwar period. This becomes apparent with regard to the connection of both sectors in education and the participation of doctors in public health research. Yet, as in other countries, health policymaking moved toward more subordination of health care under public health, which means that most health policies focused on individuals rather than on population health. In Australia, the situation was similar, but there was more evidence of political activity by the medical profession, who participated in a large public health coalition that advocated more population health policies. For the United States, there is less evidence of political responsiveness.

What do these results imply for the argument of this book? Previous chapters hypothesized that there should be a decoupling of health care and public health in the United States because the context changed in the sense that demands for public health policies were reduced. This analysis confirms this hypothesis, at least to some degree. Overall, health care and public health remained institutionally and organizationally separate. The reason for this was that the federal government did not succeed in passing comprehensive national health insurance, which had been on the political agendas of at least the Truman, Johnson, and Nixon administrations. In each case, however, the combination of a politically active medical profession and the absence of a political majority in support of universal health care in Congress blocked such a reform. However, there were some incremental reforms. The addition of Medicaid and Medicare in 1965 shifted the relationship of health care and public health toward more institutional and organizational unification. Concerning professionalism, there is little responsiveness between health care and public health. Doctors and public health officers did not openly forge a public health coalition, but the medical profession did not oppose new public health policies, such as tobacco control measures. The political activity in that field mostly came from public health officials themselves.

9.4 Toward Integration of Health Care and Public Health (1980–2010)

During t3, the contextual condition for the coevolution of health care and public health changed. Demands for more public health policies increased because noncommunicable diseases, such as diabetes and cancer, became more prevalent. At the same time, new infectious diseases, such as HIV, appeared. According to this book's expectations, these developments should have drawn more attention of policymakers to public health and lead to responsiveness between health care and public health in the United States.

9.4.1 Toward Institutional Unification

During the 1980s, health care policy in the United States underwent similar changes to those in other countries, namely an increased demand for more cost containment and reforms to make the provision of health care more efficient. Demands for universal health care, which had been prevalent in the debate in the United States since the 1930s, calmed down. During the presidencies of Ronald Reagan and George Bush Senior, budgetary deficits in the health care sector dominated the political debate. Reform suggestions mostly concerned the realignment of the bureaucracy in order to rationalize the provision of Medicare and to introduce DRG payments in hospitals (Marmor, 2012). The reforms of the American health care system in the 1980s came along with the rise of health maintenance organizations (HMOs), which are profitable organizations in health care (Gottweis et al., 2004, 15).

During the 1980s, the federal government changed the grant structure of state funding by introducing block grants and left it to the states to deal with the budgetary implications. In this phase, state health departments had to manage budget cuts along with Medicaid programs, emergency health services, and a growing poor population with problems, including alcoholism, drug abuse, teenage pregnancy, and family violence (Fee, 1994, 216). Health insurance in the United States had been dominated by employer-based insurance schemes because attempts to introduce health insurance legislation failed in the 1930s and thereafter. The company health insurance plans worked as long as workers were young and healthy. However, during the 1960s, most of the beneficiaries had already become older and needier, and health care expenses for companies increased. For instance, in 1965, the spending of American businesses on health benefits increased from 2.2 to 8.3 percent of salary costs and from 8.4 to 56.4 percent of pre-tax profits (Porter, 1999, 262). This development began to have negative effects on the competitiveness of American firms from the 1970s onward and they began to introduce measures to save money – for instance, by shifting costs to older employees, dropping coverage, imposing managed care through HMOs, and stopping the hiring of employees with known medical conditions (Porter, 1999, 262). In addition, companies had cross-subsidized contributions for the low-insured or the underinsured. This changed after the end of the postwar economic growth and the new jobs that were created in the 1970s and thereafter allowed for no fringe benefits (Tuohy, 1999).

In this context of reduced coverage regarding medical, the cost of health care in the United States continued to rise during the 1980s. In contrast to other countries in the OECD, which kept health expenditures at a stable level (around or slightly above 10 percent of the gross domestic product [GDP]), the United States was the only country in which expenditures for health – mostly for individual health care – rose above 15 percent of the GDP after 2000 (OECD, 2017). Consequently, Medicare costs became subjected to debates about budgetary issues. Coverage for private health care insurance and Medicare for services per capita was reduced during the 1980s, but, at the same time, out-of-pocket payments for health care augmented steeply, shifting the cost for Medicare to the private sector and consequently to consumers (Marmor and McKissick, 2012).

In 1993, a legal project trying to introduce comprehensive health insurance and to nationalize health policy failed (Tuohy, 1999; Uhlmann and Braun, 2011; Marmor, 2012) – although the AMA was in favor of the legislation but was not strong enough to win decisive support (Porter, 1999, 265–267). It was only during the recent financial and economic crisis that the US government passed a major overhaul of its health care system, the Patient Protection and Affordable Care Act of 2011. The law intended to include almost universal health care coverage by sharing responsibilities for this between employers and employees, improve fairness and affordability, improve the value of health care, make the system more accountable, increase access to primary health care, and make better investments in public health by expanding investments in the community as well as preventive care (Rosenbaum, 2011; Beaussier, 2012).

From the perspective of public health, the period since the 1980s has been one of cost containment and restriction as well as the continuing encroachment of individual health care along with the increasing unification of the two sectors. The institutional combination of preventive programs with health care or social welfare policies threatened original public health programs, which focused on prevention of diseases. During the 1970s, for instance, state and local public health programs began to provide individual care to uninsured patients and those who were rejected by private practitioners (Fee, 1994, 214). The public health community agreed that a coordinated national effort was needed to educate about and prevent these diseases. Public health departments also became a part of the cost-containment debates of the 1980s and had to defend their expenditures; they became institutions that were oriented toward the poor and the needy, with the challenge of providing care for these groups. Nevertheless, public health officials did not manage to lobby effectively for encompassing public health programs and policies at the national level in order to jump the high hurdles of veto players for national policies. By 1988, more than two-thirds of the budgets of state and local health departments went to personal health services; medical care absorbed more and more of the resources of the health departments. Legislators preferred meeting needy people's urgent care needs over having a basic infrastructure of public health (Fee, 1994, 215–217).

The 1990s and 2000s also saw some dynamics with regard to the relationship of public health and public health care programs. Health policies strengthened support for children, for example, with the State Children's Health Insurance Programs under which the federal government provided matching funds for state programs (Volden, 2006). Other reforms unify health care and public health, such as the Breast and Cervical Cancer Treatment and Prevention Act of 2000. In the wake of the economic and financial crisis of 2007, the federal government put into place the Patient Protection and Affordable Care Act (2010), which not only created a national health care framework law but also included funding for various prevention and public health measures, notably through the Prevention and Public Health Fund (Haberkorn, 2012; Rice et al., 2013).

Organizationally, national is under the control of the Department of Health and Human Services (DHHS). Along with the Department of Veterans Affairs and the Department of Defense, it is responsible for many public health-related programs. In addition, the Department of Agriculture, the Environmental Protection Agency, and the Department of Labor (Occupational Health and Safety) hold health-related responsibilities. Within the DHHS are eleven divisions that are responsible for health; eight among them are under the supervision of the USPHS. The others are the centers for Medicare and Medicaid, the Administration for Children and Families, and the Administration on Aging (Jonas, Goldsteen, and Goldsteen, 2007).

With regard to concrete policy issues in the field of public health, the United States faced new challenges during the 1980s. The appearance of AIDS again shifted the focus of policymakers to the problem of infectious diseases (Avery, 2004). The public health community agreed that a coordinated national effort to educate on and prevent these diseases was needed, but the money mostly went to research and medical initiatives rather than prevention and education. It seems that at the political level, it was easier to find money for research than for programs that deal directly with problems of the impoverished middle class; politicians seem likely to avoid very emotional issues such as drug use and AIDS (Fee, 1994, 215–216). The USPHS was revived in the wake of the AIDS epidemic. Surgeon General Everett C. Kopp demanded that Reagan publicly recognize the disease, which turned the attention of the public back to the service. Before that, the USPHS was largely preoccupied with health care issues within medical care provision and only partially focused on environmental health (Mullan, 1989; Porter, 1999, 288). Furthermore, tobacco control policy played an important role in the United States. For example, in 1997, the Master Settlement Agreement between the tobacco companies and the state governments promoted compensation payments as well as the disclosure of information concerning industry lobbying activities (Sung et al., 2005; Clegg Smith, Wakefield, and Nichter, 2003; Schroeder, 2004). The smoking ban legislation at the national level (for buildings of the federal government) followed in 1998, when the Master Settlement Agreement between the tobacco industry and the American states was reached (Gilardi et al., 2014).

To sum up, in the United States, the institutional relation of health care and public health moved toward more institutional unification, as health care and public health are organized under the same institutional umbrella. However, the lack of powerful public health institutions at the national level as well as more veto points against public health policies (Mayes and Oliver, 2012) did not lead to the same institutional unification of both sectors but rather the contin-uation of institutional separation and a strong interaction of actor groups. Not until the establishment of the national health insurance legislation in 2011 did the institutional distinctiveness of health care and public health vanish and the United States fulfill (somewhat) the criteria of the institutional unification of health care and public health.

9.4.2 Responsiveness Regarding HIV and Tobacco

Regarding responsiveness between health care and public health, there was interaction between both sectors. First of all, concerning infectious diseases, such as AIDS, there was a large coalition of actors and public health officials as well as doctors and medical organizations that demanded a coordinated approach to responding to the disease. What is more, the Surgeon General played an important role in underlining the need for a public health intervention.

AIDS appeared as a clinical condition in 1983. Consequently, debates arose on what the response to the disease should be. Gay leaders, civil libertarians, physicians, and public health officials argued that the disease needed to be dealt with in an exceptional way and were against using the classical public health approach, which would entail a tight control of the disease and those infected with it. However, the opinion of medical organizations changed during the 1980s and they demanded recognizing HIV as an infectious disease that can be sexually transmitted (Bayer, 1991).

Generally speaking, the debate on AIDS in the United States was conflictual with regard to screening, testing, needle exchange, and research on drugs and treatment. Yet eventually the policy was made by those who were in charge of health policy over the last fifty years in the country. Despite the typical rhetorical debates in the United States regarding this type of interventionist policy, there was a certain agreement that a comprehensive reaction to the sickness was necessary. Interestingly, Surgeon General Everett C. Kopp was appointed with the support of the political right although he insisted on a progressive AIDS policy despite his political and religious beliefs (Fox, Day, and Klein, 2012). In spite of these rhetorical differences, there was a large public health coalition supporting AIDS policy, which consisted of the medical profession, public health doctors, and members of the public health administration, underlining the responsiveness of health care and public health in the matter.

The same had occurred with regard to tobacco advertising during the 1980s. In 1985, the AMA publicly demanded a complete ban of tobacco advertising and the Surgeon General agreed publicly. Other public health actors, such as the American Heart Association and the American Lung Association, joined in on this issue. In public statements, the organizations emphasized that the ban of tobacco advertising was a very important step in reducing smoking prevalence (Bayer and Colgrove, 2004). With regard to policies, restrictions on tobacco advertising had been in effect concerning advertising on TV since the 1950s and 1960s. However, it was only after the Master Settlement Agreement of 1998 that outdoor and billboard advertising was banned in forty-six states (Bayer and Colgrove, 2004).

Despite mutual suspicions of the American Medical Association and the public health services, both sectors joined in and argued in favor of political activity concerning the most important public health issues (Institute of Medicine, 1988). The responsiveness of the two sectors is also underscored and cultivated by the inclusion of different professions in the USPHS, which employs doctors, engineers, and other professionals in order to attack public health issues broadly.

These two examples show that health care and public health responded to each other on the level of actors. Apart from responsiveness with respect to specific policy problems, such as HIV and tobacco, this also led to demands for a more general integration of health care and public health policies. For example, one suggestion entailed creating health trusts to provide individual medical care and to implement this in tandem with population-based health policies (Chernichovsky and Leibowitz, 2010). However, the main problem with this is that formal policy integration and far-reaching reforms are difficult in the US political system, which is also valid for the area of public health. Therefore, policy integration – across all states but also in between different policy sectors – should occur by stealth, as in the area of tobacco control. This means that there is a more informal network of organizations and cooperations that coordinates public health policies as much as possible (Studlar, 2014).

To sum up, there has been responsiveness between the health care and the public health sectors since the 1980s in the United States. Regarding HIV and tobacco, actors from the health care and public health sectors were politically active in supporting an encompassing public health strategy with regard to these problems but also concerning a more encompassing strategy for connecting both fields. This did not happen without differences of opinions, but there was no general disagreement or ignorance of public health problems on the side of the medical profession. This coalition also demanded more policy integration for public health, but such reforms are difficult to implement due to the political constraints at the national level.

What do these results imply for the discussed hypotheses regarding the US case? This book has expressed the hypothesis that there should be a loose coupling of health care and public health in the US because the government is fragmented and professionalism is high. What is more, the contextual condition was positive for sectoral responsiveness and the unification of both sectors. The results of this analysis confirm these expectations for the most part. Until 2011, health care and public health were institutionally separated because all attempts to create comprehensive national health insurance failed. During the financial and economic crisis, the Obama government succeeded at passing health care reform despite the magnitude of institutional veto points in the country. Since then, health care and public health have been institutionally unified. With regard to responsiveness, we find politically active professions in the health care and the public health sectors that have commonly advocated important policies, such as those concerning tobacco control and HIV. Globally speaking, actors from the health care and public health sectors worked together. Concerning policy integration, there were concepts and suggestions to better connect both fields. However, to actually implement these plans in more coordinated policy programs proved difficult, given the mentioned veto structures.

9.5 Discussion

This chapter analyzed the coevolution of health care and public health in the United States. The most notable results are (a) the institutional separation of health care and public health and slow movement toward unification and (b) some actor responsiveness of professional actors from both sectors (Table 9.1). In addition, the case study reveals the well-known dynamic toward an increasingly important role of the state in the organization, financing, and provision of individual health care throughout the course of the twentieth century. In the first time period under observation, both sectors were institutionally separated: health care was largely in private hands, whereas the state focused on the provision of public health. At the same time, there was responsiveness between both sectors in the sense that the medical profession and the public health professionals commonly supported public health policies. During the interwar period, the aforementioned institutional separation was retained, as was the responsiveness of health care and public health on the professional level. However, conflicts between the USPHS and the AMA increased with regard to a universal health service and compulsory health insurance, where the former demanded both and the latter opposed any large role of the state in individual health care. In that period, the relationship of both sectors shifted from the loose coupling to the decoupling of health care and public health.

In the postwar time period, health care and public health remained institutionally distinctive. There was an increasing focus on health policy toward individual health care, which led to a strengthening of

Table 9.1. *Coevolution of health care and public health in the United States.*

1850–1918 (t0)	1918–1945 (t1)	1945–1980 (t2)	1980–2010 (t3)
Loose coupling: Separation of sectors at the national level and between the national government and the states (public–private); responsiveness between professions and interest groups	*Decoupling (Loose coupling):* Separation of sectors at the national level and between the national government and the states (public–private); responsiveness between professions concerning health education	*Loose coupling (Decoupling):* Separation of sectors at the national level and between the national government and the states (public–private); more unification due to Medicare; responsiveness between professions with regard to public health issues	*Loose coupling (Tight coupling):* National health insurance legislation 2011 – institutional unification; responsiveness between professions with regard to public health issues

229

private health care but also an increasing role of the state in individual health care with the establishment of Medicaid and Medicare. Yet, in contrast to Australia, this did not result in the establishment of national compulsory health insurance. On the contrary, in the 1970s, when the context for health policy turned once again to population-based health policies, compulsory health insurance dropped from the political agenda and the state public health departments had to deal with increasing demands for Medicaid and Medicare services. It was only during the global financial and economic crisis that national health insurance passed. With regard to public health issues such as tobacco use and HIV, the medical and public health professionals played an important role in that they both advocated more state activity in the matter. This was more unanimous with regard to tobacco, whereas there were some conflicts on how to respond to the HIV epidemic. Overall, however, my results give the impression that a large coalition of actors from health care and public health support public health issues.

9.5.1 Unified Government and Professionalism in the United States

What does this empirical analysis imply for the discussed hypotheses? The book has expressed the hypothesis that there should be loose coupling of health care and public health because of a fragmented government and high professionalism, given that the contextual condition is favorable to responsiveness between both sectors.

Concerning the strength of the national government, the results turned out as expected. As there are many more veto possibilities at the national level in the United States, the institutions of both sectors remained separate from each other until 2011. Health care, notably individual health insurance, was privately governed. Throughout the twentieth century, there were many attempts to introduce compulsory health insurance, but these projects often failed in Congress. Nonetheless, there was an incremental growth of publicly funded health care schemes that focused on indigent groups. On the side of public health, however, the role of the national government remained stronger. Yet, the sectors were inherently fragmented as a result of the distribution of legislative competences between the states and municipal governments.

Regarding professionalism, the analysis found strong evidence for politically active professions, which can lead to political responsiveness between the health care and public health sectors. Most importantly in that regard is the professional organization of doctors, the AMA, which successfully opposed the implementation of a national health insurance system and defended the freedom of practice for its members. However, it supported public health activities at the same time, such as sanitary measures in the late nineteenth century, health promotion actions in the 1920s, and tobacco control policies as well as a coordinated response to HIV, especially after the 1980s. It jealously guarded the rights and privileges of its members, notably the doctoral monopoly on medical practice and individual health care. There were also conflicts with public health reformers, especially during the interwar period, about the question of whether a comprehensive public health service should be created or not. During the postwar period, when the first new public health issues appeared on the agendas of policymakers, the most prominent advocates of these measures were public health reformers but not the medical profession.

The context played an important role regarding the coevolution of the health care and public health sectors in the United States. As theoretically expected, responsiveness between actors of the health care and public health sectors occurred the most when the contextual conditions were favorable for it. This was the case in t0, in the late nineteenth century, when the demand for public health policies was high. However, there is also evidence for this during t3, which is the period after 1980s, when noncommunicable diseases and new infections led to the demand for public health regulation.

9.5.2 Competing Explanations

In addition to the mentioned explanatory factors, the book has referred to other theoretical elements in the previous case studies, which has come out as potentially important findings. The remainder of this section will discuss these elements for the United States before presenting a comparative discussion in the concluding chapter.

1. *Complementarity*: In the United States, health care and public health coevolved toward complementarity during the time periods under observation in this report. This is empirically visible with

regard to the demands for more policy integration in the post-1980 period. However, in some ways, the two sectors were compatible before this period, because health care and public health were largely complementing one another in the sense that the market governed individual health care and the state governed public health and population-based health policies. During the course of the twentieth century, the state absorbed more and more bad risks in that it provided health care policies for indigent groups. In other words, it compensated for the externalities of the private health care system. At first, these measures only applied to mothers and children, then also to the elderly and handicapped (Medicare and Medicaid, 1965), until the national government created a universal national health insurance guarantee in 2011. However, actual health strategies that combined elements of prevention and cure with regard to specific health problems had existed since 1980, long before universal health care.

2. *Policy learning*: The results of this case study confirm to some extent the additional result of the other case studies that responsiveness between health care and public health comes along with a learning process – first, in the broad sense that professions and interest groups learn from one another, notably the public health and the medical care profession. More narrowly, I found evidence for policy learning, namely that the political activity of the medical profession has an impact on putting public health topics in the political agendas of policymakers. However, this did not always lead to reforms because the US political system makes it difficult to transfer the result of these learning processes into actual policy outputs.

In contrast to some of the other case studies, the analysis did not reveal evidence for partisan differences regarding the relationship of the health care and public health sectors. Notably, there were conflicts between parties regarding the introduction of a universal health insurance plan but not concerning the direct relationship of the two sectors under observation in this chapter.

9.6 Summary

Selecting the United States as a case study allowed me to examine the configuration of a fragmented government and high professionalism (i.e., politically active professions). The results largely confirm these hypotheses. Due to the many veto points and the decentralization of the political system, health care and public health were institutionally separated for a long time, compared to other countries in this sample. At the same time, the strong professionalism and competitive system of interest intermediation in the United States transferred into politically active health professions, notably the medical profession. This resulted in the common political activism of interest groups and professions from the health care and public health sectors – for example, regarding health promotion and tobacco control policy. However, this also led to conflicts, especially regarding the distribution of resources and competences, such as the right of doctors to free practice.

10 | Coevolution of Policy Sectors

Health Care and Public Health in a Comparative Perspective

This chapter will compare the results of the case studies and discuss the hypotheses proposed in the theoretical section against the background of the empirical analysis. This chapter begins with a comparison of the coupling and the coevolution of the two policy sectors in the five countries based on the case studies (Australia, Germany, Switzerland, United Kingdom, and United States). Then follows a discussion of the main hypotheses after which I present a revised theoretical model, which includes additional theoretical elements according to a strategy of inductive iterative refinement (Yom, 2015). After that, the chapter will argue that the health care and the public health sectors coevolved toward complementarity, i.e., policy integration of health care and public health, and will illustrate this argument by comparing reform activity in the two sectors based on a quantitative empirical assessment of reforms related to the two sectors.

10.1 Overview: Coupling of Health Care and Public Health in Five Countries

The case studies revealed that there are differences in coupling of health care and public health between countries and time periods. Most striking is that there are discrepancies between English-speaking countries, Australia, the United Kingdom, and the United States, on the one hand, because they coevolved from noncoupling and loose coupling to tight coupling of health care and public health. On the other hand, in non-English-speaking Germany and Switzerland, health care and public health are rather decoupled; i.e., there is less responsiveness between the health care and the public health sectors (Figure 1.2).

Nevertheless, there are also differences within these two groups. Concerning institutional distinctiveness, in the United Kingdom, health care and public health were institutionally unified early on whereas instances of actual policy integration – in the sense of integrated solutions (6 et al., 2002, 33–34) that denote policy responsiveness – appeared at a later point in time; in Australia, institutional unification occurred in the mid-twentieth century; in the United States, institutional distinctiveness remained until the early twenty-first century. In Australia, health care and public health were institutionally separated in colonial times and coevolved toward more tight coupling in the interwar and the postwar period. This is because the national government took more and more responsibility for health care; in 1921, a national ministry for health was founded; in 1944, the Pharmaceutical Benefits Scheme; and, in 1974, a national health insurance was put into place, which shifted the country's health care system toward more institutional unification of health care and public health. In the United States, health care and public health were separated into the public health sector and the health care sector, which was based on private health care organization and provision. At the same time, there were primary health care services for indigent groups. At first, these were only for soldiers and mothers, but with the introduction of Medicare and Medicaid in 1965, these services increased to include pensioners and the poor. This development came along with institutional drift in the sense that the state public health departments had to implement primary care instead of doing preventive health policies. During the same time, the USPHS was subordinated under a new department of health. Nevertheless, there was a shift toward more institutional unification during the 1960s, but – other than for example in Australia – it did not result in more reforms or institutional unification of health care and public health. Therefore, readers should keep in mind that the sectors were much more institutionally separated in the United States than in Australia and the United Kingdom. Even though the Patient Protection and Affordable Care Act of 2010 shifted health care and public health toward more institutional unification, private health care has still played a very important role. In the United Kingdom, institutional unification of both sectors occurred in the early twentieth century after the establishment of a national health insurance, which was the means for the national government to control individual health care as well as public health. At the latest, with the establishment of the NHS, health care and public health were unified institutionally in 1946.

Whereas the degree of institutional distinctiveness varies among Australia, the United Kingdom, and the United States, the responsiveness of health care and public health has been a rather constant element in the relations of both sectors in all three countries, except for the interwar period. Doctors and other actors responded to one another with regard to the professionalization of public health in the late nineteenth and early twentieth centuries, as well as with regard to the politicization of public health issues in the sense that the professions in both sectors supported public health policies. In the interwar period, there were conflicts between public health scholars, activists, and professionals, such as social hygienists on the one hand and the medical professions on the other. Social hygienists demanded the creation of national health services to combine matters of population health and prevention as well as individual health care. These struggles occurred in all three countries. In Australia and the United States, they were connected to the opposition of the medical profession against compulsory health insurance, whereas in the United Kingdom, the British Medical Association sought to keep its prerogatives under the existing health care legislation and (successfully) opposed a national health service based on the style proposed by social hygienists. During the postwar period, individual health care became more prominent in health policy as a result of the changes in contextual factors. Yet, in all three countries the medical profession and public health professionals advocated further public health action, for instance, with regard to immunization campaigns, cancer screening, and tobacco and alcohol control policies as well as obesity prevention. In the wake of the return of public health since the late 1970s, the public health agenda continued to receive support from the medical profession.

The results are different regarding Germany and Switzerland. In Germany, health care and public health have been institutionally separated since the emergence of both sectors. This situation only changed during the Nazi period, when reforms unified public health with health care at the national level. Nevertheless, after the Second World War, policymakers restored institutional distinctiveness of health care and public health in the FDR. Individual health care became again the main paradigm for health policy at the national level, whereas the subnational and municipal governments retained competencies for most areas of public health. The federal agency for preventive health (BZfGA), which is a subordinate agency to the national ministry of health, retained most competencies for public health at the national level. In Switzerland, health care and public health were decoupled at the national level from the outset because the national health insurance administration was in the ministry of social insurance, whereas prevention and public health was a responsibility of the Federal Office for Public Health, which was, however, under the supervision of the Department of Domestic Affairs. This sectoral distinction at the national level remained present until 2003, when the national health insurance law was transferred to the Federal Office for Public Health. In Switzerland, health care and public health are separated between the national and the subnational level of government. The cantons are quite competent in health policy, specifically health care and public health.

Regarding the responsiveness between health professions and interest groups, Germany and Switzerland are similar to one another and different from Australia, the United Kingdom, and the United States. For Germany, the analysis does not reveal significant responsiveness between both sectors during the late nineteenth century with regard to the professionalization of public health and I find little evidence concerning a common politicization of public health issues by actors belonging to different sectors. This changed in the interwar period as there were conflicts between social hygienists and the medical profession concerning the creation of a national public health service which would have combined health care and public health. The conflict was resolved with the expulsion and incarceration of many members of the public health profession after 1933 and the continuing empowerment of the medical profession. Doctors and those public health experts that had remained participated in the design and the implementation of racist public health policies. After the war, health policy in Germany turned toward individual health care, as in many countries, but there were barely any public health stakeholders to whom the medical profession could have responded in order to politicize health policy as a public health issue; and the profession itself eventually did not see the necessity to do so. This situation has remained prevalent until today, although the public health professionals – as well as related stakeholders – have become more politically active in Germany since the 1980s. The federal government even included leading public health researchers in its expert committee on health policy issues (*Sachverständigenrat*). Yet, this did not have the same impact as a politically active professional organization in health policy.

The absence of responsiveness in Switzerland occurred in a different way. There was no strong public health profession in the late nineteenth century, but rather occasional activities of interested individuals and cantonal health foundations as opposed to organized pressure groups. At the same time, the medical profession did not play a significant role in the politicization and professionalization of public health topics. It was only during the 1960s that public health started to professionalize nationally, but there has been little responsiveness between the medical profession and public health professionals concerning public health issues, which is still the case today. This became even clearer with regard to the development of a national response to HIV in which the main national doctoral organizations played no substantial role as political stakeholders. Since the cantonal governments are important for public health policy, they took some action to put the issue on the national political agenda and coordinated some public health responses in the Conference of Cantonal Directors of Public Health (CDP). At the same time, they became an important agenda setter for public health at the national level, as opposed to the medical and public health professions.

Despite the differences mentioned, there are two similarities between all countries. The first is the reduced responsiveness and increasing conflicts between the medical profession and public health specialists during the interwar and Second World War period. This was due to conflicts between health policymakers about the role of the state in health policies in general. In all countries, public health reformers proposed to create national health services, which would have combined public health and health care. But in all countries discussed in this book, the medical profession successfully opposed these proposals. Against this political background and the context of new medical technologies, changing health problems and economic prosperity health policy evolved toward a dominance of the individual health care over the public health approach – especially in Western democracies. Nevertheless, in Anglo-Saxon countries, responsiveness between both sectors continued in the shadow of this development. The second similarity between the five countries is the increase of actual policy integration – in addition to institutional unification – of health care and public health, which began mainly after 1980. Again,

Australia, the United States, and the United Kingdom were forerunners in this regard, but in Germany and recently in Switzerland the governments also created national health strategies that combine preventive and curative instruments for specific diseases and risk factors.

10.2 Causal Pathways of the Coevolution of Policy Sectors

How do these results fit with the hypotheses that I presented in the theoretical section? In the following, I discuss causal pathways of the coevolution of the health care and the public health sectors, which resulted from the empirical analysis of the five countries. Thereby, I adapt the previously made argument in light of the findings, following a strategy of inductive refinement (Yom, 2015). I specifically take into consideration the temporal dimension and the impact of additional explanatory factors, such as regime types, policy learning, and diffusion.

To generalize the findings that my empirical analysis revealed, Figure 10.1 shows the causal pathways of the coevolution of policy sectors in the five countries under consideration in this book. After the case studies, I propose to change the theoretical model that I have presented previously and to present more nuanced causal pathways instead of the more linear hypothesis that I have put forward before. I specifically changed the "unified government" variable that I have used to combine elements of federalism and veto points. The empirical results suggest that the difference of federal and unitary states matters particularly for the explanation of differences in the coevolution of the two sectors between countries. Furthermore, the results suggest that we need to add the regime type dimension (democracy–autocracy), diffusion, and policy learning to the explanation. The revised causal model accounts explicitly for temporal factors and suggests some interaction between different elements of the dependent variable over time, namely institutional unification, responsiveness, and policy integration. It is therefore important to distinguish between "unification," which refers to the principal consolidation health care and public health under the same institution but without necessarily resulting in policy coordination or integration, and "policy integration," which denotes that there is evidence for actual coordination and integration of health care and public health policies.

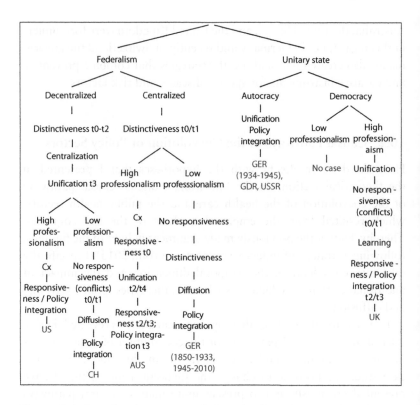

Figure 10.1 Causal pathways: coevolution of policy sectors.

10.2.1 Unified Government, Professionalism and Context

In a nutshell, my hypothesis regarding the impact of professionalism and related institutions of interest intermediation on responsiveness between sectors can be upheld. In countries with high professionalism, there was responsiveness between health care and public health professions and interest groups in the political arena if the context was favorable. In cases where the federation was centralized, it led to an earlier institutional unification of health care and public health than in decentralized federations. However, light of the empirical findings, it is difficult to uphold the hypothesis on unified government. The presence of a federal state essentially plays a more important role. The subnational governments have historically grown, own legislative powers, which seems to have an important impact on how the health care and the public health sectors coevolve.

Federalism Counts, not Unified Government

Originally, I had hypothesized that unified government should lead to institutional unification of the health care and the public health sectors. I defined a country as having a unified government either when there are few veto points or players at the national level (Lijphart, 2012; Tsebelis, 2002) or when the country is a centralized federation (Hueglin and Fenna, 2006; Watts, 1996). In fact, decentralized federations and many veto points are signs of a fragmented government.

My results show that it is necessary to revise this hypothesis. Above all, the difference between federal and unitary states is important for the coevolution of policy sectors. The fact that subnational governments are sovereign units (different from municipalities) (Hueglin and Fenna, 2006, 30–33) and possess their own legislative powers in health care and public health policy has an impact on the coevolution of policy sectors, especially in the early time periods (t0 and t1). This came along with the absence of institutional unification, especially until the interwar period. Also, my results show it is necessary to distinguish centralized from decentralized federations with regard to the institutional coevolution. Both Australia and Germany are centralized federations and in the two countries there is no unification of health care and public health at t0 or t1 as in the other two federal countries, but in the following time periods this changes, along with differences in professionalism. On the other hand, decentralized federations – in this case Switzerland and the United States – slowly coevolve toward institutional unification, independently of high or low professionalism. This is no surprise as health policy evolves toward more national legal frameworks in many federal states. Regarding the coevolution of policy sectors, this implies there should be a development toward institutional unification in all federal countries. Yet, such a dynamic does not necessarily need to accompany an absolute centralization of powers. Even if there is a new national framework, subnational governments might retain considerable powers in implementation or gain own legislative powers in other areas.

The presence of a unitary state leads to institutional unification of the two sectors, because another level of government was lacking. My results show that, in this case, governments tend to unify policy sectors institutionally. However, it is important to keep in mind that my results are based on the health care and public health sectors, two fields that are very close with regard to their origin and actor constellations. The extent to which this finding is valid for other cases – such as energy policy, for example – remains to be seen. What is more, in Germany the *Länder* were abolished legally between 1934 and 1945. However, in this instance there was indeed a change from institutional separation to unification.

Professional Activism, Context and the Politicization of Health
The second part of my argument starts from the hypothesis that high professionalism and a system of competitive interest aggregation would lead to political activism and, consequently, the responsiveness of professions and interest groups of the health care and the public health sectors. High professionalism means that professional organizations – in the case of this book, the medical profession – are important political actors (Freidson, 1983, 23–26; Macdonald, 1995, 30). In countries with high professionalism, professional organizations are politically active and need legitimacy and clout to effectively advocate their special interests. To obtain such legitimacy clout, they will also demonstrate political activity in matters beyond their special interests, such as the medical profession does regarding public health matters. High and low professionalism (i.e., the general inclination of professional actors to be politically active) covaries with the distinction of corporatist and pluralist institutions of interest intermediation. According to this logic, in pluralist systems of interest intermediation, the medical profession should also act as a pressure group for public health matters because it needs the legitimacy clout. Alternatively, corporatist interest intermediation comes with less political activity of the medical profession regarding public health because doctors do not need to gain additional legitimacy clout.

Overall, the results confirm my hypothesis that strong professionalism leads to politically active health professions and in turn to responsiveness between the health care and the public health sectors. In the countries in my sample where professionalism was high – Australia, the United Kingdom and the United States – health professions were politically active and respond to one another (discourse coalitions, cooperation, coordination) with regard to health policy problems, notably public health issues. The medical profession, understood as GPs and the medical organizations, are active in politicizing important problems together with actors from the health care sector. These include issues such as tobacco and HIV as well as health education. On the other hand, health professions in Germany and Switzerland are not very politically active, especially not with regard to agenda setting of policy problems. Other than in the countries with high professionalism, doctors do not play an important role in publicly politicizing problems of the public health sector. In this context, the medical profession focuses only on scientific exchange, not on political activism.

High professionalism and responsiveness come along with policy integration of health care and public health. Due to the large coalition of actors in health policy that connects the health care and public health professions and interest groups, governments are more likely to integrate policies from both fields – even though I also find policy integration of health care and public health in countries where professionalism is low. In addition to policy integration, high professionalism contributes to the institutional unification of health care and public health in Australia. Due to the political activity of the medical profession as well as the general centralizing tendency of the Australian federation, health policy has been a high priority for the national government since the foundation of the Commonwealth. The medical profession successfully opposed national health insurance legislation and was partly responsible for the fact that universal health care was only created during the 1970s. Nonetheless, the consequence of doctor's political activism is a strong national health policy, which includes the NHMRC, the PBS, and a centralized coordination of the Commonwealth and state governments.

However, my findings regarding the impact of professionalism on responsiveness need to be qualified in at least two ways. First, contextual elements play an important role in some countries. The responsiveness of health care and public health actors – especially in the United States – is most visible during t0 and t3, which means it correlates highly with the contextual conditions. In times when the contextual conditions are favorable to responsiveness and there is a demand for coordination of both sectors, interest groups and professions from health care and the public health sector commonly advocate public health issues, but not in times when the contextual conditions change. Second, the earlier there is institutional unification and broad legislation of the state in matters of health care and public health, the more conflicts occur between the health care and the public health sectors, which are resolved by learning over the course of time. This mechanism took shape in the United Kingdom. Although professionalism is high, there are conflicts between medical and public health doctors on posts and responsibilities in the public health services and the national health insurance scope of coverage, even when contextual conditions are favorable to sectoral unification (t0). Other than in the United States, health professions and interest groups from both sectors do not demand more state action, but fought for resources. This changed in a gradual and linear manner throughout the twentieth century because there is responsiveness of both sectors regarding new public health problems in t3.

On the other hand, the situation is different in Germany and Switzerland. In these countries, low professionalism and corporatist interest intermediation led to less politicization of the medical profession compared to the United States, Australia, and the United Kingdom. The German national government introduced a national health insurance in 1883, and delegated regulative powers in health policy to interest groups that administered it in a corporatist manner. Medical doctors and health insurance organizations are part of this arrangement. The power of the medical profession increased continuously as far as its involvement in the health insurance was concerned. Things are different in Switzerland, though with a similar outcome for the professionalization of the medical profession. In the late nineteenth century, health insurance was organized locally and compensated only for income losses; patients paid for treatment themselves. In the course of the twentieth century, health insurance was organized more regionally and wage agreements were closed between doctors and health insurance carriers. During this process, the medical profession improved its position compared to the health insurance carriers. At the national level, a health insurance law passed, however, only in 1994. Due to this inclusion of doctors in administrative matters of health insurance, doctors became a profession of office. As a consequence, the medical profession was less politicized and did not need to be politically active beyond its core interests, such as in the framing of public health policies.

In Germany and Switzerland, health professions and interest groups, specifically the medical profession, acted as administrators rather than as political entrepreneurs. Therefore, they did not politicize problems beyond their immediate interests, as did the professional organizations in Australia, the United Kingdom, and the United States. In these last three countries, professional organizations played an important role in politicizing problems because they needed political legitimacy clout for their special interests. This book shows how professional organizations link the public and the private sphere of society by combining their special interests with the concerns of the public.

The examination of professionalism and its impact on the politicization of health care and public health issues reveals interesting insights about political parties. I have argued that if the political activism of health professions is low, partisan differences play a more important role regarding politics of health care and public health. My results show this is especially the case for policies integrating health care and public health, or public health policies as such, because a politically active medical profession can forge alliances across political parties. This is particularly important for public health problems, such as tobacco, because among the target groups and negatively affected beneficiaries of this policy are often powerful corporate interest groups, such as the tobacco industry. These groups mobilize liberal and conservative parties to oppose regulative public health policies. This mechanism becomes clear regarding Germany and Switzerland, where health professions are politically weak and therefore parties are divided on comprehensive public health. This is different in Australia and the United Kingdom. However, this does not mean there are no party conflicts regarding the relationship of health care and public health in these countries. In Australia and the United Kingdom, there have been conflicts on the coordination of both sectors and public health policymaking. Yet, there is a basic consensus that these issues are important, not in the least due to the support by the medical profession for regulative public health policies. On the contrary, conservative and liberal parties in Germany and Switzerland have successfully opposed broad public health laws for a long time because they have argued that the health care system as it is provides sufficient prevention and public health and that the state does not need to intervene any further in this matter.

I have also argued that responsiveness between health professions depends on contextual elements, notably if there is a demand for actor coordination and policy integration of health care and public health due to pressing health problems. Specifically, I hypothesized that in the post-First World War period as well as after the Second World War, demands for institutional unification of the two sectors should have been low. My results partially confirm this hypothesis. In the United States, contextual elements have mostly the expected effect, whereas they do to a lesser extent in Australia. To the contrary, in the United Kingdom, responsiveness of health care and public health does not seem to follow the business cycle of public health. The reason for this is that the state has already controlled health policy early on in this country, which puts the focus of health professions and interest groups on political fights for the distribution of resources rather than on political cooperation for public health matters. Alternatively, the results in Germany and Switzerland turned out as expected; there was no responsiveness due to the absence of professionalism. The changing contextual conditions influence the health policy agenda by circulation and learning from others.

10.2.2   Regime Type, Policy Diffusion, and Policy Learning

During my analysis, a number of theoretical elements which I had not discussed in the theoretical section appear as important factors during the empirical analysis. Following a strategy of inductive iterative refinement, I include them in the analysis. Notably, these factors are the regime type, policy learning, and diffusion effects.

1. *Regime type*: My results show that the presence of an autocratic regime, which often comes along with the presence of central-ized government, has an impact on the institutional unification and policy integration of the health care and the public health sectors (Figure 10.1). During its time under the Nazi regime, Germany was a unitary state with strict centralization of legislative and administrative competences. This context had an impact on the institutional unification of both sectors. During that time, a national public health service was created and administrated together with the national health insurance. What is more, there were common policies connecting health care and public health, namely the racist health policies aimed at excluding "inferior races" (mainly, Jews). Whether there is "responsiveness" – in the sense of political coordination – between the health care and the public health sector is difficult to say because political advocacy is not possible as it is in democratic times. Doctors supported public

health issues, but I did not analyze whether the majority were afraid of negative consequences for opposition or truly adhered to Nazi ideas. However, in the USSR and in the GDR, which were both autocratic regimes, policymakers institutionally unified the health care and the public health sectors. However, it remains open whether there is also responsiveness between professions and interest groups. Based on the empirical analysis in this book, I hypothesize that there was no political coordination between interest groups from both sectors due to the lack of democratic structures. However, this hypothesis needs to be confirmed by further empirical analyses.

2. *Policy diffusion and policy learning*: A second element that turned out to be important is the role of learning and diffusion. My argument about the political importance of professions and the differences they make for the coupling of policy sectors includes an implicit assumption about policy learning: namely, that if doctoral professional organizations are politically active, they will not only take note of new public health problems and policies as part of the scientific debate but also help to put them on the agenda of policymakers – unless they are not against their own interests. Therefore, a highly politicized medical profession has an important impact on the politicization of innovations in the field of health policy, including public health, and contributes to the connection of both sectors.

Policy diffusion is another important element. I hypothesized that in countries where professionalization is low that the political activism of the medical profession should also be low. Therefore, it should be unlikely that policies of health care and public health are unified. However, my analysis shows that governments learn about policy integration from other countries. For example, although health care and public health are decoupled and noncoupled, the German government put into place policy integration that connected both sectors, such as health strategies that combine care and prevention because it learned about these policies from other governments, notably in English-speaking countries.

10.2.3 Complementarity and Coevolution of Policy Sectors

In addition to professionalism, unified government, regime type, and policy learning, my analysis provides another important theoretical lesson, especially for the analysis of comparative public policy. My results show a pattern of drift and layering with regard to the institutional change of health care and public health over time, as well as – and this is a particularly interesting finding – a pattern of coevolution toward complementarity independent of the type of coupling. What is more, my results reveal that noncoupling and decoupling of health care and public health coincide with "tight coupling" of health care to other institutions of the welfare state.

Learning and Complementarity in the Coevolution of Policy Sectors

Regarding complementarity, the first part of my results refer to the temporal dimension. In the theoretical chapter (Chapter 3), I discuss the literature and present an innovative argument to explain the coupling between policy sectors by referring to configurations of professionalism and unified government. I frame this argument as a complement to some of the arguments in the literatures on historical institutionalism and institutional complementarity. Based on my case studies, I show how political activism of health professions and federalism lead to the coupling of policy sectors. However, my results also show that the coevolution of policy sectors ties into the historical institutionalism literature.

First, the coevolution of health care and public health is a story of institutional drift and layering. Jacob Hacker argued that institutional drift occurs with regard to retrenchment in health policy. This means costs were cut by changing existing policies rather than through formal "legislative reform" (Hacker, 2004a, 2004b, 723). I find dynamics of drift and layering also with regard to the coevolution of the health care and the public health sectors. For example, in Germany, and much later in Switzerland, national health insurance has been the guiding principle of health policy. In these countries, policymakers integrate prevention and public health into the national health insurance when the demand for such policies increases. The consequence is that preventive health policies focus mainly on individuals in these countries. In the United States, policy drift took a different form. Once medical services for the elderly and the poor are established in the 1960s, the state public health services have the task of implementing these reforms – although their original mission is to provide preventive and population-based health services. Yet, there are also instances of layering, which refers to formal legislative reforms in the health sector. Notably, the introduction of a national health insurance (Medicare/Medibank) in Australia, in 1975, and the Patient Protection and Affordable Care Act of 2011 in the United States, are instances of layering because new health care policies were placed onto existing legal arrangements of private health care and public health care for indigent groups. Although the latter shows that health policy reform does not only happen through mechanisms of drift, these results are not surprising theoretically because the findings remain largely similar to what previous papers argue.

A second finding connects to the literature on institutional complementarity with comparative public policy analysis. My results show there is a coevolution of the health care and the public health sectors toward more complementarity, independent of the type of coupling between the two sectors. In the literature on institutional complementarity, some authors put forward the hypothesis that capitalist institutions emerge randomly and that they coevolve toward complementarity under historical and political constraints of their time (Crouch et al., 2005, 364–366). In that sense, complementarity means an improvement of the two sectors' common output as a result of coordination (Boyer, 2005).

There is a coevolution of health care and public health toward complementarity in all of the countries that I have analyzed in this book. During t0, the institutions of the health care and the public health sectors emerged regarding the demands and the specific conditions of each country. The guiding principles that impacted the relationship of the two sectors were centralized government and professionalism, as I have explained previously. During t1, conflicts dominated and during t2, individual health care was most important. Yet, in t3, complementarity, i.e., policy integration, of health care and public health gained importance because there are policies that combine both sectors. These patterns are visible if we compare the reform activity on health care and public health in the five countries, by taking a look at the quantity of laws that have passed in the two fields across the five countries (Figure 10.2).[1] Since the late 1970s and early 1980s, health policy reforms have combined – or integrated – prevention and cure into common health policies. This entails strategies to improve population health in general but also policies and strategies against specific diseases, such as cancer or

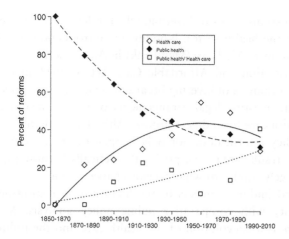

Figure 10.2 Coevolution and complementarity of health care and public health.

diabetes, or risk factors, such as smoking or drinking. The case studies show that there is no planned "grand design" (Crouch et al., 2005, 364–366) that creates complementary institutions, which in turn combine health care and public health. Instead, the institutions of the health care and the public health sectors emerge uncoordinated and coevolve toward complementarity in the course of a learning process. Policymakers have learned – also from the other sector and from other countries – on how to solve specific problems.

If we take a look at the reform activity on health care and public health in the single countries, the quantitative overview shows that, overall, there was a coevolution toward more complementarity of the two sectors in all countries. Nevertheless, there are also differences between the countries, which correspond to what the case studies reveal (Figure 10.3).[2] In the United Kingdom – a unitary state with politically active health professions – the temporal variance of the coevolution of health care and public health follows the cumulated curves, i.e., first there was a period of public health reforms, then a time of health care reforms, and, eventually, a policy integration of health care and public health dominated. In Australia, which combines a centralized federation with politically active health professions, the dynamics are similar, although the share of reforms integrating health care and public health is lower over time than in the United Kingdom.

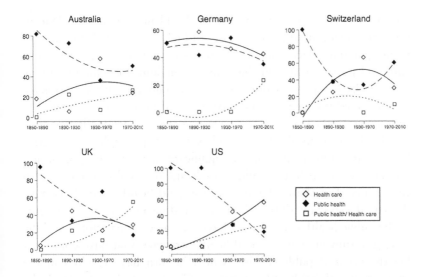

Figure 10.3 Coevolution and complementarity per country (percentage of reforms).

In the United States, which has a configuration of a decentralized federation with high professionalism, the coevolution of the reform activity is similar, but the share of health care reforms has increased more in the last half of the twentieth century than in Australia and the United Kingdom. Nevertheless, the tendency of reform activities evolves toward more policy integration of the two sectors. In Germany, which necessitates the conditions of a centralized federation and politically inactive health professions, the data on reform activity shows a parallel evolution of the health care and the public health sectors with less importance of the policy integration dimension. In Switzerland, which provides us with the marriage of decentralized federalism and low professionalism, national health-related legislation first deals with public health matters, then with health care matters, and then again with public health matters. Similar to Germany, policy integration of health care and public health play a less important role.

The case studies (Chapters 5–9) show that health care and public health coevolve toward complementarity in all the countries of this sample, although in very different ways depending on the coupling of the health care and the public health sectors. In Australia and the United Kingdom, where both sectors are more tightly coupled, coevolution have occurred in a unified and integrated way. Due to the rather centralized government and high professionalism, governments put into place complementary policies that integrated health care and public health. In the United Kingdom, for example, many conflicts between the health care and the public health sectors have accompanied this process and have resulted in mutual learning. The two sectors in the United States have coevolve independently from one another because, until 2011, there has been, in principle, no universal health care system, although a significant share of the population has access to Medicare and/or Medicaid or employer-paid health care plans. The share of the employer-paid health care plans have decreased, especially during the 1980s, and the number of dependents in the public health care services have increased. The national and the state governments have created health strategies that have combined health care and public health, which in turn have resulted in the creation of a global health strategy. In Germany and Switzerland, the coevolution of health care and public health toward complementarity is different because the two sectors are decoupled or noncoupled due to the lack of actor responsiveness. In these countries, public health remains subordinate to individual health care because there is less responsiveness between the two sectors. Nonetheless, the governments in Germany and Switzerland also implement complementary health policies due to diffusion processes, such as direct and indirect EU pressure and policy learning from other countries.

As mentioned before, the coevolution of health care and public health proceeded incrementally and not as the consequence of a "grand institutional design." Exceptions are autocratic regimes, where the national government seeks to create complementary institutions to improve population health, especially in Germany. Among the democratic states, the United Kingdom is the closest to this ideal, but it also shows a pattern of coevolution toward complementarity. First, the government put into place national public health laws and preventive measures in the late nineteenth century and then an encompassing national health care policy (a national health insurance in 1911 and the NHS in 1946) in order to respond to the most pressing health problems. Although policymakers have quickly unified both sectors, there are many conflicts between health professions and interest groups of the two sectors – particularly conflicts about resources during t1 and t2. Actors from both sectors only began to learn from one another and to cooperate in the post-Second World War period, for example, on health inequalities, tobacco, and HIV. This learning process is part of the coevolution toward complementarity.

Apart from the mutual learning processes between the health care and public health sectors, contextual factors contribute to policy convergence and therefore increasing complementarity of the two sectors. Noncommunicable diseases, rising health expenditure, and returning infections have increased the demand for policy integration of health care and public health since the 1980s. This has led to the increasing policy convergence regarding countries, which I discuss in this book, irrespective of the political activity of health professions and the fragmentation of government.

Coupling of Health Care and Public Health with other Institutions

A second finding related to complementarity deals with the coupling of health care and public health with other institutions of the welfare state. In short, in countries where health care and public health are tightly or loosely coupled, health care is decoupled from other institutions of the welfare state. At the same time, in countries where health care and public health are decoupled or noncoupled, health care is tightly or loosely coupled with other institutions of the welfare state, such as unemployment or retirement insurance.

As I have explained before, coupling has traditionally been understood with regard to the connection of institutions in general and, more specifically, with regard to political economies (Benz, 2013; Hall and Soskice, 2001; Mayntz and Scharpf, 1995), European politics (Jachtenfuchs, 2001; Papadopoulos, 2007), and welfare states (Hemerijck and Van Kersbergen, 1999). These authors distinguish a dichotomy mostly between loosely and tightly coupled welfare states, institutions, or political economies. I use coupling in a more fine-grained way in order to analyze the relationship between the sectors at the microlevel, such as the responsiveness between health professions and interest groups. In a nutshell, my findings are that in Australia, the United Kingdom, and the United States, health care and public health are tightly and loosely coupled, whereas in Germany and Switzerland the two sectors are decoupled and noncoupled, respectively.

However, my results are also interesting regarding the broader level of coupling, namely the connection of health to other institutions of the welfare state. In Australia, the United Kingdom, and the United States, health care and public health are tightly and loosely coupled. This was the case even though Australia and the United Kingdom have national health insurance and a national health service and the United States had, until 2011, a mostly private health care system (Wendt, Frisina, and Rothgang, 2009; Böhm et al., 2013; Trein, 2017a). In all the countries, the control of the state over health care policy increases continuously in the course of the twentieth century, although this process went faster in the United Kingdom than in Australia and the United States. Health in these countries is considered a "benefit in kind" (Barr, 2012), which means the state takes a crucial role in providing it. The United States was slightly different since public health care entitlements have focused on indigent groups for a long time, but the principle remains the same. Health care and public health consequently are tightly or loosely coupled and the common policy output of the two sectors is high in the sense that policy integration appears early on and in an encompassing way. At the same time, all three countries have a liberal welfare state (Esping-Andersen, 1990) and a liberal market economy (Hall and Soskice, 2001). This entails a decoupling or noncoupling of health care from other social insurance pillars, since cash transfers (unemployment and retirement benefits) have a very limited scope compared to other political economies, such as Germany and Sweden.

In Germany and Switzerland, which are conservative welfare states and coordinated market economies, health insurance is originally part of the cash transfer system of social policies. The founding principle of health policy in Germany and Switzerland is health insurance, which – in its first form – provides sickness benefits but does not pay for treatment. This has changed considerably over the course of the twentieth century. Today, health insurance carriers pay above all for the treatment of sicknesses, and in Switzerland sickness benefits are even privatized. However, as a consequence, health care and health insurance were coupled with other social policies – such as unemployment and accidental insurance, which also provide cash benefits – but decoupled from public health. I explain this outcome by referring to the microlevel, arguing that the politicization of doctors in Germany is low and that the medical profession does not object to the introduction of a national health insurance but rather regards it as an advantage. In Switzerland, although the medical profession resists national legislation in the field of health insurance, it is involved in the voluntary and cantonal governance of health insurance. Consequently, the state makes a deal with the medical profession and other interest groups, who then participate formally and permanently in health governance. The state withdraws from health policy, except for issues of public security, such as epidemics. Consequently, professions and interest groups involved in health care governance do not need additional legitimacy and clout and have no interest in advocating public health policy in the sense that I have defined it in Chapter 2 (prevention and population focused). Responsiveness of health care and public health therefore remains low as public health does not receive political support from the medical profession.

This book forges a link between health care and public health by conceptualizing them as two different but overlapping policy sectors. The analysis makes a contribution to health policy research because it underlines how preventative and curative as well a individual- and population-related elements are linked in the institutionalization and the politics of health. Furthermore, this book demonstrates how coevolution and coupling can be used to analyze coordination and policy integration between related policy fields in a comparative historical manner. Nevertheless, there remains room for further research. One possible next step could be to conceptualize the distinction of health care and public health in a more systematic quantitative manner, such as expenses and policy capacities. In addition, the concepts of coupling and coevolution should be transferred to the analysis of other policy challenges such as immigration or environmental protection.

Appendix A

List of Interviews

Three of the case studies in this book are based on interviews with experts and stakeholders in health policy and, above all, in public health policy. I conducted the interviews as part of the previously mentioned research project which the Swiss National Science Foundation (SNSF) supported generously. I conducted most of the interviews together with my colleagues Wally Achtermann, Dorte Hering, and Björn Uhlmann. Without their help in tracking down interview partners, it would have been difficult for me to properly complete this project. We tried to find interview partners based on three categories: experts, interest groups, and politicians from different parties in order to have different voices. The selection of interview partners occurred according to the research design of the SNSF project, which aimed at understanding the coordination of actors in tobacco control policy and pharmaceutical policy in Australia, Germany, and Switzerland. The interviews were conducted as semistructured interviews according to the following broad guidelines:

1. Legal basis for public health.
2. Main actors in public health (state and nonstate).
3. Coordination of interest groups with parties; coordination between levels of government.
4. Timing in the institutionalization of health care and public health.
5. Connection of health care system and public health policymaking in general.
6. Opposition to public health, i.e., tobacco industry.
7. Laws to connect health care and public health, i.e., diabetes, cancer, HIV, and so on.
8. Institutional relation of health care and public health.
9. Actor connection of health care and public health with regard to political activity as well as professionalization.

10. Learning between health care and public health actors.
11. Relation of professions in health care and public health.
12. International dimension of public health policy.

Interviews Australia

1. Int-AUS-1: Senator, Liberal Party, Melbourne, October 17, 2011.
2. Int-AUS-2: Former Minister of Health of South Australia, Canberra, October 5, 2011.
3. Int-AUS-3: Senior Tobacco Policy Officer, Tasmanian Department of Health, Tasmania, May 13, 2011.
4. Int-AUS-4: Associate Professor, LaTrobe University, Skype Interview, August 2011.
5. Int-AUS-5: Associate Professor, LaTrobe University, Melbourne, October 18, 2011.
6. Int-AUS-6: Professor of Health Prevention, Cancer Council Victoria and University of Melbourne, Melbourne, October 13, 2011.
7. Int-AUS-7: Former Prime Minister Victoria, Melbourne, October 18, 2011.
8. Int-AUS-8: Principal Policy Officer at South Australian Department of Health Demographic, South Australia.
9. Int-AUS-9: Professor of Public Health, University of Sydney, October 7, 2011.
10. Int-AUS-10: Former Head of ACoSH, Skype Interview, April 28, 2011.
11. Int-AUS-11: Professor of Public Health, University of Sydney, October 19, 2011.
12. Int-AUS-12: Former Director, Cancer Council Victoria, Melbourne, October 17, 2011.
13. Int-AUS-13: Director of ASH, Skype Interview, May 3, 2011.
14. Int-AUS-14: Director of ASH, Sydney, October 7, 2011.
15. Int-AUS-15: Professor of Public Health, Skype Interview, May 13, 2011.
16. Int-AUS-16: Professor of Public Health, Geneva, August 25, 2011.
17. Int-AUS-17: MP, Liberal Party, Skype Interview, September 12, 2011.

18. Int-AUS-18: Former Commonwealth Minister (Defense/Education, Science and Training) former President of the AMA, Skype Interview, October 28, 2011.
19. Int-AUS-19: CEO of Cancer Council Australia, Skype Interview, April 18, 2011.
20. Int-AUS-20: CEO of Cancer Council Australia, Skype Interview, September 12, 2011.
21. Int-AUS-21: Acting Director, Drug Policy and Population Health Division, South Australia, Skype Interview, May 27, 2011.
22. Int-AUS-23: Researcher, Cancer Council Victoria, Melbourne, October 12, 2011.
23. Int-AUS-24: Former CEO Australian National Preventive Health Agency; former Policy Advisor Commonwealth Minister of Health, Canberra, October 6, 2011.
24. Int-AUS-25: Researcher, Heart Foundation Western Australia, Skype Interview, May 5, 2011.
25. Int-AUS-26: Researcher, Heart Foundation Western Australia, Skype Interview, September 8, 2011.
26. Int-AUS-27: Professor of Public Health, University of New South Wales, Sydney, Skype Interview, May 3, 2011.
27. Int-AUS-28: Professor of Public Health, University of New South Wales, Sydney, October 19, 2011.
28. Int-AUS-29: Former Commonwealth Minister for Health, Sydney, October 20, 2011.

Interviews Germany

1. Int-GER-1: Professor of Health Policy, University of Braunschweig, Skype Interview, October 9, 2012.
2. Int-GER-2: Professor of Public Health, University of Fulda, Skype Interview, October 3, 2012.
3. Int-GER-3: MP of CDU, Berlin, November 27, 2012.
4. Int-GER-4: Professor of Public Health, University of Kiel, Skype Interview, September 28, 2012.
5. Int-GER-5: Professor of Public Health, Hertie School of Governance, Skype Interview, September 16, 2012.
6. Int-GER-6: Researcher, Law School, University of Hamburg, Skype Interview, November 13, 2012.
7. Int-GER-7: Professor of Health Policy, University of Bielefeld, Skype Interview, November 5, 2012.

8. Int-GER-8: MP Social Democratic Party, Berlin, December 10, 2012.
9. Int-GER-9: Employee Society for Health Promotion, Skye Interview, October 2, 2012.
10. Int-GER-10: Professor of Political Science, University of Siegen, Skype Interview, October 22, 2012.
11. Int-GER-11: Lobby Control Germany, Skype Interview, October 26, 2012.
12. Int-GER-12: Adviser of former Federal Minister for Health, Berlin, October 2012.
13. Int-GER-13: Head of the Non-Smoker's Initiative in Germany, Skype Interview, October 22, 2012.
14. Int-GER-14: Professor of Public Policy, University of Hannover, October 2012.
15. Int-GER-15: Professor of Health Policy, University of Braunschweig, Skype Interview, Braunschweig, September 2012.
16. Int-GER-16: Researcher DKFZ (German Cancer Research Centre), Skype Interview, October 8, 2012.
17. Int-GER-17: Head of Federal Organization for Health Promotion and Prevention, Skype Interview, October 10, 2012.
18. Int-GER-18: Professor of Public Health, WZB, Skype Interview, October 9, 2012.
19. Int-GER-19: Professor of Health Policy, University of Bremen, October 2012.
20. Int-GER-20: Professor of Medicine, Helmholtz Research Centre for Health and Environment, University of Munich, Skype Interview, October 9, 2012.
21. Int-GER-21: MP Social Democratic Party, Skype Interview, December 2012.
22. Int-GER-22: MP Social Democratic Party, Heidelberg, December 3, 2012.
23. Int-GER-23: Former Employee Municipal Public Health Service, Berlin, Skype Interview, October 19, 2012.
24. Int-GER-24: Organization of German Health Insurers, Berlin, October 2012.

Interviews Switzerland

1. Int-CH-1: Former Secretary of the CDP, Bern, November 24, 2011.

2. Int-CH-2: Former Head of the Federal Office for Public Health, Bern, December 15, 2011.
3. Int-CH-3: Health Policy Lobbyist, Bern, December 22, 2012.
4. Int-CH-4: Member of the Federal Office for Public Health, Bern, January 17, 2012.
5. Int-CH-5: Head of Oxy-Romandie, Geneva, January 26, 2012.
6. Int-CH-6: Head of the Swiss Working Group on Tobacco Prevention, Lausanne, February 9, 2012.
7. Int-CH-7: MP Liberal Party, Bern, February 2, 2012.
8. Int-CH-8: Law Division Federal Office of Public Health, Bern, January 25, 2012.
9. Int-CH-9: Member Federal Office of Public Health, Bern, February 3, 2012.
10. Int-CH-10: Member of Federal Commission on Addictive Substances, Skype Interview, February 13, 2012.
11. Int-CH-11: Member of Federal Commission on Addictive Substances, Zurich, February 7, 2012.
12. Int-CH-12: MP Cantonal Parliament Bern, February 24, 2012.
13. Int-CH-13: Former Professor of Public Health University of Bern, Lausanne, March 3, 2012.
14. Int-CH-14: Member of Department of Health, Canton of Argau.
15. Int-CH-15: Former Head of the Swiss Working Group on Tobacco Prevention, Lausanne, March 3, 2012.
16. Int-CH-16: MP Liberal Party, Bern, February 21, 2012.
17. Int-CH-17: Head of Cantonal Office of Public Health Lucerne, Skype Interview, February 17, 2012.
18. Int-CH-18: Head of Cantonal Office of Public Health Geneva, Skype Interview, February 17, 2012.
19. Int-CH-19: Former Head of the Federal Department of Domestic Affairs, Martigny, March 19, 2012.
20. Int-CH-20: Members of the Cantonal Office of Public Health of the Canton de Vaud, Lausanne, March 20, 2012.
21. Int-CH-21: Head of Cantonal Office of Public Health St. Gall, Winterthur, March 30, 2012.
22. Int-CH-22: Former Member of the Law Division, Federal Office of Public Health, Lausanne, March 22, 2012.
23. Int-CH-24: Head of Cantonal Government of Thurgau, Frauenfeld, March 26, 2012.

24. Int-CH-25: Former Head of Cantonal Office of Public Health St. Gall, Geneva, March 8, 2012.
25. Int-CH-26: Minister of Health Canton of Zurich, Zurich, April 5, 2012.
26. Int-CH-27: Health Economist Zurich, Skype Interview, March 14, 2012.
27. Int-CH-28: Former Deputy Secretary General of Federal Office of Domestic Affairs, Bern, April 4, 2012.
28. Int-CH-29: Former MP Social Democratic Party, Geneva, June 6, 2012.
29. Int-CH-30: Professor of Health Economics, University of Neuchatel, Skype Interview, February 27, 2012.
30. Int-CH-32: Health Economist, Bern, March 28, 2012.
31. Int-CH-33: Head of Swiss Cancer League, Bern, March 23, 2012.
32. Int-CH-34: Member Federal Office for Public Health, Bern, June 28, 2012.

Appendix B

Institutional Development

Institutional Development, UK

- 1848: Nuisances Removal and Disease Prevention Act (Public Health)
- 1848: City of London Sewers Act (Public Health)
- 1848: Metropolitan Sewers Act (Public Health)
- 1850: Lodging Houses Act (Public Health)
- 1851: Common Lodging Houses Act (Public Health)
- 1853: Vaccination Act (Public Health)
- 1854: General Board of Health Act (Public Health)
- 1855: Disease Prevention Act (Public Health)
- 1855: Metropolis Local Management Act (Public Health)
- 1860: Nuisances Removal Act (Public Health)
- 1861: Vaccination Act (Public Health)
- 1863: Nuisance Removal Act (Public Health)
- 1865: Sewage Utilisation Act (Public Health)
- 1866: Nuisance Removal Act (Public Health)
- 1866: Sanitary Act (Public Health)
- 1867: Sewage Utilisation Act (Public Health)
- 1867: New Vaccination Act (Public Health)
- 1868: Sanitary Act (Public Health)
- 1871: Government Act (Public Health)
- 1872: Public Health Act (Public Health)
- 1883: Disease Prevention (metropolis) Act (Public Health)
- 1883: The Medical Relief (disqualification removal) Act (Health Care)
- 1889: Infectious Disease Notification Act (Public Health)
- 1906: Local health authorities received the rights to feed children (Public Health)

- 1907: Education Act granted local health authorities powers to perform medical inspections (Public Health)
- 1908: Medical examinations of school children began in England (Public Health and Health Care)
- 1911: Health Insurance Act (Health Care)
- 1918: The Education Act of 1918 made treatment of certain diseases mandatory, i.e., skin problems and dental disease in schoolchildren (Health Care)
- 1919: National Ministry of Health established (Public Health and Health Care)
- 1919: Public Health (tuberculosis) Act (Public Health)
- 1923–1924: Legislation permitted subsidies to facilitate improvements in the housing (Public Health)
- 1929: Creation of national assistance scheme, which was a medical-tested welfare scheme (Health Care)
- 1934: "Milk in schools" scheme (Public Health)
- 1934: Public Health Act (Public Health)
- 1939: Emergency Medical Service created (Health Care)
- 1942: Beveridge Plan (Public Health)
- 1944: Education Act (Public Health)
- 1946: National Health Service (Health Care and Public Health)
- 1956: Clean Air Act (Public Health)
- 1967: Legalization of abortion under certain conditions (Health Care)
- 1967: New cars need seatbelts (Public Health)
- 1973: Management reorganizations for the NHS (Health Care)
- 1973: NHS reorganization (Public Health and Health Care)
- 1979: Conservative government encouraged privatization of ancillary services (Health Care)
- 1980: NHS reform – district health authorities (DHA) replaced area health authorities (AHA) (Public Health and Health Care)
- 1984: Health and Social Security Act received royal assent (Health Care)
- 1987: HIV public health campaign (Public Health)
- 1987: Plan promoting better health published (Public Health)
- 1988: Screening for breast cancer launched (Public Health and Health Care)
- 1988: Cervical screening program launched (Public Health and Health Care)

- 1990: New GP contract created in the NHS (Health Care)
- 1990: National Health Service and community care act receives royal assent (Health Care)
- 1992: Private Finance Initiative (PFI) schemes introduced (Health Care)
- 1992: Health of the Nation white paper published (Public Health and Health Care)
- 1992: Health authority act received royal assent (Health Care)
- 1992: Health of the Nation Strategy (1992–1997) (Public Health and Health Care)
- 1996: UK national screening committee founded (Public Health and Health Care)
- 1997: Minister for Public Health (Public Health)
- 1999: New national strategy for health in England published: "Saving Lives: Our Healthier Nation" (Public Health)
- 1999: Primary care groups established (Health Care)
- 2000: Health Development Agency (Public Health and Health Care)
- 2001: Publication of NHS plan (Public Health and Health Care)
- 2001: National targets on health inequalities published (Public Health and Health Care)
- 2002: Strategy for combating infectious diseases published (Public Health and Health Care)
- 2002: National Health Service Reform and Health Care Professionals Act (Health Care)
- 2002: Department of Health introduced the concept of payment by result (Health Care)
- 2003: National campaign for healthy eating launched (Public Health and Health Care)
- 2003: Health protection agency set up (Public Health and Health Care)
- 2004: NHS improvement plan (Public Health and Health Care)
- 2004: NHS employers established (Health Care)
- 2004: White paper "The Choosing Health" published (Public Health and Health Care)
- 2006: National child measurement programme created as part of efforts against childhood obesity (Public Health and Health Care)
- 2006: "Our Health, Our Care, Our Say" white paper published (Public Health and Health Care)

- 2006: Bowel screening programs launched (Public Health and Health Care)
- 2006: Health Care Act 2006 passed (Public Health and Health Care)
- 2007: Smoking ban came into force (Public Health)
- 2008: Government published the strategy "Healthy Weight, Healthy Lives" (Public Health)
- 2008: HPV vaccinations for 12–13 year old girls introduced (Public Health and Health Care)
- 2009: Government launched anti-obesity strategy (Public Health)
- 2009: Corporation and competition plan panel for NHS services established (Health Care)
- 2009: Health Act 2009 received royal assent (Public Health and Health Care)
- 2009: NHS check program launched (Public Health and Health Care)

Institutional Development Australia

- 1847: Public Health Act (English Act) (Public Health)
- 1853: VIC English Act (created a Central Board of Health) (Public Health)
- 1871: QUE Health Board (temporary board if a formidable epidemic was threatening, caused by smallpox in NZ, VIC, NSW) (Public Health)
- 1871: VIC Medical treatment for the cure of alcohol and drug addicts introduced (Health Care)
- 1880: NSW Infectious Diseases Supervision Act (Public Health)
- 1882: VIC Amendment of Public Health Act (notification of malignant, infectious, or contagious diseases) (Public Health)
- 1883: QUE and SA Public Health Act (Public Health)
- 1884: TAS Public Health Act (Public Health)
- 1885: WA Public Health (reaction to the bad sanitary conditions in Perth) Act (Public Health)
- 1885: NSW Dairies Supervision Act (Public Health)
- 1889/1900: Legislation to treat alcohol problems all over Australia (Health Care)
- 1896: NSW Comprehensive Public Health Act Public Health)
- 1897: Public Health Laboratory in the Department of Bacteriology at the Melbourne University (Public Health)

- 1897: NSW Microbiological Lab (Public Health)
- 1898: NSW first sanitary courses started (Public Health)
- 1900: First Royal Sanitary Examination and VIC Meet Supervision Act (Public Health)
- 1905: VIC Pure Food Act and Dairy Supervision Act (Public Health)
- 1906: Start of Diploma in Public Health at the University in Melbourne (Public Health)
- 1907: Medical inspections of school children in Sydney and Newcastle (Public Health and Health Care)
- 1908: NSW Pure Food Act (Public Health)
- 1909: SA Food and Drug's Act (Public Health)
- 1910: TAS Food and Drugs Act (Public Health)
- 1910: Start of Diploma in Public Health at the University in Sydney (Public Health)
- 1911: QUE General Health Act regarding the control of quality and purity of food (Public Health)
- 1911: WA Health Act (establishment of advisory committee for questions of health) (Public Health)
- 1915: WA establishment of compulsory notification of venereal diseases. Reaction to the CW urging the states to do that) (Public Health)
- 1919: Repatriation Pharmaceutical Benefit Scheme (RPBS). Arrangement between Repatriation Commission and various Australian pharmaceutical societies concerning medication for veterans of the First World War and the Boer War (Health Care)
- 1921: Commonwealth Department of Health (Public Health and Health Care)
- 1926: Federal Health Council (Public Health and Health Care)
- 1930: School of Public Health at the University of Sydney (Public Health)
- 1938: Enactment of National Health and Pensions Insurance Bill (Health Care)
- 1941: Plan for National Health Service. An NHMRC subcommittee report proposed the establishment of a national system of hospitals and clinics, which is staffed by salaried doctors and officially supervises preventive work of private practitioners. (Public Health and Health Care)
- 1944: Pharmaceutical Benefits Act (Health Care)

- 1945/1948: National campaign against tuberculosis (Public Health)
- 1947–1948: Hospital Benefits Act (coverage for pensioners) (Health Care)
- 1947: Pharmaceutical Benefits Act (coverage for pensioners; small fee of charge for elderly) (Health Care)
- 1952: Hospital Benefits Scheme (co-payment for wage earners) (Health Care)
- 1953: National Health Act (Immunization) (Public Health)
- 1956: Mass vaccinations against poliomyelitis begin (Public Health)
- 1956: Foundation for Research and Treatment of Alcoholism and Drug Dependence of NSW (Health Care)
- 1959: Langton Clinic Sydney created (treat alcoholism) (Health Care)
- 1960: PBS reform (expanded range of drugs for the general public and the introduction of a patient contribution – or co-payment) (Health Care)
- 1960s/1970s: ACCV ran several campaigns against skin cancer in Victoria (Public Health)
- 1970s: First local and state tobacco control policies (Public Health)
- 1973: Tobacco advertisement on TV begun to be phased out (Public Health)
- 1963: South Australian Foundation on Alcoholism and Drug Dependence (Health Care)
- 1965: Wacol Clinic in Brisbane opened (treat alcoholism) (Health Care)
- 1968: St. Anthony's Hospital Adelaide opened (treat alcoholism) (Health Care)
- Mid-1970s: Federal Body on Alcohol and Drug Dependence (Health Care)
- 1971: First Community Health Centre opened (Public Health and Health Care)
- 1971/1972: Introduction of compulsory use of seat belts; VIC first, other MS followed within a year (Public Health)
- 1974: Medibank (Health Care)
- 1975: Free hospital services introduced (Coordination of CG with states) (Health Care)
- 1978/1979: Dismantling of Medibank (Liberal Fraser Government) (Health Care)

- 1980: Warnings on cigarette packs (Liberal Government) (Public Health)
- 1980–1988: Slip-Slop-Slap campaign against skin cancer (Public Health)
- 1984: Resurrection of Medibank Scheme (Health Care)
- 1984: National Campaign against Drug Abuse (NCADA) (Public Health)
- 1986: Better Health Commission (Response to WHOs Health for All 2000 Policy) (Public Health and Health Care)
- 1986: Prohibition of smoking on all domestic aircraft flights; Health Ministers agree to introduce stronger health warnings (Public Health)
- 1987: Transfer of the public health functions of the National School of Public Health to the University of Sydney's Faculty of Medicine: Australian Institute on Health became a statutory authority (Public Health and Health Care)
- 1987: First Health Promotion Foundation created (VIC, other states followed) (Public Health)
- 1988–2001: Sun-Smart Program against skin cancer (Public Health)
- 1991–1995: National AIDS Strategy (Public Health and Health Care)
- 1992: Tobacco Advertising Prohibition Act (CW) (Public Health)
- 1992: National Drug Strategy (NDS) (Public Health and Health Care)
- 1996: NPHP created (National Partnership for Public Health) (Public Health)
- 1997: Strategic Plan against Obesity (Public Health and Health Care)
- Since 1999: National Tobacco Strategy (Coordination of national and state tobacco policies as well as coordination of various policy instruments) (Public Health and Health Care)
- 2001–2010: National Road Safety Strategy (Public Health)
- 2006: NHMRC becomes independent (independent statutory agency within the portfolio of the Australian Government Minister for Health and Ageing) (Public Health)
- 2006: AHPC (Australian Health Protection Committee) and APHDPC (Australian Population Health Development Principal Committee) replace NPHP (Public Health)

- 2007: Indoor smoking bans started to be introduced (Public Health)
- 2007: Integration of National Institute of Clinical Studies into the NHMRC (Public Health and Health Care)
- 2009: National Preventive Health Strategy (Public Health)
- 2011: ANPHA Australian National Preventive Health Agency (Public Health)
- 2011: National Cancer Strategy (Public Health and Health Care)

Institutional Development Germany

- 1860s: Cities such as Berlin and Munich begin to construct sewage systems (Public Health)
- 1869: Liberalization of medical occupations in Prussia. Everyone could have medical services (Health Care)
- 1871: Factory inspection became compulsory (Public Health)
- 1873: Foundation of the National Society for Public Health (Public Health)
- 1876: Legalization of local voluntary health insurances (Health Care)
- 1883: Creation of Public Health Insurance (Health Care)
- 1884: Creation of Accident Insurance (Health Care)
- 1889: Creation of Invalidity and Retirement Insurance
- 1899: Full time employment for public health doctors (*Kreisärzte*) (Public Health)
- 1899: Extension of public health doctors' (*Kreisärzte*) competencies to oversee medical and sanitary (Public Health)
- 1911: Unification of existing social insurances (Health Care)
- 1913: Health insurances loose discretion in the appointment of doctors (Health Care)
- 1914: Non-doctors can no longer be reimbursed by the health insurance (Health Care)
- 1925: Preventive measures become part of the Public Health Insurance (Public Health)
- 1931: Public health insurances are transferred into statutory organizations (Health Care)
- 1933: Sterilization law (Public Health)
- 1934: Unification of the municipal and state level public health services (Public Health)

- 1935: Marriage health legislation (Public Health)
- 1938: Jewish doctors lose their right to practice
- 1951: Central Health Administration created (GDR) (Public Health and Health Care)
- 1953: Law regarding the protection of infectious diseases (Public Health)
- 1954: Increase of health care expenditures (Health Care)
- 1955: Strengthening of panel doctors (Health Care)
- 1956: Failed attempt to introduce a federal law regarding preventive health (Public Health)
- 1958–1961: Failed attempt to introduce a federal law regarding cost containment in the health insurance sector (Health Care)
- 1958–1961: Failed attempt to introduce a federal law regarding co-payments in the health care sector (Health Care)
- 1960: Federal law passed regarding epidemics (Public Health)
- 1964: Failed attempt to introduce a federal law regarding dental care for kids (Public Health)
- 1968: First university professorship in workplace medicine established (Public Health)
- 1969: Ministry of Health established (Public Health)
- 1972: Preventive exams in national health insurance (Public Health)
- 1972: Changes in hospital financing legislation (Health Care)
- 1974: Law on workplace security passed (Public Health)
- 1976: Cost containment legislation in the health care sector
- 1977: Coordination body in the health care sector established (*Koordinierte Aktion im Gesundheitswesen*) (Health Care)
- 1989: Competences of the national health insurances concerning preventive exams extended (Public Health)
- 1991: Cost containment legislation in the health care sector (Health Care)
- 1993: Reform of health insurance legislation (Health Care)
- 1996: Prevention transferred to accident insurances away from health insurances, which came along with a drastically reduction in nonmedical preventive services (Public Health)
- 1996–2000: Restructuring of public health insurances (Health Care)
- 1998: Failed attempt to introduce a national smoking ban (Public Health)
- 2000: DRGs for hospital payments established (Health Care)

- 2000: Prevention reintroduced in the public health insurances (Health Care)
- 2000: National strategy on diabetes (Public Health and Health Care)
- 2003: National strategy on breast cancer (Public Health and Health Care)
- 2003: National strategy on tobacco control (Public Health and Health Care)
- 2003/2010: National strategy on healthy education, stress reduction, health nutrition, and movement (Public Health and Health Care)
- 2003/2011: National strategy on improvement of patient competencies (Public Health)
- 2005: Failed attempt to introduce a national smoking ban (Public Health)
- 2005: Failed attempt to introduce a federal law on preventive health (Public Health)
- 2006: National strategy on depression (Public Health and Health Care)
- 2007: Primary prevention reintroduced in the public health insurances (Health Care)
- 2007: National smoking ban introduced (in the areas where such legislation by FG is possible; MS followed) (Public Health)
- 2007: Strengthening of competition amongst the health insurances (Health Care)
- 2008: Occupational and public health insurances merged
- 2012: National strategy on healthy aging (Public Health and Health Care)

Institutional Development Switzerland

- 1877: Federal law regarding work safety in factories (Public Health)
- 1887: National law on epidemics (Public Health)
- 1893: Creation of the federal office for public health (Public Health)
- 1900: Unified health insurance failed in referendum (Health Care)
- 1911: Federal law on health insurances (Health Care)
- 1914: Second law on workplace regulation (Public Health)
- 1918: SUVA founded (Public Health and Health Care)

- 1919: Foundation of the CDP (Public Health and Health Care)
- 1924: Foundation of the Centre Anticancereux Romand (CACR), Lausanne
- 1928: National law regarding TB (Public Health)
- 1935: National law to control alcohol (Public Health)
- 1948: Creation of AHV (retirement insurance) (Welfare)
- 1949: Law to implement mandatory TB exams failed (Public Health)
- 1951: Creation of the federal law on narcotics (Public Health)
- 1959: Creation of the invalidity insurance (Health Care)
- 1962: Federal legislation on counteracting of rheumatism (Health Care)
- 1964: Revision of the national health insurance law (Health Care)
- 1969: "Giftgesetz" – National law regarding drugs and toxic substances (Health Care)
- 1974: Opening of the rehabilitation clinic in Bellikon (Health Care)
- 1976: "Sezione sanataria" was created in Ticino (Public Health)
- 1978: Proposal for a national ban of tobacco and alcohol advertisement failed in referendum (Public Health)
- 1979: An office for preventive health was created in St. Gallen (Public Health)
- 1981: Revision of the national health insurance by creating a separate accidental insurance (Health Care)
- 1984: Law regarding prevention failed (Public Health)
- 1985: National program to prevent AIDS (Public Health)
- 1986: Foundation for public health created (Public Health)
- 1990: First HMO in Europe opens in Zurich (Health Care)
- 1992: Proposal for a national ban of tobacco and alcohol advertisement failed in referendum (Public Health)
- 1993: Drug-prevention law (Public Health)
- 1994: National health insurance law (Health Care)
- 1995: Federal law on narcotics (Public Health)
- 1995: National program for tobacco prevention (Public Health)
- 1997: National program for alcohol prevention (Public Health)
- 1998–2004: Thirteen cantons renewed their legislation on health. (The term prevention has mostly been used in the cantons of Western Switzerland, whereas the German-speaking constituencies prefer to use "*Gesundheitsschutz*".) (Public Health and Health Care)
- 1999: Start of influenza immunization campaigns (Public Health)

- 2001: Revision of the national health insurance law. Substitution with generics are allowed (Health Care)
- 2003: Creation of the tobacco prevention fund (Public Health)
- 2004: Creation of the dialog on a national health policy, replacing the informal consultations between cantons and the federal government (Public Health and Health Care)
- 2004: First national cancer program (Public Health)
- 2007: Unified health insurance failed in referendum (Health Care)
- 2010: National law on smoking bans (exceptions possible) (Public Health)
- 2012: National law on prevention failed in parliament (Public Health)
- 2012: Managed care project failed in referendum (Health Care)
- 2014: Unified health insurance failed in referendum (Health Care)

Institutional Development United States

- As of 1866, sanitary bureau established in the state of New York, as well as laboratories; Similar development in other eastern cities such as Newark, Chicago, Louisville (Kentucky), Cleveland (Ohio), and St. Louis (Public Health)
- 1879: National Board of Health, which put the task to control public health acts in the states. Repealed in 1883 (Public Health)
- 1900: Public health expedition to Cuba (Public Health)
- 1909: Creation of the Rockefeller Sanitary Commission (Public Health)
- 1912: Congress passed a measure that transferred the Marine Hospital Service into the United States Public Health Service (Public Health)
- 1919: School of Hygiene and Public Health at the Rockefeller School of Public Health was established (Public Health)
- 1921: Sheppard-Towner Act, which provided federal grants for maternal and child health. Repealed in 1929 (Public Health)
- 1935: New Deal Legislation (Public Health and Health Care)
- 1935: Interdepartmental Committee to coordinate Health and Welfare Activities (Public Health and Health Care)
- 1937: Technical Committee on Medical Care established (Health Care)

- 1938: Federal grants for the control of venereal disease (Public Health)
- 1939: Department of Health and Human Services created (Public Health and Health Care)
- 1940: USPHS greatly expanded its program of grants to states and counties (Public Health)
- 1944: Federal grants for the control of tuberculosis (Public Health)
- 1946: Hill-Burton Act (Hospital Survey and Construction Act) (Health Care)
- 1950s: Polio vaccination campaign developed; mass scale implementation of polio vaccination (Public Health)
- 1951: Joint Commission on the Accreditation of Hospitals formed (Health Care)
- 1953: Federal Security Agency made a cabinet level agency, which was renamed Department of Health Education and Welfare (Health Care)
- 1956: Military medicare program enacted (Health Care)
- 1960: Federal Employees Health Benefit Plan provides coverage to federal workers (Health Care)
- 1960: Kerr-Mills Act passes using federal funds in support of state programs providing medical care to the poor (Health Care)
- 1963: Clean Air Act established (Public Health)
- 1965: Neighborhood Health Centers established (Health Care and Public Health)
- 1965: Medicare and Medicaid (Health Care)
- 1967: Amendment to Medicare Act adds optional Medicare categories, such as early screening (Health Care and Public Health)
- 1970: Occupational health legislation (Public Health)
- 1972: Social Security amendments extend Medicare to under 65 with terminal diseases (Health Care)
- 1972: Federal Water Pollution Control Amendments (Public Health)
- 1974: Health Planning Resource Development Act (Health Care)
- 1974: Safe Drinking Water Act (Public Health)
- 1977: Health Care Financing Administration established in the Department of Health and Welfare (Health Care)
- 1981: Federal Budget Reconciliation Act requires states to pay more Medicaid payments are established for hospitals with a disproportionate share of low income patients/waivers (Health Care)

- 1981: States allowed to expand Medicaid to children with disabilities (Health Care)
- 1983: Medicare introduces DRGs. HMO become prominent (Health Care)
- 1986: Emergency Medical Treatment and Active Labor Act requires hospitals participating in Medicare to screen and stabilize all persons who use their emergency services (Health Care)
- 1986: Federal Budget Reconciliation Act provides to states the Medicaid option to cover infants, young children, and pregnant women who are poor (Health Care)
- 1988: Medicare Catastrophic Coverage Act (MCCA) (Health Care)
- 1988: Federal Health Aviation Act (smoking ban on flights longer than two hours) (Public Health)
- 1988: Family Support Act (Health Care)
- 1988: National Committee on Quality Assurance (NCQA) forms to accredit managed care health plans (Health Care)
- 1990: Healthy People 2000 (Health Care and Public Health)
- 1993: Vaccines for Children program established (Public Health and Health Care)
- 1996: Health Insurance Portability and Accountability Act (HIPAA) established (Health Care)
- 1996: Personal Responsibility and Work Opportunity Act (Health Care)
- 1997: Balanced Budget Act (BBA), the State Children's Health Insurance Program (S-CHIP) is enacted (Health Care)
- 1998: Master Settlement Agreement (Public Health)
- 2000: Breast and Cervical Cancer Treatment and Prevention Act (Public Health and Health Care)
- 2000: Healthy People 2010 (Health Care and Public Health)
- 2002: President Bush launches Health Center Growth Initiative (Public Health and Health Care)
- 2003: Drug, Improvement, and Modernization Act (Health Care)
- 2003: Medicare legislation creates Health Savings Accounts (Health Care)
- 2005: The Centers for Disease Control and Prevention (CDC) created the National Center for Public Health Informatics (NCPHI) (Public Health and Health Care)
- 2009: Children's Health Insurance Program (CHIP) reauthorized (Health Care)

- 2009: Family Smoking Prevention and Tobacco Control Act (Public Health)
- 2009: The American Reinvestment and Recovery Act (ARRA) entails investments in health information technology, expans the primary care workforce, and conducts research on comparative effectiveness for health care treatment options (Health Care)
- 2010: Patient Protection and Affordable Care Act (Health Care and Public Health)
- 2010: Healthy People 2020 (Health Care and Public Health)

Notes

1 Introduction

1 Another important strand of social science research referring to coevolution concerns the coevolution of individual behaviors and social institutions (Bowles, Choi, and Hopfensitz, 2003), or of firms along with their institutional environment. Thereby, the research has yielded results about the coevolution of strategic alliances between firms (Koza and Lewin, 1998) and between firms and their environment (Krug and Hendrischke, 2008; Cantwell, Dunning, and Lundan, 2009). Additionally, sociologists have proposed a general theoretical approach to coevolutionary systems (Hird, 2010; Hodgson, 2010; Gual and Norgaard, 2010). Eventually, authors referred to coevolution in the literature on institutional complementarity (Boyer, 2005; Campbell, 2011). Boyer even put forward a *coevolutionary hypothesis*, which contends that in capitalist systems technologies, organizations, and institutions coevolve and are selected according to a fitness criterion and that these systems subsequently evolve by learning as well as by trial and error (Boyer, 2005, 45). This book does not use such a specific understanding of coevolution.

2 No distinctiveness does not mean that one sector ceases to exist. The sectoral paradigm and the related actors and professions remain intact.

2 Sectoral Coupling of Health Care and Public Health

1 However, most of the pharmaceutical industry's profits are in the area of health care and individual treatment (Berndt, 2001; Reinhardt, 2001; Abraham, 2009).

2 I have discussed this point in Trein (2017c).

3 Administrative coordination, such as the common implementation of policies (D. Braun, 2008), is a problematic area because it entails some common output with regard to coordination, but excludes political coordination. So, where should we place it in this logic of responsiveness? Since the main interest of this book is political coordination, I am not going to pursue this concept further, but it might be necessary for any author attempting to adapt this concept of coupling to a logic of policy implementation.

3 Theoretical Priors

1 The sections presented in this book refer to important following contextual dimensions: philosophy, psychology, ideas, culture, history, place, population, technology, as well as "old and new" (Goodin and Tilly, 2006).
2 Layering, drift, conversion, and displacement (Mahoney and Thelen, 2010).
3 To be precise, there are also instances of abrupt institutional change. For instance, the introduction of the Patient Protection and Affordable Care Act of 2011 shows (Beaussier, 2012) that institutional path dependencies can be overcome in health care policy. The same conclusion could be made concerning the Swiss health care reform in 1994/1996 (Uhlmann and Braun, 2011).
4 A subsequent application of the typology in an empirical analysis shows that five of these health care systems exist in 30 OECD countries: National Health Service, National Health Insurance, Social Health Insurance, Private Health System, and Etatist Social Health Insurance (Böhm et al., 2012, 2013).
5 In the administrative type of federalism, this is the case anyway (Hueglin and Fenna, 2006).

4 Global Context and Case Selection

1 It is important to mention that in terms of ideas, the distinction between population and individual-based health policies has already existed for a long time (Rosen, 1993 [1959]; Porter, 1999). However, it was in the late nineteenth century when they emerged as two different policy sectors, with different health professions and interest groups as well as modern policy instruments, such as public health legislation covering large territories using the latest scientific advancements.
2 If we compare the introduction of health insurance in twenty-three countries, the mean year of introduction is 1924 (Germany first in 1883 and the US last in 1965) (M. Schmidt, 2005b, 182).
3 The International Health Board had already been established in 1908 in Paris. Its main task was to distribute and collect information between health departments across the world. It became the foundation for the establishment for the League of Nations Health Organization, although the two bodies were not integrated because of problems between the United States and some member states (www.who.int/archives/fonds_collections/bytitle/fonds_3/en/, accessed August 11, 2014).
4 The source for Figures 4.1 and 4.2 is OECD data (OECD, 2017).

5 Source of data: The Maddison-Project, 2013, www.ggdc.net/maddison/
  maddison-project/home.htm, accessed May 5, 2015. See Bolt and Zanden
  (2014) for the method in which data have been collected.
6 The respective figures can be found in the following sources. Australia:
  ABS (2011). Germany: Sensch ((1875, 2013 [2006]). Switzerland:
  Database of historical statistics of Switzerland online: www.fsw.uzh
  .ch/hstat/nls_rev/ls_files.php?chapter_var=./d, accessed May 5, 2015.
  United Kingdom: Griffiths and Brock (2003). United States: US Public
  Health Service (1900–1970); www.cdc.gov/tb/statistics/tbcases.htm,
  accessed May 05, 2015.
7 "Multilevel Governance in Health Policy: Comparing Australia, Germany and Switzerland," research project funded by the Swiss National
  Science Foundation (Ref: 26041044). I am especially grateful to Wally
  Achtermann, Dorte Hering, and Björn Uhlmann who helped me with the
  interviews.
8 The research project focused on the analysis of tobacco control policies,
  which means that many of the experts that we interviewed in this context
  knew the most about this issue. Nonetheless, we discussed public health
  and health care in general and I did complementary interviews with other
  actors who could provide more information regarding the relationship of
  health care and public health.

6 Australia: Politicized Professions and Tight Coupling of Health Care and Public Health

1 www.nhmrc.gov.au/about/organisation-overview/history-nhmrc, accessed
  March 6, 2014.
2 www.health.gov.au/internet/main/publishing.nsf/Content/health-history
  .htm, accessed September 22, 2014.
3 ID of information on the legislation: BILLS DIGEST NO. 86, 2013-14 16
  JUNE 2014.

7 Germany: Dominance of Individual Health Care and Decoupling from Public Health

1 www.bmfsfj.de/BMFSFJ/Ministerium/geschichte, accessed June 9, 2015.
2 www.bzga.de/die-bzga/aufgaben-und-ziele/, accessed, June 9, 2015.
3 Gesetz zur Stärkung der Gesundheitsförderung und der Prävention
  (Präventionsgesetz PrävG) Vom 17. Juli 2015. [Law on strengthening
  health promotion and prevention (prevention law) of July 17, 2015]
4 The first important publication concerning the negative impact of smoking on health had already been published in 1964 (Surgeon General's
  Advisory Committee, 1964).

8 Switzerland: Institutional Fragmentation, Depoliticized Health Professions, and Noncoupling

1 www.geschichtedersozialensicherheit.ch/institutionen/bundesamt-fuer-sozialversicherungen-bsv/, accessed October 16, 2014.
2 www.ispm.ch/index.php?id=150, accessed October 20, 2014; Int-CH-13.
3 Indications for this is the publication of a newspaper for doctors (*Schweizerische Ärztezeitung*) in 1920 and the establishment of a General Secretariat in 1923: www.fmh.ch/ueber_fmh/portraet/geschichte.html, accessed October 22, 2014.
4 www.ispm.ch/index.php?id=150, accessed June 29, 2015.
5 Parliamentary Motion 93.3673 of the federal parliament of Switzerland.
6 It is named AWMP (Allianz der Wirtschaft für eine massvolle Präventionspolitik [Alliance of economic organizations for a restrained preventative health policy) www.awmp.ch/mitglieder-awmp.html, accessed December 9, 2014.
7 Federal Government 09.076 in the database of the federal parliament of Switzerland.
8 Federal Government 10.107 in the database of the federal parliament of Switzerland.
9 An overview of the strategies can be found at: www.nationalegesundheit .ch/nc/de/uebersicht/index.html, www.bag.admin.ch/bag/de/home/ themen/strategien-politik/nationale-gesundheitsstrategien.html, accessed November 3, 2014.

9 United States: Politicized Professions and Loose Coupling of Health Care and Public Health

1 In the following years, the Surgeon General published reports on the health of the nation. These reports focused mostly on the consequences of smoking but also on the effect of certain medical technologies, such as radiation and smog. Other reports evaluated health promotion efforts (1979). Again, another group of reports focused on special diseases, such as chronic lung disease (1984), or the needs of indigent groups, such as children (1987). More recent reports had been focusing on AIDS and nutrition and health (1988) as well as physical activity (1996). Most importantly, however, were the repeated contributions concerning smoking and health, as the latest report showed (2014: "The Health Consequences of Smoking 50 Years of Progress: A Report of the Surgeon General." All reports are available at www.surgeongeneral.gov/library/ reports/, accessed November 19, 2014.

10 Coevolution of Policy Sectors: Health Care and Public Health in a Comparative Perspective

1 A list of the reforms (that were considered) and their coding can be found in the appendix to this book. The figure is illustrative, and neither contains all reforms in a period nor is a statistically representative sample. Nevertheless, the list contains the most significant reforms, according to the secondary literature.
2 Figure 10.3 uses the same data as Figure 10.2.

References

6, Perri. 2004. "Joined-up Government in the Western World in Comparative Perspective: A Preliminary Literature Review and Exploration." *Journal of Public Administration Research and Theory* 14(1):103–138.
    2005. Joined-up Government in the West beyond Britain: A Provisional Assessment. In *Joined-Up Government*, ed. Vernon Bogdanor. New York: Oxford University Press, pp. 43–106.
6, Perri, Diana Leat, Kimberley Setzler, and Gerry Stoker. 2002. *Towards Holistic Governance: The New Reform Agenda*. Houndmills, UK: Palgrave.
Abbott, Andrew. 1988. *The System of Professions: An Essay on the Division of Expert Labor*. Chicago: University of Chicago Press.
    2005. "Linked Ecologies: States and Universities as Environments for Professions*." *Sociological Theory* 23(3):245–274.
Abel-Smith, Brian. 1992. "The Beveridge Report: Its Origins and Outcomes." *International Social Security Review* 45(1–2):5–16.
Abraham, John. 2009. "Partial Progress: Governing the Pharmaceutical Industry and the NHS, 1948–2008." *Journal of Health Politics, Policy and Law* 34(6):931–977.
ABS (Australian Bureau of Statistics). 2011. "Australian Social Trends March 2011: Life Expectancy Trends – Australia" Report no. 4102.0, Canberra, Australia.
Acheson, Donald. 1988. *Public Health in England*. London: Department of Health.
Achtermann, Wally and Christel Berset. 2006. *Gesundheitspolitiken in der Schweiz: Potential für eine nationale Gesundheitspolitik. Volume 1: Analyse und Perspektiven*. Bern: Bundesamt für Gesundheit.
Adler, Rolf H. 2009. "Engel's Biopsychosocial Model Is Still Relevant Today." *Journal of Psychosomatic Research* 67(6):607–611.
Albaek, Erik, Christoffer Green-Pedersen, and Lars Beer Nielsen. 2007. "Making Tobacco Consumption a Political Issue in the United States and Denmark: The Dynamics of Issue Expansion in Comparative Perspective." *Journal of Comparative Policy Analysis: Research and Practice* 9(1):1–20.

Alber, Jens. 1982. *Vom Armenhaus zum Wohlfahrtsstaat: Analysen zur Entwicklung der Sozialversicherung in Westeuropa*. Frankfurt: Campus.

Alber, Jens and Brigitte Bernardi Schenkluhn. 1992. *Westeuropäische Gesundheitssysteme im Vergleich: Bundesrepublik Deutschland, Schweiz, Frankreich, Italien, Grossbritannien*. Frankfurt: Campus.

Alford, R. R. 1975. *Health Care Politics: Ideological and Interest Group Barriers to Reform*. Chicago: University of Chicago Press.

Anderiesz, Cleola, Mark Elwood, and David J. Hill. 2006. "Cancer Control Policy in Australia." *Australia and New Zealand Health Policy* 3(1):12–25.

APHTF. 2009. "Australia: The Healthiest Country by 2020." Discussion paper, Australian Preventative Health Task Force, Canberra, Australia.

Askim, Jostein, Åge Johnsen, and Knut-Andreas Christophersen. 2008. "Factors behind Organizational Learning from Benchmarking: Experiences from Norwegian Municipal Benchmarking Networks." *Journal of Public Administration Research and Theory* 18(2):297–320.

Avery, George. 2004. "Bioterrorism, Fear, and Public Health Reform: Matching a Policy Solution to the Wrong Window." *Public Administration Review* 64(3):275–288.

BAG. 2014. "Basisinformation zur Tabakwerbung – Februar 2014." Technical report, Bundesamt für Gesundheit BAG.

Baggott, Rob. 2011. *Public Health Policy and Politics*, 2nd edn. New York: Palgrave Macmillan.

2013. *Partnerships for Public Health and Well-Being: Policy and Practice*. Houndmills, UK: Palgrave Macmillan.

Baldwin, Peter. 1999. *Disease and Democracy: Contagion and the State in Europe, 1830–1930*. Cambridge: Cambridge University Press.

Bandelow, Nils. 2004. "Akteure und Interessen in der Gesundheitspolitik: Vom Korporatismus zum Pluralismus." *Politische Bildung* 37(2): 49–63.

1998. *Gesundheitspolitik : Der Staat in der Hand einzelner Interessengruppen? Probleme, Erklärungen, Reformen*, vol. 60. Opladen, Germany: Leske und Budrich.

Barber, Bernard. 1963. "Some Problems in the Sociology of the Professions." *Daedalus* 92(4):669–688.

Barr, Nicholas A. 2012. *The Economics of the Welfare State*. 5th edn. Oxford: Oxford University Press.

Bashford, Allison and Philippa Levine, eds. 2010. *The Oxford Handbook of the History of Eugenics*. New York: Oxford University Press.

.

Baum, Fran. 1998. *The New Public Health: An Australian Perspective.* Melbourne: Oxford University Press.

———. 2008. *The New Public Health.* Melbourne: Oxford University Press.

———. 2016. *The New Public Health.* Melbourne: Oxford University Press.

Baumgartner, Frank R. and Bryan D. Jones. 2009. *Agendas and Instability in American Politics.* 2nd edn. Chicago: University of Chicago Press.

Bayer, Ronald. 1991. "Public Health Policy and the AIDS Epidemic: An End to HIV Exceptionalism?" *New England Journal of Medicine* 324:1500–1504.

Bayer, Ronald and James Colgrove. 2004. Children and Bystanders First: The Ethics and Politics of Tobacco Control in the United States. In *Unfiltered: Conflicts over Tobacco Control and Public Health*, ed. Eric A. Feldman and Ronald Bayer. Cambridge, MA: Harvard University Press, pp. 9–37.

Beaussier, Anne-Laure. 2012. "The Patient Protection and Affordable Care Act: The Victory of Unorthodox Lawmaking." *Journal of Health Politics, Policy and Law* 37(5):741–778.

Bednar, Jenna. 2009. *The Robust Federation: Principles of Design.* Cambridge: Cambridge University Press.

Béland, Daniel. 2005. "Ideas and Social Policy: An Institutionalist Perspective." *Social Policy & Administration* 39(1):1–18.

Bell, Kirsten, Amy Salmon, and Darlene McNaughton. 2011. "Alcohol, Tobacco, Obesity and the New Public Health." *Critical Public Health* 21(1):1–8.

Bennett, Colin J. and Michael Howlett. 1992. "The Lessons of Learning: Reconciling Theories of Policy Learning and Policy Change." *Policy Sciences* 25(3):275–294.

Benz, Arthur. 2013. "Balancing Rigidity and Flexibility: Constitutional Dynamics in Federal Systems." *West European Politics* 36(4):726–749.

Benz, Arthur and Burkard Eberlein. 1999. "The Europeanization of Regional Policies: Patterns of Multi-level Governance." *Journal of European Public Policy* 6(2):329–348.

Berndt, Ernst R. 2001. "The U.S. Pharmaceutical Industry: Why Major Growth in Times of Cost Containment?" *Health Affairs* 20(2):100–114.

Bero, Lisa. 2003. "Implications of the Tobacco Industry Documents for Public Health and Policy." *Annual Review of Public Health* 24(1):267–288.

Berridge, Virginia. 2003. "Post-war Smoking Policy in the UK and the Redefinition of Public Health." *Twentieth Century British History* 14(1):61–82.

Bertozzi, Fabio and Fabrizio Gilardi. 2008. The Swiss Welfare State: A Changing Public–Private Mix? In *Public and Private Social Policy: Health and Pension Policies in a New Era*, ed. Daniel Béland and Brian Gran. Basingstoke: Palgrave Macmillan, pp. 207–227.

Bijker, Wiebe E. 2006. Why and How Technology Matters. In *Oxford Handbook of Contextual Political Analysis*, ed. R.E. Goodin and C. Tilly. New York: Oxford University Press, pp. 681–706.

Blank, Robert H. and Viola Burau. 2007. *Comparative Health Policy*. 2nd edn. Basingstoke, UK: Palgrave Macmillan.

2013. *Comparative Health Policy*. 4th edn. Basingstoke, UK: Palgrave Macmillan.

Blatter, Joachim K. 2001. "Debordering the World of States: Towards a Multi-level System in Europe and a Multi-polity System in North America? Insights from Border Regions." *European Journal of International Relations* 7(2):175–209.

2008. "In Search of Co-variance, Causal Mechanisms or Congruence? Towards a Plural Understanding of Case Studies." *Swiss Political Science Review* 14(2):315–356.

Blatter, Joachim and Markus Haverland. 2012. *Designing Case Studies*. Basingstoke: Palgrave Macmillan.

Bogdanor, Vernor. 2005. *Joined-Up Government*. New York: Oxford University Press.

Böhm, Katharina, Achim Schmid, Ralf Götze, Claudia Landwehr, and Heinz Rothgang. 2012. "Classifying OECD Healthcare Systems: A Deductive Approach." TranState Working Papers, no. 165.

2013. "Five Types of OECD Healthcare Systems: Empirical Results of a Deductive Classification." *Health Policy* 113(3):258–269.

Bolt, Jutta and Jan Luiten Zanden. 2014. "The Maddison Project: Collaborative Research on Historical National Accounts." *The Economic History Review* 67(3):627–651.

Bonoli, Giuliano, Dietmar Braun, and Philipp Trein. 2013. "Country Document 2013 Pensions, Health and Long-Term Care Switzerland." ASISP/EU Commission.

Bornhäuser, A., J. McCarthy, and S. A. Glantz. 2006. "German Tobacco Industry's Successful Efforts to Maintain Scientific and Political Respectability to Prevent Regulation of Secondhand Smoke." *Tobacco Control* 15(2):e1.

Börzel, Tanja. 2010. "European Governance: Negotiation and Competition in the Shadow of Hierarchy." *Journal of Common Market Studies* 48(2):191–219.

Bowles, Samuel, Jung-Kyoo Choi, and Astrid Hopfensitz. 2003. "The Co-evolution of Individual Behaviors and Social Institutions." *Journal of Theoretical Biology* 223(2):135–147.

Boxall, Anne-Marie and James Gillespie. 2013. *Making Medicare: The Politics of Universal Health Care in Australia.* Sydney: UNSW Press.

Boyer, Robert. 2005. "Coherence, Diversity, and the Evolution of Capitalisms – The Institutional Complementarity Hypothesis." *Evolutionary Institutional Economics Review* 2(1):43–80.

Brändli, Sebastian. 2008. "Gesundheitswesen." HLS (Historisches Lexikon der Schweiz) pp. www.hls–dhs–dss.ch/textes/d/D16593.php, accessed April 15, 2018.

Brauchbar, Mathis, Philippe Chastonay, and Thomas Mattig. 2014. "Zukunft wagen: Gesundheitsförderung und Prävention in der medizinischen Ausbildung." *Schweizerische Ärztezeitung – Bulletin des médecins suisses – Bollettino dei medici svizzeri* 94(35):1317–1320.

Braun, Dietmar. 1993. "Who Governs Intermediary Agencies? Principal–Agent Relations in Research Policy-Making." *Journal of Public Policy* 13(2):135–162.

1994. *Structure and Dynamics of Health Research and Public Funding: An International Institutional Comparison.* Dordrecht Boston London: Kluwer Academic.

2000. The Territorial Divison of Power in Comparative Public Policy Research: An Assesment. In *Public Policy and Federalism*, ed. Dietmar Braun. Burlington, VT: Ashgate, pp. 27–56.

2008. "Organising the Political Coordination of Knowledge and Innovation Policies." *Science and Public Policy* 35:227–239.

Braun, Dietmar and Philipp Trein. 2014. "Federal Dynamics in Times of Economic and Financial Crisis." *European Journal of Political Research* 53(4):803–821.

Braun, Dietmar and Björn Uhlmann. 2009. "Explaining Policy Stability and Change in Swiss Health Care Reform." *Swiss Political Science Review* 15(2):205–240.

Braun, Rudolf. 1985. Zur Professionalisierung des Ärztestandes in der Schweiz. In *Bildungsbürgertum im 19. Jahrhundert; Teil I: Bildungssystem und Professionalisierung in internationalen Vergleichen*, ed. Werner Conze and Jürgen Kocka. Stuttgart, Germany: Klett-Cotta, pp. 332–357.

Brößkamp-Stone, Ursel. 2003. Institutionen, Systeme und Strukturen in der Gesundheitsförderung und Prävention. In *Das Public Health Buch: Gesundheid und Gesundheitswesen*, ed. F. Schwartz, B. Badura, R. Busse, R. Leidl, H. Raspe, J. Siegrist, and W. Ulla, 2nd edn. Münich: Urban und Fischer, pp. 243–268.

Bryder, Linda. 1988. *Below the Magic Mountain: A Social History of Tuberculosis in Twentieth-Century Britain.* Oxford: Oxford University Press.

———. 1994. "A New World? Two Hundred Years of Public Health in Australia and New Zealand." In *The History of Public Health and the Modern State,* ed. Dorothy Porter. Amsterdam: Rodopi, pp. 313–334.

Burau, Viola and Robert H. Blank. 2006. "Comparing Health Policy: An Assessment of Typologies of Health Systems." *Journal of Comparative Policy Analysis: Research and Practice* 8(1):63–76.

Burgess, Michael. 2006. *Comparative Federalism: Theory and Practice.* New York: Routledge.

Burstein, Paul. 1991. "Policy Domains: Organization, Culture, and Policy Outcomes." *Annual Review of Sociology* 17:327–350.

Busse, Reinhard, Miriam Blümel, David Scheller-Kreinsen, and Annette Zentner. 2010. *Tackling Chronic Disease in Europe: Strategies, Interventions and Challenges.* Copenhagen: WHO Regional Office Europe.

Campbell, John L. 2011. "The US Financial Crisis: Lessons for Theories of Institutional Complementarity." *Socio-Economic Review* 9(2):211–234.

Candel, Jeroen J. L. and Robbert Biesbroek. 2016. "Toward a Processual Understanding of Policy Integration." *Policy Sciences* 49(3):211–231.

Cantwell, John, John H. Dunning, and Sarianna M. Lundan. 2009. "An Evolutionary Approach to Understanding International Business Activity: The Co-evolution of MNEs and the Institutional Environment." *Journal of International Business Studies* 41(4):567–586.

Capie, Forrest and Geoffrey Wood. 1997. Great Depression of 1873–1896. In *Business Cycles and Depressions: An Encyclopedia,* ed. Thomas F. Glasner and David Cooley. New York: Garland Publishing, pp. 148–149.

Carey, Gemma and Pauline McLoughlin. 2016. "The Powerful Pull of Policy Targeting: Examining Residualisation in Australia." *Critical Public Health* 26(2):147–158.

Carline, J. D. and D. G. Patterson. 2003. "Characteristics of Health Professions Schools, Public School Systems, and Community-based Organizations in Successful Partnerships to Increase the Numbers of Underrepresented Minority Students Entering Health Professions Education." *Academic Medicine* 78(5):467–482.

Carrera, Percivil M., Karen K. Siemens, and John Bridges. 2008. "Health Care Financing Reforms in Germany: The Case for Rethinking the Evolutionary Approach to Reforms." *Journal of Health Politics, Policy and Law* 33(5):979–1005.

Castles, Francis G., Stefan Leibfried, Herbert Obinger, and Christopher Pierson, eds. 2010. *The Oxford Handbook of the Welfare State.* New York: Oxford University Press.

Chapman, Simon and Melanie Wakefield. 2001. "Tobacco Control Advocacy in Australia: Reflections of 30 years of Progress." *Health Education and Behavior* 28(3):274–289.

Cheng, Tsung-Mei. 2010. "Understanding the 'Swiss Watch' Function of Switzerland's Health System." *Health Affairs* 29(8):1442–1451.

Chernichovsky, D. and A. A. Leibowitz. 2010. "Integrating Public Health and Personal Care in a Reformed US Health Care System." *American Journal of Public Health* 100(2):205–211.

Christensen, Tom and Per Lægreid. 2007. "The Whole-of-Government Approach to Public Sector Reform." *Public Administration Review* 67(6):1059–1066.

Clavier, C. and E. de Leeuw. 2013. *Health Promotion and the Policy Process.* New York: Oxford University Press.

Clegg Smith, K. M., M. A. Wakefield, and M. Nichter. 2003. "Press Coverage of Public Expenditure of Master Settlement Agreement Funds: How Are Non-Tobacco Control Related Expenditures Represented?" *Tobacco Control* 12(3):257–263.

Colgrove, James. 2002. "The McKeown Thesis: A Historical Controversy and Its Enduring Influence." *American Journal of Public Health* 92(5):725.

Cornuz, J., B. Burnand, I. Kawachi, F. Gutzwiller, and F. Paccaud. 1996. "Why Did Swiss Citizens Refuse to Ban Tobacco Advertising?" *Tobacco Control* 5(2):149–153.

Crouch, Colin. 1993. *Industrial Relations and European State Traditions.* Oxford: Oxford University Press.

Crouch, Colin, Wolfgang Streeck, Robert Boyer, Bruno Amable, Peter A. Hall, and Gregory Jackson. 2005. "Dialogue on 'Institutional Complementarity and Political Economy.'" *Socio-Economic Review* 3(2):359–382.

Curson, P. and K. McCracken. 1989. *Plague in Sydney: The Anatomy of an Epidemic.* Sydney: New South Wales Press.

Cusack, Thomas, Torben Iversen, and David Soskice. 2010. "Coevolution of Capitalism and Political Representation: The Choice of Electoral Systems." *American Political Science Review* 104(2):393–403.

Czarniawska, Barbara. 2005. "Karl Weick: Concepts, Style and Reflection." *The Sociological Review* 53(s1):267–278.

Daube, Mike. 2006. "Public Health Needs a Strong, Well-Planned Advocacy Program." *Australian and New Zealand Journal of Public Health* 30(5):405–406.

Day, Patricia and Rudolph Klein. 1992. "Constitutional and Distributional Conflict in British Medical Politics: The Case of General Practice, 1911–1991." *Political Studies* 40(3):462–478.

Deeg, Richard. 2007. "Complementarity and Institutional Change in Capitalist Systems." *Journal of European Public Policy* 14(4):611–630.

Degen, Bernhard. 2006. Entstehung und Entwicklung des schweizerischen Sozialstaates. In *Geschichte der Sozialversicherungen*, ed. Schweizerisches Bundesarchiv. Zurich: Chronos, pp. 17–48.

2008. "Krankenversicherung." HLS (Historisches Lexikon der Schweiz) www.hls-dhs-dss.ch/textes/d/D16608.php, accessed April 16, 2018.

DGfPH. 2012. "Situation und Perspektiven von Public Health in Deutschland." Unpublished paper, Deutsche Gesellschaft fr Public Health e.V.

Dick, W. Allan. 2001. *Fighting Cancer: Anti-Cancer Council of Victoria*. Carlton, Australia: The Cancer Council Victoria.

Diederichs, C., K. Klotmann, and F. Schwartz. 2008. "Zur historischen Entwicklung der deutschen Gesundheitsversorgung und ihrer Reformansätze." *Bundesgesundheitsblatt – Gesundheitsforschung – Gesundheitsschutz* 51(5):547–551.

DiMaggio, Paul and Walter W. Powell. 1991. *The New Institutionalism in Organizational Analysis*. Chicago: University of Chicago Press.

Dingwall, Robert and Philipp Lewis, eds. 1983. *The Sociology of the Professions: Lawyers, Doctors and Others*. London: Sage.

Dodds, Anneliese. 2012. *Comparative Public Policy*. New York: Palgrave Macmillan.

Döhler, Marian. 1993. "Comparing National Patterns of Medical Specialization: A Contribution to the Theory of Professions." *Social Science Information* 32(2):185–231.

1997. *Die Regulierung von Professionsgrenzen: Struktur und Entwicklungsdynamik von Gesundheitsberufen im internationalen Vergleich*. Frankfurt am Main: Campus.

Domenighetti, G., N. Florio, F. Gutzwiller, and M. Krafft. 1993. Gesundheitsförderung auf schweizerischer Ebene: Aktionsprogramm 1993–1997. Technical report Schweizerische Stiftung für Gesundheitsförderung.

Dubos, René. 1987. *The White Plague: Tuberculosis, Man and Society*. New Brunswick, NJ: Rutgers University Press.

Duckett, Stephen J. 2007. *The Australian Health Care System*. 3rd edn. Oxford: Oxford University Press.

Duina, Francesco and Paulette Kurzer. 2004. "Smoke in Your Eyes: The Struggle over Tobacco Control in the European Union." *Journal of European Public Policy* 11(1):57–77.

Dundas, E. A. 1952. "The National Campaign against Tuberculosis." *Australian Journal of Public Administration* 11(2):79–84.

Dunlop, Claire, Claudio Radaelli, and Philipp Trein, eds. 2018. *Learning in Public Policy: Analysis, Modes and Outcomes.* Basingstoke, UK: Palgrave Macmillan.

Eberle, Gudrun. 2002. Prävention in der Gesetzlichen Krankenversicherung von 1970 bis heute. In *Prävention im 20. Jahrhundert: Historische Grundlagen und aktuelleste Entwicklung in Deutschland,* ed. Sigrid Stoeckl and Ulla Walter. Munich: Juventa, pp. 237–249.

Eckart, Wolfgang U. 2011. *Illustrierte Geschichte der Medizin: Von der französischen Revolution bis zur Gegenwart.* Berlin: Springer.

Egger, Matthias and Razum Oliver. 2012. *Public Health: Zentrale Begriffe, Disziplinen und Handlungsfelder.* Berlin: De Gruyter, pp. 1–22.

Eichengreen, Barry. 1992. *Golden Fetters: The Gold Standard and the Great Depression, 1919–1939.* New York: Oxford University Press.

Ellerbrock, Dagmar. 2002. Prävention in der US-Zone: Zielsetzung, Konzeption und Reichweite von Präventionsmassnahmen nach dem Zweiten Welkrieg. In *Prävention im 20. Jahrhundert: Historische Grundlagen und aktuelleste Entwicklung in Deutschland,* ed. Sigrid Stoeckl and Ulla Walter. Munich: Juventa, pp. 152–164.

Engel, George L. 1977. "The Need for a New Medical Model: A Challenge for Biomedicine." *Science* 196(4286):129–136.

——— 1978. "The Biopsychosocial Model and the Education of Health Professionals?" *Annals of the New York Academy of Sciences* 310(1):169–181.

——— 1980. "The Clinical Application of the Biopsychosocial Model." *American Journal of Psychiatry* 137(5):534–544.

Enthoven, Alain C. 1988. *Theory and Practice of Managed Competition in Health Care Finance.* Amsterdam: Elsevier.

——— 1993. "The History and Principles of Managed Competition." *Health Affairs* 12(suppl):24–48.

Ernst, E. 2001. "Commentary: The Third Reich – German Physicians between Resistance and Participation." *International Journal of Epidemiology* 30(1):37–42.

Esping-Andersen, Gøsta. 1990. *The Three Worlds of Welfare Capitalism.* Princeton, NJ: Princeton University Press.

Evans, David. 2003. "'Taking Public Health out of the Ghetto': The Policy and Practice of Multi-Disciplinary Public Health in the United Kingdom." *Social Science & Medicine* 57(6):959–967.

Fava, G. A. and N. Sonino. 2008. "The Biopsychosocial Model Thirty Years Later." *Psychotherapy and Psychosomatics* 77(1):1–2.

Federal Council of Switzerland. 2010. Botschaft zur Revision des Bundesgesetzes über die Bekämpfung übertragbarer Krankheiten des Menschen (Epidemiengesetz, EpG). Technical report, Federal Council of Switzerland. www.admin.ch/opc/de/federal-gazette/2011/311.pdf, accessed April 6, 2018.

Fee, Elizabeth. 1987. *Disease and Discovery: A History of the Johns Hopkins School of Hygiene and Public Health, 1916–1939*. Baltimore, MD: Johns Hopkins University Press.

⸻. 1994. Public Health and the State: The United States. In *The History of Public Health and the Modern State*, ed. Dorothy Porter. Atlanta, GA: Rodopi, pp. 180–232.

⸻. 2008. "Divorce between Theory and Practice: The System of Public Health Training in the United States." *Ciencia & Saude Coletiva* 13(3):841–851.

Feldstein, Paul. 2011. *Health Care Economics*. New York: Cengage Learning.

Field, Mark G. 1973. "The Concept of the 'Health System' at the Macrosociological Level." *Social Science & Medicine* 7:763–785.

Fischer, Frank, Gerald J. Miller, and Mara S. Sidney, eds. 2006. *Handbook of Public Policy Analysis: Theory, Politics, and Methods*. Boca Raton, FL: CRC Press.

Foucault, Michel. 1963. *Naissance de la clinique: Une archéologie du regard médical*. Paris: Presses universitaires de France.

Fox, Daniel M., Patricia Day, and Rudolf Klein. 2012. "The Power of Professionalism: Policies for AIDS in Britain, Sweden, and the United States". In *Politics, Health, and Health Care: Selected Essays*, ed. Theodore R. Marmor and Rudolf Klein. New Haven, CT: Yale University Press, pp. 464–480.

Freeman, Richard and Heinz Rothgang. 2010. Health. In *The Oxford Handbook of the Welfare State*, ed. Jane Lewis, Herbert Obinger, Christopher Pierson, Francis G. Castles, and Stephan Leibfried. New York: Oxford University Press, pp. 368–377.

Freidson, Eliot. 1970. *Professional Dominance: The Social Structure of Medical Care*. New York: Aldine.

⸻. 1983. "The Theory of Professions: State of the Art." In *The Sociology of the Professions: Lawyers, Doctors and Others*, ed. Robert Dingwall and Philipp Lewis. London: Sage, pp. 19–37.

⸻. 1986. *Professional Powers: A Study of the Institutionalization of Formal Knowledge*. Chicago: University of Chicago Press.

⸻. 1990. *Profession of Medicine: A Study of the Sociology of Applied Knowledge*. Chicago: University of Chicago Press.

Frenk, Julio and Avedis Donabedian. 1987. "State Intervention in Medical Care: Types, Trends and Variables." *Health Policy and Planning* 2(1):17–31.

Garton, Stephen. 1994. "Sound Minds and Healthy Bodies: Re-Considering Eugenics in Australia, 1914–1940." *Australian Historical Studies* 26(103):163–181.

2010. "Eugenics in Australia and New Zealand: Laboratories of Racial Science." In *The Oxford Handbook of the History of Eugenics*, ed. Allison Bashford and Philippa Levine. New York: Oxford University Press, pp. 243–257.

Geddes, Barbara. 2003. *Paradigms and Sand Castles: Theory Building and Research Design in Comparative Politics*. Ann Arbor: University of Michigan Press.

George, Alexander L. and Andrew Bennett. 2005. *Case Studies and Theory Development in the Social Sciences*. Cambridge, MA: MIT Press.

Gerlinger, Thomas and Klaus Stegmüller. 2009. "Ökonomisch-rationales Handeln als normatives Leitbild der Gesundheitspolitik." In *Normativität und Public Health: Vergessene Dimensionen gesundheitlicher Ungleichheit*, ed. Uwe H. Bittlingmayer, Diana Sahrai, and Peter-Ernst Schnabel. Wiesbaden: VS Verlag für Sozialwissenschaften, pp. 135–161.

Gerring, John. 2007. *Case Study Research: Principles and Practices*. Cambridge: Cambridge University Press.

Giaimo, Susan and Philip Manow. 1999. "Adapting the Welfare State: The Case of Health Care Reform in Britain, Germany, and the United States." *Comparative Political Studies* 32(8):967–1000.

Gilardi, Fabrizio, Katharina Füglister, and Stéphane Luyet. 2009. "Learning from Others: The Diffusion of Hospital Financing Reforms in OECD Countries." *Comparative Political Studies* 42(4):549–573.

Gilardi, Fabrizio, Manuela Giovanoli, Charles R. Shipan, and Bruno Wüest. 2014. "Measuring Policy Diffusion with Automated Content Analysis." Paper presented at Political Context Matters: Content Analysis in the Social Sciences Conference, Mannheim, October 10–11.

Gilardi, Fabrizio and C. Radaelli. 2012. Governance and Learning. In *Oxford Handbook of Governance*, ed. David Levi-Faur. Oxford: Oxford University Press, pp. 155–168.

Givel, Michael. 2007. "A Comparison of the Impact of U.S. and Canadian Cigarette Pack Warning Label Requirements on Tobacco Industry Profitability and the Public Health." *Health Policy* 83(2–3):343–352.

Goodin, Robert E. and Charles Tilly, eds. 2006. *The Oxford Handbook of Contextual Politics*. New York: Oxford University Press.

Gostin, Lawrence O. 2014. *Global Health Law*. Cambridge, MA: Harvard University Press.

Gottweis, Herbert, Wolfgang Hable, Barbara Prainsack, and Doris Wydra. 2004. *Verwaltete Körper: Strategien der Gesundheitspolitik im internationalen Vergleich*. Vienna: Böhlau Verlag.

Grant, Wyn and Anne MacNamara. 1995. "When Policy Communities Intersect: The Case of Agriculture and Banking." *Political Studies* 43(3):509–515.

Griffiths, Clare and Anita Brock. 2003. "Twentieth Century Mortality Trends in England and Wales." *Health Statistics Quarterly* 18:5–17.

Grüning, Thilo and Anna Gilmore. 2007. "Germany: Tobacco Industry Still Dictates Policy." *Tobacco Control* 16(1):2.

Grüning, Thilo, Anna Gilmore and Martin McKee. 2006. "Tobacco Industry Influence on Science and Scientists in Germany." *American Journal of Public Health* 96(6):20–32.

Gual, Miguel A. and Richard B. Norgaard. 2010. "Bridging Ecological and Social Systems Coevolution: A Review and Proposal." *Ecological Economics* 69(4):707–717.

Haberkorn, J. 2012. "Health Policy Brief: The Prevention and Public Health Fund." *Health Affairs* February 23.

Hacker, Jacob S. 1998. "The Historical Logic of National Health Insurance: Structure and Sequence in the Development of British, Canadian, and US Medical Policy." *Studies in American Political Development* 12(1):57–130.

2004a. "Privatizing Risk without Privatizing the Welfare State: The Hidden Politics of Social Policy Retrenchment in the United States." *American Political Science Review* 98(2):243–260.

2004b. "Review Article: Dismantling the Health Care State? Political Institutions, Public Policies and the Comparative Politics of Health Reform." *British Journal of Political Science* 34(4):693–724.

2005. "Policy Drift: The Hidden Politics of US Welfare State Retrenchment." In *Beyond Continuity: Institutional Change in Advanced Political Economies*, ed. Wolfgang Streeck and Kathleen Thelen. New York: Oxford University Press, pp. 40–82.

Haines, Michael R. 2001. "The Urban Mortality Transition in the United States, 1800–1940." *Annales de démographie historique* 1:33–64.

Hall, Jane. 1999. "Incremental Change in the Australian Health Care System." *Health Affairs* 18(3):95–110.

Hall, Peter A. 1993. "Policy Paradigms, Social Learning, and the State: The Case of Economic Policymaking in Britain." *Comparative Politics* 3(25):275–296.

Hall, Peter and David Soskice. 2001. *Varieties of Capitalism: The Institutional Foundations of Comparative Advantage*. New York: Oxford University Press.

Hancock, Linda. 1999. Policy, Power and Interests. In *Health Policy in the Market State*, ed. Linda Hancock. St. Leonards, Australia: Allen & Unwin, pp. 19–47.

Hancock, Trevor. 1986. "Lalonde and Beyond: Looking Back at 'A New Perspective on the Health of Canadians.'" *Health Promotion International* 1(1):93–100.

Hassenteufel, Patrick. 1997. *Les médecins face à l'État: Une comparaison européenne*. Paris: Les Presses de sciences po.

Hawe, Penelope, Melanie Wakefield, and Don Nutbeam. 2001. "Policy and System-Level Approaches to Health Promotion in Australia." *Health Education & Behavior* 28(3):267–273.

Heinz, John P. and Edward O. Laumann. 1978. "The Legal Profession: Client Interests, Professional Roles, and Social Hierarchies." *Michigan Law Review* 76(7):1111–1142.

Hemerijck, Anton and Kees van Kersbergen. 1999. Negotiated Policy Change: Towards a Theory of Institutional Learning in Tightly Coupled Welfare States. In *Public Policy and Political Ideas*, ed. Dietmar Braun and Andreas Busch. Cheltenham, UK: Edward Elgar, pp. 168–185.

Henisz, Witold J. 2000. "The Institutional Environment for Economic Growth." *Economics & Politics* 12(1):1–31.

Hennock, Ernest Peter. 1987. *British Social Reform and German Precedents: The Case of Social Insurance, 1880–1914*. Oxford: Clarendon Press.

Herman, Joseph. 1989. "The Need for a Transitional Model: A Challenge for Biopsychosocial Medicine?" *Family Systems Medicine* 7(1):106–111.

Hird, Myra J. 2010. "Coevolution, Symbiosis and Sociology." *Ecological Economics* 69(4):737–742.

Hirschhorn, Norbert. 2000. "Shameful Science: Four Decades of the German Tobacco Industry's Hidden Research on Smoking and Health." *Tobacco Control* 9(2):242–248.

Hockerts, Hans-Günther. 1991. Sozialpolitik in der Bundesrepublik Deutschland. In *Staatliche, städtische, betriebliche und kirchliche Sozialpolitik vom Mittelalter bis zur Gegenwart: Referate der 13. Arbeitstagung der Gesellschaft für Sozial-und Wirtschaftsgeschichte vom 28. März bis 1. April 1989 in Heidelberg*, ed. Hans Pohl. Stuttgart: Steiner, pp. 359–379.

Hodgson, Geoffrey M. 2010. "Darwinian Coevolution of Organizations and the Environment." *Ecological Economics* 69(4):700–706.

Holland, Walter W. 2004. Overview of Policies and Strategies. In *The Oxford Textbook of Public Health*, ed. Robert Beaglehole, Mary Ann Lansang, Martin Gulliford, and Roger Detels. 5th edn. New York: Oxford University Press, pp. 257–280.

Holland, Walter W. and Susie Stewart. 1998. *Public Health: The Vision and the Challenge*. London: The Nuffield Trust.

Hooghe, Liesbet, Gary Marks, Arjan H. Schakel, Sandra Chapman-Osterkatz, Sara Niedzwiecki, and Sarah Shair-Rosenfield. 2016. *Measuring Regional Authority. Volume I: A Postfunctionalist Theory of Governance*. Oxford: Oxford University Press.

Howlett, Michael. 2005. What Is a Policy Instrument? Policy Tools, Policy Mixes, and Policy-Implementation Styles. In *Designing Government: From Instruments to Governance*, ed. Pearl Eliadis, Margaret M. Hill, and Michael Howlett. Montreal: McGill-Queen's University Press, pp. 31–50.

Howlett, Michael, M. Ramesh, and Anthony Pearl. 2009. *Studying Public Policy: Policy Cycles and Policy Subsystems*. 3rd edn. New York: Oxford University Press.

Huber, Evelyne and John D. Stephens. 2001. *Development and Crisis of the Welfare State: Parties and Policies in Global Markets*. Chicago: University of Chicago Press.

Hueglin, Thomas O. and Alan Fenna. 2006. *Comparative Federalism: A Systematic Inquiry*. Peterborough, Canada: Broadview Press.

Huerkamp, Claudia. 1985. Die preussisch-deutsche Ärzteschaft als Teil des Bildungsbürgertums: Wandel in Lage und Selbstverständnis vom ausgehenden 18. Jahrhundert bis zum Kaiserreich. In *Bildungsbürgertum im 19. Jahrhundert. Volume I: Bildungssystem und Professionalisierung in internationalen Vergleichen*, ed. Werner Conze and Jürgen Kocka. Stuttgart: Klett-Cotta, pp. 358–387.

Hunter, David J. 2003. Public Health Policy. In *Public Health for the Twenty-first Century: New Perspectives on Policy, Participation and Practice*, ed. Pat Taylor, Judy Orme, Jane Powell, and Melanie Grey. Maidenhead, UK: Open University Press, pp. 25–41.

Hunter, David J., Linda Marks, and Katherine E. Smith. 2010. *The Public Health System in England*. Bristol, UK: Policy Press.

Immergut, Ellen M. 1990. "Institutions, Veto Points, and Policy Results: A Comparative Analysis of Health Care." *Journal of Public Policy* 10(4):391–416.

1992. *Health Politics: Interests and Institutions in Western Europe*. New York: Cambridge University Press.

1998. "The Theoretical Core of the New Institutionalism." *Politics & Society* 26(1):5–34.

Indra, Peter, Reto Januth, and Stephan Cueni. 2010. *Krankenversicherung.* Bern, Switzerland: Hans Huber, pp. 177–196.

Institute of Medicine. 1988. *The Future of Public Health.* Washington, DC: National Academic Press.

Jachtenfuchs, Markus. 2001. "The Governance Approach to European Integration." *Journal of Common Market Studies* 39(2):245–264.

Janzen, Daniel H. 1980. "When is it Coevolution?" *Evolution* 34(3): 611–612.

Jochim, Ashley E. and Peter J. May. 2010. "Beyond Subsystems: Policy Regimes and Governance." *Policy Studies Journal* 38(2):303–326.

Jonas, Steven, Raymond L. Goldsteen, and Karen Goldsteen. 2007. *An Introduction to the US Health Care System.* New York: Springer.

Joossens, Luk and Martin Raw. 2014. *The Tobacco Control Scale 2014 in Europe.* Brussels: Associations of European Cancer Leagues.

Jordan, Andrew and Adriaan Schout. 2006. *The Coordination of the European Union.* Oxford: Oxford University Press.

Kaufmann, Stefan. 2010. *Krankenversicherer.* Bern: Hans Huber, pp. 167–175.

Kauz, Daniel. 2010. *Vom Tabu zum Thema? 100 Jahre Krebsbekämpfung in der Schweiz 1910–2010.* Basel: Schwabe Verlag.

Kay, Adrian and Anne-Marie Boxall. 2015. "Success and Failure in Public Policy: Twin Imposters or Avenues for Reform? Selected Evidence from 40 Years of Health-care Reform in Australia." *Australian Journal of Public Administration* 74(1):33–41.

Kingdon, John W. 1995. *Agendas, Alternatives, and Public Policies.* 2nd edn. New York: Longman.

Kleinman, A. 1978. "Concepts and a Model for the Comparison of Medical Systems as Cultural Systems." *Social Science and Medicine* (12):85–93.

Knoepfel, Peter, Corinne Larrue, Frédéric Varone, and Michael Hill. 2011. *Public Policy Analysis.* Bristol: The Policy Press.

Kocher, Gerhard. 1967. *Verbandseinfluss auf die Gesetzgebung: Aerzteverbindung, Krankenkassenverbände und die Teilrevision des Kanken- und Unfallversicherungsgesetzes.* Bern, Switzerland: W. Dürrenmatt.

2010. Kompetenz- und Aufgabenteilung Bund – Kantone – Gemeinden. In *Gesundheitswesen Schweiz 2010–2012: Eine aktuelle Übersicht,* ed. Gerhard Kocher and W. Oggier, 4th edn. Bern: Hans Huber, pp. 133–144.

Korpi, Walter and Joakim Palme. 2003. "New Politics and Class Politics in the Context of Austerity and Globalization: Welfare State Regress in 18 Countries, 1975–1995." *American Political Science Review* 97(3):425–446.

Koza, Mitchell P. and Arie Y. Lewin. 1998. "The Co-Evolution of Strategic Alliances." *Organization Science* 9(3):255–264.

Krug, Barbara and Hans Hendrischke. 2008. "Framing China: Transformation and Institutional Change through Co-evolution." *Management and Organization Review* 4(1):81–108.

Kübler, Daniel. 2001. "Understanding Policy Change with the Advocacy Coalition Framework: An Application to Swiss Drug Policy." *Journal of European Public Policy* 8(4):623–641.

Kübler, Daniel, Peter Neuenschwander, and Yannis Papadopoulos. 2001. "Evaluation der Aidspräventionsstrategie des Bundes Aidspolitik in der Schweiz: Welche Normalisierung? Normalisierungsszenarien und Neue Partnerschaften in der HIV/Aidsprävention auf Bundesebene und in fünf Kantonen." Technical report University of Lausanne/University of Zurich Lausanne, Zurich.

Kübler, Daniel and Sonja Wälti. 2001. "Drug Policy-making in Metropolitan Areas: Urban Conflicts and Governance." *International Journal of Urban and Regional Research* 25(1):35–54.

Labisch, Alfons. 1982. "Entwicklungslinien des öffentlichen Gesundheitsdienstes in Deutschland: Vorüberlegungen zur historischen Soziologie öffentlicher Gesundheitsvorsorge." *Oeffentliches Gesundheitswesen* 44:745–761.

1985. "Doctors, Workers and the Scientific Cosmology of the Industrial World: The Social Construction of 'Health' and the 'Homo Hygienicus.'" *Journal of Contemporary History* 20(4):599–615.

Labisch, Alfons and Florian Tennstedt. 1991. Prävention und Prophylaxe als Handlungsfelder der Gesundheitspolitik im Deutschen Reich (1871–1945). In *Prävention und Prophylaxe: Theorie und Praxis eines gesundheitspolitischen Grundmotivs in zwei deutschen Staaten 1949–1990*, ed. Thomas Elkeles, Jens-Uwe Niedhoff, Rolf Rosenbrock, and Frank Schneider. Berlin: WZB/Edition Sigma, pp. 13–28.

Labisch, Alfons and Wolfgang Woelk. 2012. Geschichte der Gesundheitswissenschaften. In *Handbuch Gesundheitswissenschaften.* 5th edn. Klaus Hurrelmann and Oliver Razum. Weinheim, Germany: Beltz Juventa, pp. 55–98.

Lalonde, M. 1974. "A New Perspective on the Health of Canadians." Technical report, Ottawa.

Larson, Magali Sarfatti. 1977. *The Rise of Professionalism: A Sociological Analysis*. Berkeley, CA: University of California Press.

Leeder, Stephen. 2007. "The Scope, Mission and Method of Contemporary Public Health." *Australian and New Zealand Journal of Public Health* 31(6):505–508.

Lehmbruch, Gerhard. 1977. "Liberal Corporatism and Party Government." *Comparative Political Studies* 10(1):91–126.

1988. Der Neokorporatismus der Bundesrepublik im internationalen Vergleich und die "Konzertierte Aktion im Gesundheitswesen." In *Neokorporatismus und Gesundheitswesen: Symposium der Medizinisch-Pharmazeutischen Studiengesellschaft e.V. (MPS), Bonn,* ed. Gérard Gäfgen. Baden-Baden, Germany: Nomos, pp. 11–32.

Levi-Faur, David. 2014. "The Welfare State: A Regulatory Perspective." *Public Administration* 92(3):599–614.

Levy, Barry S. and Victor W. Sidel, eds. 1997. *War and Public Health.* Oxford University Press.

Lewis, Jenny M. 1999. "The Durability of Ideas in Health-Policy-Making." In *Public Policy and Political Ideas,* ed. Dietmar Braun and Andreas Busch Cheltenham: Edward Elgar, pp. 152–168.

Lewis, Milton J. 2003a. *The People's Health: Public Health in Australia, 1788–1950.* Westport, CT: Praeger.

2003b. *The People's Health: Public Health in Australia, 1950 to the Present.* Westport, CT: Praeger.

2008. Public Health in Australia from the Nineteenth to the Twenty-first Century. In *Public Health in Asia and the Pacific: Historical and Comparative Perspectives,* ed. Milton J. Lewis and Kerrie L. MacPherson. New York: Routledge, pp. 222–249.

Lewis, Milton J. and Kerrie L. MacPherson. 2008. Public Health in Asia and the Pacific. In *Public Health in Asia and the Pacific: Historical and Comparative Perspectives,* ed. Milton J. Lewis and Kerrie L. MacPherson. New York: Routledge, pp. 1–9.

Lewis, Orion and Sven Steinmo. 2010. "Taking Evolution Seriously in Political Science." *Theory in Biosciences* 129(2–3):235–245.

Lijphart, Arend. 1999. *Patterns of Democracy: Government Forms and Performance in Thirty-Six Countries.* New Haven, CT: Yale University Press.

2012. *Patterns of Democracy: Government Forms and Performance in Thirty-Six Countries.* 2nd edn. New Haven CT: Yale University Press.

Lin, Vivian and Priscilla Robinson. 2005. "Australian Public Health Policy in 2003–2004." *Australia and New Zealand Health Policy* 2(1):7.

Lindner, Ulrike. 2004a. "Chronische Gesundheitsprobleme: Das deutsche Gesundheitssystem vom Kaiserreich bis in die Bundesrepublik." *Aus Politik und Zeitgeschichte* 33/34:21–28.

2004b. *Gesundheitspolitik in der Nachkriegszeit: Grossbritannien und die Bundesrepublik Deutschland im Vergleich.* Munich: Oldenbourg Wissenschaftsverlag.

Linz, Juan J. and Alfred Stepan. 1996. *Problems of Democratic Transition and Consolidation: Southern Europe, South America, and Post-Communist Europe.* Baltimore, MD: Johns Hopkins University Press.

Luhmann, Niklas. 1990. *Der medizinische Code.* Opladen, Germany: Westdeutscher Verlag.

Lupton, Deborah. 1995. *The Imperative of Health: Public Health and the Regulated Body.* London: Sage.

Lupton, Gillian M. and Jakob M. Najman, eds. 1995. *Sociology of Health and Illness: Australian Readings.* Melbourne: Macmillan Education.

Ma, Shu-Yun. 2016. "Taking Evolution Seriously, or Metaphorically? A Review of Interactions between Historical Institutionalism and Darwinian Evolutionary Theory." *Political Studies Review* 14(2):223–234.

Macdonald, Keith M. 1995. *The Sociology of the Professions.* London: Sage.

Mackenbach, Johan P. and Martin McKee. 2013. "A Comparative Analysis of Health Policy Performance in 43 European Countries." *The European Journal of Public Health* 23:195–201.

Mahoney, James. 2000. "Path Dependence in Historical Sociology." *Theory and Society* 29(4):507–548.

2001. *The Legacies of Liberalism: Path Dependence and Political Regimes in Central America.* Baltimore, MD: Johns Hopkins University Press.

Mahoney, James and Dietrich Rueschemeyer. 2003. Comparative Historical Analysis: Achievements and Agendas. In *Comparative Historical Analysis in the Social Sciences,* ed. James Mahoney and Dietrich Rueschemeyer. Cambridge: Cambridge University Press, pp. 3–38.

Mahoney, James and Kathleen Thelen. 2010. *A Theory of Gradual Institutional Change.* Cambridge: Cambridge University Press, pp. 1–37.

Marmor, Theodore R. 2012. "American Health Care Policy and Politics: The Promise and Perils of Reforms." In *Politics, Health, and Health Care: Selected Essays,* ed. Theodore R. Marmor and Rudolf Klein. New Haven, CT: Yale University Press, pp. 37–52.

Marmor, Theodore R. and Rudolf Klein, eds. 2012. *Politics, Health, and Health Care: Selected Essays.* New Haven, CT: Yale University Press.

Marmor, Theodore R. and Gary J. McKissick. 2012. "Medicare's Future: Fact, Fiction and Folly." In *Politics, Health, and Health Care: Selected*

Essays, ed. Theodore R. Marmor and Rudolf Klein. New Haven, CT: Yale University Press, pp. 53–88.

Maschewsky-Schneider, Ute. 2005. "The Current Public Health Situation in Germany." *Bundesgesundheitsblatt - Gesundheitsforschung - Gesundheitsschutz* 48(10):1138–1144.

Maschewsky-Schneider, U., G. Klärs, L. Ryl, D. Sewöster, A. Starker, and A.-C. Saß. 2009. "gesundheitsziele.de: Ergebnisse der Kriterienanalyse für die Auswahl eines neuen Gesundheitsziels in Deutschland." *Bundesgesundheitsblatt - Gesundheitsforschung - Gesundheitsschutz* 52(7):764–774.

Mavrot, Céline and Fritz Sager. 2017. "Vertical Epistemic Communities and Multilevel Goverance." Policy and Politics

May, Peter J. 1992. "Policy Learning and Failure." *Journal of Public Policy* 12(04):331–354.

May, Peter J., Ashley E. Jochim, and Joshua Sapotichne. 2011. "Constructing Homeland Security: An Anemic Policy Regime." *Policy Studies Journal* 39(2):285–307.

May, Peter J, Joshua Sapotichne, and Samuel Workman. 2009. "Widespread Policy Disruption: Terrorism, Public Risks, and Homeland Security." *Policy Studies Journal* 37(2):171–194.

Mayes, Rick and Thomas R. Oliver. 2012. "Chronic Disease and the Shifting Focus of Public Health: Is Prevention Still a Political Lightweight?" *Journal of Health Politics, Policy and Law* 37(2):182–200.

Mayntz, Renate. 1993. Policy-Netzwerke und die Logik von Verhandlungssystemen. In *Policy-Analyse: Kritik und Neuorientierung* (PVS-Sonderheft 24), ed. Adrienne Héritier. Opladen, Germany: Westdeutscher Verlag, pp. 39–56.

Mayntz, Renate and Fritz W. Scharpf. 1995. Der Ansatz des akteurzentrierten Institutionalismus. In *Gesellschaftliche Selbstregulierung und politische Steuerung*, ed. Renate Mayntz and Fritz W. Scharpf. Frankfurt am Main: Campus Verlag, pp. 39–72.

McDaid, David, Franco Sassi, and Sherry Merkur, eds. 2015. *Promoting Health, Preventing Disease: The Economic Case*. Copenhagen: World Health Organization.

McKeown, Thomas. 1979. *The Role of Medicine: Dream, Mirage or Nemesis?* Oxford: Basil Blackwell.

McLaren, N. 1998. "A Critical Review of the Biopsychosocial Model." *Australian and New Zealand Journal of Psychiatry* 32(1):86–92.

McQueen, David V., Ilona Kickbusch, Louise Potvin, Jürgen M. Pelikan, Laura Balbo, and Thomas Abel. 2007. *Health and Modernity: The Role of Theory in Health Promotion*. New York: Springer Science & Business Media.

Metcalfe, Les. 1994. "International Policy Co-ordination and Public Management Reform." *International Review of Administrative Sciences* 60(2):271–290.

Milles, Dietrich and Rainer Müller. 2002. "Auftrag und Begrenzung der Gewerbehygiene: Identifikation arbeitsbedingter Erkrankungen und Begründung präventiver Massnahmen in der Geschichte der Sozialversicherung." In *Prävention im 20. Jahrhundert: Historische Grundlagen und aktuelleste Entwicklung in Deutschland*, ed. Sigrid Stöckel and Ulla Walter. Weinheim, Germany: Juventa, pp. 39–51.

Minder, Andreas. 1994. *1919–1994, 75 Jahre SDK: Notizen zur Geschichte der Schweizerischen Sanitätsdirektorenkonferenz*. Bern: Schweizerische Sanitätsdirektorenkonferenz (SDK).

Mommsen, Wolfgang J. and Wolfgang Mock, eds. 1981. *The Emergence of the Welfare State in Britain and Germany, 1850–1950*. London: Croom Helm.

Montague, Meg, Ron Borland, and Craig Sinclair. 2001. "Slip! Slop! Slap! and SunSmart, 1980–2000: Skin Cancer Control and Twenty Years of Population-Based Campaigning." *Health Education & Behavior* 28(3):290–305.

Moran, Michael. 1999. *Governing the Health Care State: A Comparative Study of the United Kingdom, the United States, and Germany*. Manchester: Manchester University Press.

Morey, Richard S. 1975. "The General Duty Clause of the Occupational Safety and Health Act of 1970." *Workmen's Compensation Law Review* 2:305.

Morgan, David and Roberto Astolfi. 2015. "Financial Impact of the GFC: Health Care Spending across the OECD." *Health Economics, Policy and Law*, 10(special issue 01):7–19.

Moser, Gabriele. 2002. "Notverordnungen und Gesundheitspolitik in der Weimarer Republik: Präventionskonzepte und Versorgungsstrukturen in der Krise." In *Prävention im 20. Jahrhundert: Historische Grundlagen und aktuelleste Entwicklung in Deutschland*, ed. Sigrid Stöckel and Ulla Walter. Weinheim, Germany: Juventa, pp. 96–109.

Mottier, Véronique. 2008. "Eugenics, Politics and the State: Social Democracy and the Swiss 'Gardening State.'" *Studies in History and Philosophy of Science, Part C: Studies in History and Philosophy of Biological and Biomedical Sciences* 39(2):263–269.

Mullan, Fitzhugh. 1989. *Plagues and Politics: The Story of the United States Public Health Service*. New York: Basic Books.

Nathanson, Constance A. 1996. "Disease Prevention as Social Change: Toward a Theory of Public Health." *Population and Development Review* 22(4):609–637.

2007. *Disease Prevention as Social Change: The State, Society, and Public Health in the United States, France, Great Britain, and Canada.* New York: Russel Sage Foundation.

Nolte, Ellen, Cécile Knai, and Richard B. Saltman. 2014. *Assessing Chronic Disease Management in European Health Systems: Country Reports.* Copenhagen: European Observatory of Health Systems and Policies.

OECD. 1987. *Financing and Delivering Health Care.* Paris: OECD Publishing.

2017. "OECD Health Statistics (database)." doi: 10.1787/data-00349-en.

OECD, WHO. 2011. *OECD-Reviews of Health Systems: Switzerland.* Paris: OECD Publishing.

Oliver, Thomas R. 2006. "The Politics of Public Health Policy." *Annual Review of Public Health* 27:195–233.

Orme, Judy, Jane Powell, Pat Taylor, and Melanie Grey. 2003. "Mapping Public Health." In *Public Health for the 21st Century: New Perspectives on Policy, Participation and Practice,* ed. Pat Taylor, Judy Orme, Jane Powell, and Melanie Grey. Maidenhead, UK: Open University Press, pp. 8–23.

Orton, J. Douglas and Karl E. Weick. 1990. "Loosely Coupled Systems: A Reconceptualization." *Academy of Management Review* 15(2):203–223.

Paccaud, Fred and Arnaud Chiolero. 2010. *Prävention, Gesundheitsförderung und Public Health.* Bern, Switzerland: Hans Huber, pp. 309–319.

Painter, Martin. 2009. *Collaborative Federalism: Economic Reform in Australia in the 1990s.* Cambridge: Cambridge University Press.

Palmer, George R. and Stephanie D. Short. 2010. *Health Care and Public Policy: An Australian Analysis.* 4th edn. Melbourne: McMillan Publishers Australia.

Papadopoulos, Yannis. 2007. "Problems of Democratic Accountability in Network and Multilevel Governance." *European Law Journal* 13(4):469–486.

Paquet, Robert. 2009. "Motor der Reform und Schaltzentrale: Die Rolle des Bundesministeriums für Gesundheit in der Gesundheitsreform 2007." In *Gesundheitsreform 2007: Nach der Reform ist vor der Reform,* ed. Wolfgang Schroeder and Robert Paquet. Wiesbaden, Germany: VS Verlag für Sozialwissenschaften, pp. 32–49.

Peters, B. Guy. 1998. "Managing Horizontal Government: The Politics of Co-ordination." *Public Administration* 76:295–311.

2015. *Pursuing Horizontal Management: The Politics of Public Sector Coordination.* Lawrence: University Press of Kansas.

Pierson, Paul. 1994. *Dismantling the Welfare State: Reagan, Thatcher, and the Politics of Retrenchment in Britain and the United States.* Cambridge: Cambridge University Press.

2000. "Increasing Returns, Path Dependence, and the Study of Politics." *American Political Science Review* 94(2):251–267.

2001. *The New Politics of the Welfare State.* New York: Oxford University Press.

2003. "Big, Slow-moving, and ... Invisible: Macrosocial Processes in the Study of Comparative Politics." In *Comparative Historical Analysis in the Social Sciences*, ed. James Mahoney and Dietrich Rueschemeyer. Cambridge: Cambridge University Press, pp. 177–207.

2004. *Politics in Time: History, Institutions and Social Analysis.* Princeton, NJ: Princeton University Press.

Pontusson, Jonas. 1995. "From Comparative Public Policy to Political Economy Putting Political Institutions in Their Place and Taking Interests Seriously." *Comparative Political Studies* 28(1):117–147.

Porter, Dorothy. 1990. "How Soon is Now? Public Health and the BMJ." *British Medical Journal* 301(6754):738.

1991. "Stratification and its Discontents: Professionalization and Conflict in the British Public Health Service." In *A History of Education in Public Health: Health that Mocks the Doctors' Rules*, ed. Elizabeth Fee and Roy Acheson. Oxford: Oxford Medical Publications pp. 83–113.

ed. 1994. *The History of Public Health and the Modern State.* Amsterdam, GA: Rodopi.

1999. *Health, Civilization, and the State: A History of Public Health from Ancient to Modern Times.* New York: Routledge.

Porter, Dorothy and Robert Porter. 1989. "The Enforcement of Health: The English Debate." In *AIDS: The Burdens of History.* Berkeley, CA: University of California Press, pp. 97–121.

Potvin, Louise and David V. McQueen. 2007. "Modernity, Public Health, and Health Promotion." In *Health and Modernity.* New York: Springer, pp. 12–20.

Pratico, Dominick. 2001. *Eisenhower and Social Security: The Origins of the Disability Program.* Lincoln, NE: iUniverse.

Princen, Sebastian. 2007. "Advocacy Coalitions and the Internationalization of Public Health Policies." *Journal of Public Policy* 27(1):13–33.

Proctor, Robert N. 1996. "The Anti-tobacco Campaign of the Nazis: A Little Known Aspect of Public Health in Germany, 1933–1945." *British Medical Journal* 313(7070):1450–1453.

Raw, Martin and Luk Joossens. 2006. "The Tobacco Control Scale: A New Scale to Measure Country Activity." *Tobacco Control* 15:247–253.

2010. *The Tobacco Control Scale 2010 in Europe*. Brussels: Associations of European Cancer Leagues.

RCP. 1962. *Smoking and Health*. London: Royal College of Physicians.

Reinhardt, Uwe E. 2001. "Perspectives on the Pharmaceutical Industry." *Health Affairs* 20(5):136–149.

Reus, Iris. 2016. "On a Successful Road to 'More Federalism' in Länder Politics? The Case of Smoking Bans after Germany's Federalism Reform." *German Politics* 25(2):210–226.

Rice, Thomas, Pauline Rosenau, Lynn Y. Unruh, and Andrew J. Barnes. 2013. *United States of America: Health System Review* (Health systems in transition, vol. 17). Copenhagen: European Observatory on Health Systems and Policies.

Rodwin, Marc A. 2011. *Conflicts of Interest and the Future of Medicine: The United States, France and Japan*. New York: Oxford University Press.

Rose, Richard. 2004. *Learning from Comparative Public Policy: A Practical Guide*. New York: Routledge.

Rosen, George. 1993 [1959]. *A History of Public Health*. Baltimore, MD: Johns Hopkins University Press.

Rosenbaum, Sara. 2011. "The Patient Protection and Affordable Care Act: Implications for Public Health Policy and Practice." *Public Health Reports* 126(1):130.

Rosenbrock, R. 2001. "Was ist New Public Health?" *Bundesgesundheitsblatt – Gesundheitsforschung – Gesundheitsschutz* 44(8):753–762.

Rosenbrock, Rolf and Thomas Gerlinger. 2009. *Gesundheitspolitik: Eine systematische Einführung*. 2nd edn. Bern, Switzerland: Hans Huber.

2014. *Gesundheitspolitik: Eine systematische Einführung*. 3rd edn. Bern, Switzerland: Hans Huber.

Rosenkrantz, Barbara Gutmann, ed. 1994. *From Consumption to Tuberculosis: A Documentary History*. New York: Garland Publishing.

Ross, E. 1991. The Origins of Public Health: Concepts and Contradictions. In *Health through Public Policy*, ed. P. Draper. London: Green Print, pp. 26–40.

Rothgang, Heinz. 2010. *The State and Healthcare: Comparing OECD Countries*. New York: Palgrave McMillan.

Rueschemeyer, Dietrich. 1973a. *Lawyers and their Society: A Comparative Study of the Legal Profession in Germany and in the United States*. Cambridge, MA: Harvard University Press.

1973b. "Professions: Historisch und kulturell vergleichende Überlegungen." In *Soziologie (Festsschrift für René König)*, ed. G. Albrecht, H. Daheim, and F. Sack. Opladen, Germany: Westdeutscher Verlag, pp. 250–260.

Russell, Louise B. 1986. *Is Prevention Better than Cure?* Washington, DC: Brookings Institution Press.

——— 2009. "Preventing Chronic Disease: An Important Investment, but Don't Count on Cost Savings." *Health Affairs* 28(1):42–45.

Sabatier, Paul A. 1993. *Policy Change and Learning: An Advocacy Coalition Approach* (Theoretical lenses on public policy). Boulder, CO: Westview Press.

Saetren, Harald. 2005. "Facts and Myths about Research on Public Policy Implementation: Out-of-Fashion, Allegedly Dead, But Still Very Much Alive and Relevant." *Policy Studies Journal* 33(4):559–582.

Sager, Fritz. 2003. "Kompensationsmöglichkeiten föderaler Vollzugsdefizite: Das Beispiel der kantonalen Alkoholpräventionspolitiken." *Swiss Political Science Review* 9(1):309–333.

——— 2004. "Verwaltung, Politik und Wissenschaft in der kantonalen Alkoholprävention." *Sozial-und Präventivmedizin* 49(3):208–215.

Saks, Mike. 1995. *Professions and the Public Interest: Medical Power, Altruism and Alternative Medicine.* New York: Routledge.

Saltman, Richard B., Reinhard Busse, and Josep Figueras, eds. 2004. *Social Health Insurance Systems in Western Europe.* Maidenhead, UK: Open University Press.

Santésuisse. 2014. "Geschichte: Von KSK zu santésuisse - von KUVG zu KVG." www.santesuisse.ch/de/unternehmen/geschichte, accessed April 17, 2018.

Sax, Sidney. 1984. *A Strife of Interests: Politics and Policies in Australian Health Services.* Sydney: George Allen & Unwin.

Scharpf, Fritz W. 1997. *Games Real Actors Play.* Boulder, CO: Westview Press.

Schild, Georg. 2003. *Zwischen Freiheit des Einzelnen und Wohlfahrtsstaat: Amerikanische Sozialpolitik im 20. Jahrhundert.* Paderborn, Germany: Schöningh.

Schleiermacher, Sabine. 2002. "Umfassende Krankenversicherung für alle? Verfassungsanspruch und Wirklichkeit im Kaiserreich und der Weimarer Republik." In *Prävention im 20. Jahrhundert: Historische Grundlagen und aktuelleste Entwicklung in Deutschland*, ed. Sigrid Stöckel and Ulla Walter. Weinheim, Germany: Juventa, pp. 52–64.

Schlesinger, Mark. 1997. "Paradigms Lost: The Persisting Search for Community in US Health Policy." *Journal of Health Politics, Policy and Law* 22(4):937–992.

Schmacke, Norbert. 1993. *Schritte in die Öffentlichkeit: Die Wiederentdeckung der kommunalen Gesundheitsämter.* Düsseldorf: Akademie für öffentliches Gesundheitswesen Düsseldorf.

1996. *Öffentlicher Gesundheitsdienst, Sozialstaat und Kommunale Selbstverwaltung: Perspektiven der Gesundheitsämter auf dem Weg ins 21. Jahrhundert.* Düsseldorf: Akademie für öffentliches Gesundheitswesen.

2002. "Die Individualisierung der Prävention im Schatten der Medizin." In *Prävention im 20. Jahrhundert: Historische Grundlagen und aktuelleste Entwicklung in Deutschland*, ed. Sigrid Stöckel and Ulla Walter. Weinheim, Germany: Juventa, pp. 178–189.

Schmid, Achim, Mirella Cacace, Ralf Götze, and Heinz Rothgang. 2010. "Explaining Health Care System Change: Problem Pressure and the Emergence of 'Hybrid' Health Care Systems." *Journal of Health Politics, Policy and Law* 35(4):455–486.

Schmidt, Manfred G. 1996. "When Parties Matter: A Review of the Possibilities and Limits of Partisan Influence on Public Policy." *European Journal of Political Research* 30(2):155–183.

2004. *Sozialpolitik der DDR.* Wiesbaden, Germany: VS Verlag für Sozialwissenschaften.

2005a. *Das politische System der Bundesrepublik Deutschland*, vol. 2371. Stuttgart: CH Beck.

2005b. *Sozialpolitik in Deutschland: Historische Entwicklung und internationaler Vergleich.* Wiesbaden, Germany: VS Verlag.

Schmidt, Vivien A. 2008. "Discursive Institutionalism: The Explanatory Power of Ideas and Discourse." *Annual Review of Political Science* 11:303–326.

Schmiedebach, Hans-Peter. 2002. "Gesundheit und Prävention in Abhängigkeit vom Gesellschaftsbegriff im 19. Jahrhundert." In *Prävention im 20. Jahrhundert: Historische Grundlagen und aktuelleste Entwicklung in Deutschland*, ed. Sigrid Stöckel and Ulla Walter. Weinheim, Germany: Juventa, pp. 26–38.

Schmitter, Philippe C. 1974. "Still the Century of Corporatism?" *The Review of Politics* 36(1):85–131.

Schneider, Nick K. and Stanton A. Glantz. 2008. "'Nicotine Nazis Strike Again': A Brief Analysis of the Use of Nazi Rhetoric in Attacking Tobacco Control Advocacy." *Tobacco Control* 17(5):291–296.

Scholten, Peter, Elizabeth Collett, and Milica Petrovic. 2016. "Mainstreaming Migrant Integration? A Critical Analysis of a New Trend in Integration Governance." *International Review of Administrative Sciences* 83(2):283–302.

Schroeder, Steven A. 2004. "Tobacco Control in the Wake of the 1998 Master Settlement Agreement." *New England Journal of Medicine* 350(3):293–301.

Schwartz, Gary E. 1977. "What is Behavioral Medicine?" *Psychosomatic Medicine* 39(6):377–381.

1982. "Testing the Biopsychosocial Model: The Ultimate Challenge Facing Behavioral Medicine?" *Journal of Consulting and Clinical Psychology* 50(6):1040–1053.

Schwoch, Rebecca. 2002. Die amtlichen Gesundheits- und Fürsorgestellen müssen für alle sorgen ... In *Prävention im 20. Jahrhundert: Historische Grundlagen und aktuelleste Entwicklung in Deutschland*, ed. Sigrid Stöckel and Ulla Walter. Weinheim, Germany: Juventa, pp. 136–151.

Seeleib-Kaiser, Martin. 1993. *Amerikanische Sozialpolitik: Politische Diskussion und Entscheidungen der Reagan-Ära*. Opladen, Germany: Leske und Budrich.

Sensch, Jürgen. (1875, 2013 [2006]). "histat-Datenkompilation online: Basisdaten zur Entwicklung der Gesundheitsverhältnisse in Deutschland." Technical report GESIS.

Shepsle, Kenneth A. 2006. "Rational Choice Institutionalism." In *The Oxford Handbook of Political Institutions*, ed. R. A. W. Rhodes, Sarah A. Binder, and Bert A. Rockman. Oxford: Oxford University Press, pp. 23–38.

Shield, Thomas W., Carolyn E. Reed, Joseph LoCicero III, and Richard H. Freins, eds. 2009. *General Thoracic Surgery*, 7th edn. Philadelphia, PA: Wolters Kluwer Health Lippincott Williams & Wilkins.

Shipan, Charles R. and Craig Volden. 2008. "The Mechanisms of Policy Diffusion." *American Journal of Political Science* 52(4):840–857.

Siaroff, Alan. 1999. "Corporatism in Twenty-four Industrial Democracies: Meaning and Measurement." *European Journal of Political Research* 36(2):175–205.

Skocpol, Theda. 1979. *States and Social Revolutions: A Comparative Analysis of France, Russia and China*. Cambridge: Cambridge University Press.

1995. *Protecting Soldiers and Mothers: The Political Origins of Social Policy in the United States*. Cambridge, MA: Harvard University Press.

Smith, G. Davey, Mel Bartley, and David Blane. 1990. "The Black Report on Socioeconomic Inequalities in Health Ten Years On." *British Medical Journal* 301(6748):373.

Soenning, Rudolf. 1957. "'Blauer Plan' für das Gesundheitswesen." *Bayerisches Aerzteblatt* 12(2):42–43.

Starr, Paul. 1982. *The Social Transformation of American Medicine: The Rise of a Sovereign Profession and the Making of a Vast Industry*. New York: Basic Books.

Starr, Paul. 2009. "Professionalization and Public Health: Historical Legacies, Continuing Dilemmas." *Journal of Public Health Management
and Practice* 15(6 suppl):S26–30.

Steindor, Marina. 2009. "Gerechte Gesundheitschancen: Von der Entwick-
lung eines gesundheitsfördernden Lebensstils für die Bürger bis hin zur
Gesundheitspädagogik für die Arbeiterschicht." In *Normativität und
Public Health: Vergessene Dimensionen gesundheitlicher Ungleichheit*,
ed. Uwe H. Bittlingmayer, Diana Sahrai, and Peter-Ernst Schnabel.
Wiesbaden, Germany: VS Verlag für Sozialwissenschaften, pp. 75–109.

Steinmo, Sven. 2010. *The Evolution of Modern States: Sweden, Japan, and
the United States*. Cambridge: Cambridge University Press.

Steinmo, Sven and Jon Watts. 1995. "It's the Institutions, Stupid! Why
Comprehensive National Health Insurance always Fails in America."
Journal of Health Politics, Policy and Law 20(2):329–372.

Stepan, Alfred. 1999. "Federalism and Democracy: Beyond the US Model."
Journal of Democracy 10:19–34.

Stewart, J. 2005. "A Review of UK Housing Policy: Ideology and Public
Health." *Public Health* 119(6):525–534.

Stöckel, Sigrid. 2002. "Gesundheitsfürsorge – von der Armenpflege zur Profession." In *Prävention im 20. Jahrhundert: Historische Grundlagen
und aktuelleste Entwicklung in Deutschland*, ed. Sigrid Stöckel and
Ulla Walter. Weinheim, Germany: Juventa, pp. 65–75.

Streeck, Wolfgang and Kathleen Thelen. 2005. "Introduction." In *Beyond
Continuity: Institutional Change in Advanced Political Economies*, ed
Wolfgang Streeck and Kathleen Thelen. New York: Oxford University
Press, pp. 3–39.

Streeck, Wolfgang and Kōzō Yamamura. 2001. *The Origins of Nonliberal
Capitalism: Germany and Japan in Comparison*. New York: Cornell
University Press.

Studlar, Donley T. 2006. "Tobacco Control Policy Instruments in a Shrink-
ing World: How Much Policy Learning?" *International Journal of
Public Administration* 29(4–6):367–396.

2014. "Cancer Prevention through Stealth: Science, Policy Advocacy, and
Multilevel Governance in the Establishment of a 'National Tobacco
Control Regime' in the United States." *Journal of Health Politics,
Policy and Law* 39(3):503–535.

Studlar, Donley T., Kyle Christensen, and Arnita Sistari. 2011. "Tobacco
Control in the EU-15: The Role of the Member States in the European
Union." *Journal of European Public Policy* 18(5):728–745.

Sung, Hai-Yen, Teh-wei Hu, Michael Ong, Theodore E. Keeler, and Mei-
ling Sheu. 2005. "A Major State Tobacco Tax Increase, the Master

Settlement Agreement, and Cigarette Consumption: The California Experience." *American Journal of Public Health* 95(6):1030–1035.

Surdez, Muriel. 2005. *Diplômes et nation: La constitution d'un espace suisse des professions avocate et artisanales (1880–1930)*. Bern, Switzerland: Peter Lang.

Surgeon General's Advisory Committee. 1964. "Smoking and Health: Report of the Advisory Committee to the Surgeon General of the Public Health Service." Washington, DC: US Department of Health, Education, and Welfare.

SUVA. 1993. "SUVA 75 Jahre: Das Menschenmögliche." *SUVA-Bulletin*, special issue.

SVRG. 1989. *Qualität, Wirtschaftlichkeit und Perspektiven der Gesundheitsversorgung: Vorschläge für die Konzertierte Aktion im Gesundheitswesen*. Baden-Baden, Germany: Nomos.

Terris, Milton. 1978. "The Three World Systems of Medical Care: Trends and Prospects." *American Journal of Public Health* 68(11):1125–1131.

Thelen, Kathleen. 2004. *How Institutions Evolve: The Political Economy of Skills in Germany, Britain, the United States and Japan*. Cambridge: Cambridge University Press.

2014. *Varieties of Liberalization and the New Politics of Social Solidarity*. Cambridge: Cambridge University Press.

Thietz, Jacqueline and Thomas Hartmann. 2012. "Das Spannungsfeld von Gesundheitszielen im Föderalismus in Deutschland." *Prävention und Gesundheitsförderung* 7(4):308–315.

Tilly, Charles. 1984. *Big Structures, Large Processes, Huge Comparisons*. New York: Russell Sage Foundation.

Tosun, Jale and Achim Lang. 2017. "Policy Integration: Mapping the Different Concepts." Unpublished paper, Heidelberg University/Zurich University of Applied Sciences.

Trampusch, Christine. 2010. "Co-evolution of Skills and Welfare in Coordinated Market Economies? A Comparative Historical Analysis of Denmark, the Netherlands and Switzerland." *European Journal of Industrial Relations* 16(3):197–220.

Trein, Philipp. 2017a. "Coevolution of Policy Sectors: A Comparative Analysis of Health Care and Public Health." *Public Administration* 95(3):744–758.

2017b. "Europeanization Beyond the EU: The Case of Tobacco Advertising Restrictions in Swiss Cantons." *Journal of Public Policy* 37(2):113–143.

2017c. "A New Way to Compare Horizontal Connections of Policy Sectors: 'Coupling' of Actors, Institutions and Policies." *Journal of Comparative Policy Analysis: Research and Practice* 19(5):419–434.

Trein, Philipp, Iris Meyer, and Martino Maggetti. 2017. "Policy Integration: A Systematic Review of the Literature." Unpublished paper, University of Lausanne.

Tsebelis, George. 2000. "Veto Players and Institutional Analysis." *Governance* 13(4):441–474.

2002. *Veto Players: How Political Institutions Work*. Princeton, NJ: Princeton University Press.

Tulchinsky, Theodore H. and Elena A. Varavikova. 1996. "Addressing the Epidemiologic Transition in the Former Soviet Union: Strategies for Health System and Public Health Reform in Russia." *American Jorunal of Public Health* 86(3):313–320.

2009. *The New Public Health*, 2nd edn. San Diego, CA: Elsevier/Academic Press.

2014. *The New Public Health*, 3rd edn. San Diego, CA: Elsevier/Academic Press.

Tuohy, Carolyn H. 1999. *Accidental Logics: The Dynamics of Change in the Health Care Arena in the United States, Britain, and Canada*. New York: Oxford University Press.

Uhlmann, Björn and Dietmar Braun. 2011. *Die schweizerische Krankenversicherungspolitik zwischen Veränderung und Stillstand*. Chur, Switzerland: Rüegger Verlag.

UN General Assembly. 2010. "Resolution 64/265: Prevention and Control of Non-Communicable Diseases." A/Res/64/265.

US Public Health Service. 1900–1970. *Vital Statistics of the United States*, annual, vol. I and vol II; 1971–2001, US National Center for Health Statistics, *Vital Statistics of the United States*, annual; *National Vital Statistics Report (NVSR)* (formerly *Monthly Vital Statistics Report*). US Public Health Service.

Varone, Frédéric, Stéphane Nahrath, David Aubin, and Jean-David Gerber. 2013. "Functional Regulatory Spaces." *Policy Sciences* 46(4):311–333.

Vatter, Adrian. 2014. *Das politische System der Schweiz*. Baden-Baden, Germany: Nomos.

Vatter, Adrian and Christian Rüefli. 2003. "Do Political Factors Matter for Health Care Expenditure? A Comparative Study of Swiss Cantons." *Journal of Public Policy* 23(3):301–323.

2014. Gesundheitspolitik. In *Handbuch der Schweizer Politik*, ed. Peter Knoepfel, Yannis Papadopoulos, Pascal Sciarini, Adrian Vatter, and Silja Häusermann Zurich: Verlag Neue Züricher Zeitung, pp. 827–854.

Volden, Craig. 2006. "States as Policy Laboratories: Emulating Success in the Children's Health Insurance Program." *American Journal of Political Science* 50(2):294–312.

Wagschal, Uwe and Georg Wenzelburger. 2008. "Roads to Success: Budget Consolidations in OECD Countries." *Journal of Public Policy* 28(3):309–339.

Wall, Ann. 1996. Australia. In *Health Care Systems in Liberal Democracies*, ed. Ann Wall. Routledge, pp. 27–46.

Watkins, Dorothy E. 1984. "The English Revolution in Social Medicine, 1889–1911." PhD thesis, University of London.

Watts, Ronald L. 1996. *Comparing Federal Systems in the 1990s*. Kingston, Canada: Institute of Intergovernmental Relations, Queens University.

2008. *Comparing Federal Systems*. 3rd edn. Montreal: McGill-Queen's University Press.

Weber, Max. 1980. *Wirtschaft und Gesellschaft: Grundriss der verstehenden Soziologie*. 5th edn. Tübingen, Germany: Mohr Siebeck.

Webster, Charles. 2002. *The National Health Service: A Political History*. New York: Oxford University Press.

Weick, Karl E. 1976. "Educational Organizations as Loosely Coupled Systems." *Administrative Science Quarterly* 21(1):1–19.

Weimer, David L. and Aidan R. Vining. 2005. *Policy Analysis: Concepts and Practice*. Upper Saddle River, NJ: Prentice Hall.

Weindling, Paul. 1989. *Health, Race and German Politics between National Unification and Nazism, 1870–1945*. Cambridge: Cambridge University Press.

1994. "Public Health in Germany." In *The History of Public Health and the Modern State*, ed. Dorothy Porter. Amsterdam, GA: Rodopi, pp. 75–87.

2002. "The Divisions in Weimar Medicine: German Public Health and the League of Nations Health Organization." In *Prävention im 20. Jahrhundert: Historische Grundlagen und aktuelleste Entwicklung in Deutschland*, ed. Sigrid Stöckel and Ulla Walter. Weinheim, Germany: Juventa, pp. 110–121.

2006. "As origens da participação da América Latina na Organização de Saúde de Liga das Nações, 1920 à 1940" [The League of Nations Health Organization and the Rise of Latin American Participation, 1920–40]." *Historia, ciencias, saude-Manguinhos* 13(9):555–570.

Weisbrod, Burton A. 1991. "The Health Care Quadrilemma: An Essay on Technological Change, Insurance, Quality of Care, and Cost Containment." *Journal of Economic Literature* 29(2):523–552.

Wendt, Claus. 2006. "Gesundheitssysteme im internationalen Vergleich." *Gesundheitswesen* 68(10):593–599.

Wendt, Claus, Lorraine Frisina, and Heinz Rothgang. 2009. "Healthcare System Types: A Conceptual Framework for Comparison." *Social Policy & Administration* 43(1):70–90.

Wenzelburger, Georg. 2013. "Die Politik der Inneren Sicherheit: Konturen eines Forschungsfelds aus Sicht der vergleichenden Politikforschung." *Zeitschrift für Vergleichende Politikwissenschaft* 7:1–25.

WHO. 1953. *The Work of the WHO 1952: Annual Report of the Director-General to the World Health Assembly and to the United Nations.* Geneva: WHO Press.

——— 2000. *The World Health Report: Health Systems: Improving Performance.* Geneva: WHO Press.

——— 2002. *The World Health Report: Reducing Risks, Promoting Healthy Life.* Geneva: WHO Press.

——— 2013a. *Global Action Plan for the Prevention of Noncommunicable Diseases 2013–2020.* Geneva: WHO Press.

——— 2013b. *Global Tuberculosis Report.* Geneva: WHO Press.

——— 2014. *Antimicrobial Resistance: Global Report on Surveillance.* Geneva: WHO Press.

Wilde, Sally. 2005. "Serendipity, Doctors and the Australian Constitution." *Health and History* 7(1):41–48.

Willis, Evan. 1989. *Medical Dominance*, rev. edn. Sydney: Allen and Unwin.

Wise, Marilyn and Louise Signal. 2000. "Health Promotion Development in Australia and New Zealand." *Health Promotion International* 15(3):237–248.

Wolf, Frieder and Thomas Pfohl. 2014. "Protecting the Population in a Multilevel System: Horizontal and Vertical Informal Governance Patterns in Germany." *Zeitschrift für Vergleichende Politikwissenschaft* 8(1):259–285.

Woodruf, P. 1984. *Two Million South Australians.* Adelaide: Peacock.

Worsham, Jeffrey. 2006. "Up in Smoke: Mapping Subsystem Dynamics in Tobacco Policy." *Policy Studies Journal* 34(3):437–452.

Yamamura, Kōzō and Wolfgang Streeck, eds. 2003. *The End of Diversity? Prospects for German and Japanese Capitalism.* Ithaca, NY: Cornell University Press.

Yom, Sean. 2015. "From Methodology to Practice: Inductive Iteration in Comparative Research." *Comparative Political Studies* 48(5):616–644.

Zafonte, Matthew and Paul Sabatier. 1998. "Shared Beliefs and Imposed Interdependencies as Determinants of Ally Networks in Overlapping Subsystems." *Journal of Theoretical Politics* 10(4):473–505.

Index

313